Florida Real Estate Postlicensing for Sales Associates

2nd Edition

PERFORMANCE PROGRAMS COMPANY

STEPHEN METTLING
DAVID CUSIC
RYAN METTLING

Material in this book is not intended to represent legal advice and should not be so construed. Readers should consult legal counsel for advice regarding points of law.

© 2025 by Performance Programs Company
6810 190th Street East, Bradenton, FL 34211
info@performanceprogramscompany.com
www.performanceprogramscompany.com

ISBN: 978-1965482261

Florida Real Estate Postlicensing for Sales Associates

Table of Contents

PREFACE

**About
the text**

Welcome to our *Florida Real Estate Postlicensing for Sales Associates (FREPSA)* course, a 45-hour review and applied principles course for newly-licensed sales associates beginning their real estate careers in Florida. Successful completion of this course will satisfy your one-time postlicense requirement as a sales associate actively practicing real estate in Florida.

**Inside
the cover**

There are three principal themes underlying the content of our FREPSA course. First is to give you a key-point review of the most critical laws and regulations impacting your current practice: license-related regulations, brokerage relationships review, disclosures and professional practices that form the foundations of professional practice. This review additionally includes a brief review of rules and regulations framing compliant practices in advertising, fair housing and brokerage operations.

Second, we wanted to give you a deeper exposure to more advanced, transaction-related brokerage practices that are critical to becoming a successful practitioner: market analysis; pricing; investment principles, construction knowledge, obtaining and marketing listings, and managing the pre-closing period.

Finally, we wanted to present several additional perspectives on real estate practice that can add valuable new dimensions to your future engagements in real estate practice: property management, real estate-related insurance, and risk management. And, for students who appreciate a brush-up in real estate math, we cap off the program with a comprehensive review of transaction-related math formulas and calculations.

**About the
authors**

For nearly fifty years, Stephen Mettling has been actively engaged in real estate education. Beginning with Dearborn in 1972, then called Real Estate Education Company, Mr. Mettling managed the company's textbook division and author acquisitions. Subsequently he built up the company's real estate school division which eventually became the country's largest real estate, insurance and securities school network in the country. In 1978, Mr. Mettling founded Performance Programs Company, a custom training program publishing and development company specializing in commercial, industrial, and corporate real estate. Over time, Performance Programs Company narrowed its focus to real estate textbook and exam prep publishing. Currently the Company's texts and prelicense resources are used in hundreds of schools in over 48 states. As of 2020, Mr. Mettling has authored over 100 textbooks, real estate programs and exam prep manuals.

David Cusic, Ph.D., has been a training consultant, author, and Performance Programs Company partner for over forty years. As an educator with international real estate training experience, Dr. Cusic has been engaged in vocation-oriented education since 1966. Specializing in real estate training since 1983, he has developed numerous real estate training programs for corporate and institutional clients nationwide. Dr. Cusic is co-author of the Company's flagship title, Principles of Real Estate Practice by Mettling and Cusic, now complemented by over 20 state supplements and 35 exam prep texts.

Ryan Mettling, partner and publisher of Performance Programs, is an accomplished online curriculum designer, author, and course developer. He is responsible for the company's strategic planning, general management, printing and production, e-pub and retail platforms, and multi-channel marketing. Mr. Mettling is a member of the Real Estate Educators Association (REEA), and graduated Valedictorian from the University of Central Florida's College of Business Administration.

1 Real Estate Specializations

Introduction to the Real Estate Business
Real Estate Brokerage
Development and Construction
Professional Organizations

INTRODUCTION TO THE REAL ESTATE BUSINESS

Real estate activities
Professional specialties
Property type specialization

In its broadest sense, the real estate industry is the largest single industry in the American economy. Within it one might include the construction industry, itself often considered our country's largest business. In addition, the real estate industry may be said to include the creation, management, and demolition of every residence and business facility in the nation: offices, warehouses, factories, stores, and special purpose buildings such as hospitals and government facilities. The real estate business would include as well the managing of all the undeveloped land in the country: national parks, forests, and the vast quantity of unused federal property.

Real estate professionals are individuals and business organizations whose *sole enterprise is performing a real estate-related service or function.* A wide range of professions is available to persons wishing to enter the real estate business.

Real estate activities

Real estate professionals perform the following property-related functions:

▶ creation and improvement
▶ management and maintenance
▶ demolition
▶ investment ownership
▶ regulation
▶ transfer

Creation and improvement. Creating real properties from raw land involves capital formation, financing, construction contracting, and regulatory approvals. The key parties involved in this aspect of the business are generally the developer, the landowner, and the mortgage lender. Also involved are market analysts, architects, engineers, space planners, interior designers, and construction subcontractors.

Experts who manage the legal aspects of the development project include real estate attorneys, title companies, surveyors, property insurance companies, and government regulatory officials. The brokerage community, with the assistance of professional appraisers, usually handles the ownership and leasing transactions that occur over the many phases of development.

Management and maintenance. All real estate, whether raw land or improved property, must be managed and maintained. The two principal types of managers are property managers and asset managers. Property managers and their staff oversee specific properties on behalf of the owners, making sure the condition of the property and its financial performance meet specific standards.

Community association managers (CAMs) manage such residential properties as mobile home parks, planned unit developments (PUDs), cooperatives, time-shares, condominiums, and homeowners' associations.

Asset managers oversee groups of properties, or portfolios. Their role is to achieve the investment objectives of the owners as opposed to managing day-to-day operations.

The scope of management work is detailed in a management agreement.

Maintenance personnel include engineers, systems technicians, janitorial staff, and other employees needed to maintain the property's condition.

Demolition. Demolition experts in conjunction with excavation and debris removal experts serve to remove properties that are no longer economically viable from the market.

Investment ownership. A specialized niche in the real estate business is the real estate investor who risks capital in order to buy, hold, and sell real properties. In contrast to property owners whose primary interest is in some other business, the real estate investor focuses on identifying and exploiting real estate investment opportunities for profit. The real estate investor provides capital and liquidity to the real estate market.

Regulation. All real estate is to some degree regulated by government. The principal areas of regulation are usage, taxation, and housing administration. Professional regulatory functions include public planners, zoning administrators, building inspectors, assessors, and administrators of specific federal statutes such as Federal Fair Housing Laws.

Transfer. Rights and interests in real estate can be bought, sold, assigned, leased, exchanged, inherited, or otherwise transferred from one owner to another. Real estate brokers and the brokers' associates are generally centrally involved in such transfers. Other professional participants are mortgage brokers, mortgage bankers, appraisers, insurers, and title companies.

Professional specialties

In summary, the six primary functional areas are populated by professionals with the following specialties.

Professions in Real Estate		
Creating	developers	market analysts
	public and private planners	surveyors
	architects	engineers
	building contractors	public and private
	inspectors	
	space planners	mortgage brokers
	mortgage lenders and bankers	securities companies
	title and escrow companies	attorneys
	insurers	appraisers
	real estate brokers and agents	
Managing & Maintaining	property managers	asset managers
	maintenance engineers	maintenance
	technicians corporate managers	
Destroying	demolition contractors	excavators
Holding	investors	corporate managers
Regulating	assessors	public planners
	zoning administrators	building inspectors
Transferring	brokers and agents	appraisers
	lenders and bankers	mortgage brokers
	title and escrow companies	attorneys
	insurers	surveyors

Property type specialization

In addition to specializing by function, many professionals also specialize in the type of property they work with. According to the purpose of ownership, properties are classified as residential, commercial, or investment properties.

Residential property refers to property that is owned and used for habitation. Such properties may be further classified in terms of how many families they are designed to house, whether they are attached to other units or detached, and so forth.

Commercial property generally refers to retail and office properties, but may also include industrial real estate. The term "commercial" relates to the fact that the property can potentially generate income from a business's usage.

Investment property refers to any property that is held by its owners for investment purposes. All classifications of property may be investment properties. Generally, however, the term does not refer to owner-occupied residences, even though such properties constitute an investment. Apartments, condominiums, cooperatives, and single-family homes may be considered as investment property if non-occupants own the property for investment purposes. These properties are also referred to as residential income properties.

According to use, the following classifications of real properties are commonly accepted.

Classifications of Real Estate by Use

residential	industrial
residential income	farm and ranch
office	special purpose
retail	land

These categories often have overlapping uses. A bank, for example, may have retail as well as office operations. An industrial distribution facility may include extensive office space. A retail center may contain offices.

Special purpose properties include publicly or privately owned recreational facilities, government buildings, churches and schools.

REAL ESTATE BROKERAGE

Forms of specialization
Skills and knowledge

Most newly licensed practitioners choose to begin their real estate careers in residential brokerage.

Primary real estate brokerage activities involve performance of one or more of the following tasks:

- ▶ locating a buyer for a seller
- ▶ locating a seller for a buyer
- ▶ locating a tenant for a landlord
- ▶ locating a landlord for a tenant

A seller, buyer, landlord or tenant hires a broker to procure the opposite party to the sale or lease transaction. To help get the job done, the broker hires licensed agents as assistants. The brokerage company, in its simplest form, consists of a broker and the broker's agents, who together work to locate buyers, sellers, tenants and landlords for the broker's clients.

Forms of specialization

In the modern brokerage environment, brokers and agents specialize along the following lines:

- ▶ property type
- ▶ geographical area

- type of transaction
- type of client
- type of relationship

One's choice of specialization is influenced by competitive factors in the market and by perceived opportunities.

Property type. Since different properties have different features and potential buyers, brokers commonly choose to specialize in a property type. Thus there are:

- residential agents
- commercial agents (office, retail)
- industrial agents
- land agents

Geographical area. Brokers and agents must maintain current, accurate data on properties. It is not possible to keep track of every property in larger markets. Therefore, one must create an area of geographical specialization. One's area may be defined by natural barriers; by streets and highways; or by a certain set of subdivisions.

Type of transaction. The principal types of transaction are sales, leases and subleases, exchanges, and options.

Each form of transaction involves particular legal documents and considerations. As a result, many agents, particularly commercial agents, specialize in a type of transaction. For example, in an urban commercial property market, agents generally specialize in either leases or sales.

Type of client. Brokers increasingly represent buyers and tenants as well as sellers and landlords. Since conflicts of interest may be involved, many brokers restrict their business to representing either buyers and tenants or sellers and landlords exclusively.

Some brokers and agents also specialize according to the type of business their clients are in or their motivations for the transaction. Thus one finds brokers who focus exclusively on hospitals, or fast-food chains, or executive relocations.

Type of relationship. In recent years, many brokers have specialized in providing advisory services to clients instead of the traditional transaction-based, commission-compensated services. In the advisory relationship, the broker works on identified real estate tasks or projects in exchange for a fee, salary, or retainer. The fee advisor may or may not focus on completing a transaction.
Some of the individual brokerage services that one might perform for a pre-set fee are:

- comparative price analysis
- database search

- ▸ prospect screening
- ▸ site analysis

Skills and knowledge

Professionals in the brokerage business must have a broad range of real estate knowledge and skills. Agents must develop a thorough awareness of their local market and the properties within it. In addition, agents must develop a proficiency with the economics of real estate: prices, financing, closing costs, and so forth. Equally important are "people" skills: communicating with clients and responding to their needs.

Skills and Knowledge in Real Estate Brokerage

Knowledge	Skills
local market conditions	financial qualification
local properties	market analysis
real estate principles	marketing practices
real estate law	ethical practices
value estimation	liability management
real estate financing	data management
investment principles	selling
license laws	time management
related math calculations	communication
closing procedures	writing
	basic computer operation

DEVELOPMENT AND CONSTRUCTION

Land acquisition
Subdividing and development
Construction

Development and construction involve a complex process consisting of many stages requiring the participation of numerous parties and entailing many financial risks. The physical process consists of a sequence of events from land acquisition through subdividing, land preparation, construction, leasing, and sale,

Land acquisition

Before land is located for a development, the developer undertakes a strategic analysis of what uses the area requires, the market demographics, potential trade areas and locational features for users, whether the use is to be commercial or residential, competitive projects in the region, supply and demand, and financing options. Careful study of the features of the potential site and a highest and best use and feasibility analysis go into creation of a master development plan.

An estimate of land and development costs representing the developer's outlays, including site preparation, engineering and design, commissions, construction, permits, financing and other items will guide how much the developer can pay for the land. These costs will vary depending on whether the developer intends to proceed with the entire development to finished product or will re-sell the land at an earlier stage of the process to another developer or builder.

Subdividing and development

A division of land into two or more lots, units, parcels or interests may or may not include a plan for streets and utilities. Subdivision is regulated by state and municipal laws concerning zoning, permissible uses, construction standards, and environmental constraints, among other things. One essential step is the creation and recording of a subdivision plat map. This map lays out the proposed building sites, streets, and public utilities. Also, improvements that will not be sold to individuals, such as parks, streets, sidewalks, and curbs, are typically donated to the local municipality or county by means of a recorded dedication. This dedication ensures that the local government will be responsible for maintaining those improvements.

Construction

Residential construction falls into three general categories.

Spec homes. Speculative or spec homes are those that are built without a prior commitment from a homebuyer.

Custom homes. When there is a contract with a buyer for a particular home before there is any construction, the builder constructs a custom home, usually according to a plan presented by the buyer or an architect.

Tract homes. Here the builder offers a choice of floor plans and designs, often represented by one or more model homes, for the buyer to choose along with a particular lot.

PROFESSIONAL ORGANIZATIONS

There are trade organizations within the real estate industry that support and promote virtually every form of business specialization. Benefits of membership include training programs, professional designations, and communication channels for keeping abreast of events and laws. Trade organization membership also generally enhances one's business image in the eyes of clients and the public at large.

Some of the major trade organizations, institutes and related professional designations are listed below.

Real Estate Trade Organizations and Designations

American Society of Appraisers
www.appraisers.org

American Society of Home Inspectors
www.ashi.com

Building Owners and Managers Association
www.boma.org

CCIM Institute
www.ccim.com

    Certified Commercial-Investment Member (CCIM)

Corenet Global
www.corenetglobal.org

    Master of Corporate Real Estate (MCR)

Counselors of Real Estate
www.cre.org

    Counselor of Real Estate (CRE)

Institute of Real Estate Management
www.irem.org

    Certified Property Manager (CPM)

International Association of Assessing Officers
www.iaao.org

International Council of Shopping Centers
www.icsc.org

Mortgage Bankers Association of America
www.mbaa.org

    Certified Mortgage Banker (CMB)

National Association of Exclusive Buyer's Agents
www.naeba.org

National Association of Home Builders
www.nahb.org

NAIOP Commercial Real Estate Development Association
www.naiop.org

National Association of Real Estate Brokers
www.nareb.com

National Association of Realtors
www.nar.realtor

    Graduate, Realtors Institute (GRI)
    Certified International Property Specialist (CIPS)

Real Estate Educators Association
www.reea.org

Realtors Land Institute
www.rliland.com

    Accredited Land Consultant (ALC)

Society of Industrial and Office Realtors

www.sior.com

The Appraisal Institute
www.appraisalinstitute.org

    Member, Appraisal Institute (MAI)
    Senior Residential Appraiser (SRA)

Women's Council of Realtors
www.wcr.org

Performance Management Network (PMN)

1 Real Estate Specializations
Snapshot Review

INTRODUCTION TO THE REAL ESTATE BUSINESS

Real estate activities
- create, improve, manage, maintain, demolish, own, regulate, and transfer real properties

Property type specialization
- residential; residential income; office; retail; industrial; farm and ranch; special purpose; land

REAL ESTATE BROKERAGE
- procure a buyer or tenant for an owner or landlord, or vice versa

Forms of specialization
- by property type; geographical area; type of transaction; type of client; by form of business organization; or by form of client relationship

Skills and knowledge
- market conditions; law; financing; marketing; ethics; selling; communications; computer basics; and other skills

DEVELOPMENT AND CONSTRUCTION

Land acquisition
- components of acquiring land for development: strategic planning, market analysis, locational features, demographics, intended use, highest and best use, financing, competition, supply and demand, feasibility, costs of site preparation, engineering, design, construction, permits to determine affordable price

Subdividing and development
- state and municipal regulation: zoning, uses, construction standards, environment, recording of plat map, dedication of non-private areas

Construction
- three types of residential construction: spec home, custom homes, tract homes

PROFESSIONAL ORGANIZATIONS
- promote interests of practitioners and enhance their professional standing real estate commission

SECTION ONE QUIZ: Real Estate Specializations

1. Property management and real estate asset management are both real estate management professions. The primary distinction between the two is that

    a. property managers always report to an asset manager.
    b. asset managers have greater knowledge of a property's finances.
    c. property managers handle day-to-day operations while asset managers manage portfolios of properties.
    d. asset managers are primarily responsible for maintenance technicians.

2. People in the real estate business who primarily focus on creating new properties are

    a. brokers.
    b. developers.
    c. zoning administrators.
    d. excavators.

3. The term "commercial property" generally refers to

    a. non-owner-occupied properties.
    b. retail, office and industrial properties.
    c. multi-tenant properties.
    d. retail properties.

4. Which of the following professionals involved in the real estate business are most concerned about procuring buyers and sellers for clients?

    a. Brokers and agents
    b. Property managers
    c. Corporate real estate managers
    d. Appraisers

5. Which of the following ways of specializing is common in the real estate brokerage business?

    a. By type of house
    b. By geography
    c. By financial background of client
    d. By type of mortgage

6. What is an advisory service provider?

    a. A broker of fee simple titles
    b. A corporate real estate broker
    c. A broker performing non-transactional services for a commission
    d. A broker who renders real estate services for a fee

7. The level of government which is most active in regulating real estate licensees is the

   a. federal government.
   b. state government.
   c. county government.
   d. municipal government where the person resides.

8. What are the two principal types of real estate managers who oversee groups of properties?

   a. Property managers and asset managers
   b. Staff managers and management managers
   c. Property managers and management managers
   d. Lead managers and asset managers

9. What is the primary focus of an asset manager compared to a property manager?

   a. Maximizing rent in a given apartment complex
   b. Reserves and avoiding excessive depreciation
   c. Financial performance of an income property portfolio
   d. Responsiveness of the HOA to the complex's tenants

10. Which of the following is a major commercial brokerage specialization area?

   a. Office leases
   b. Land sales
   c. Single family house sales
   d. Warehouse sales

2 Florida License Law Review

Key Florida Statutes and Rules
General Licensure Provisions
Application Requirements
Sales Associate License Requirements
Broker License Requirements
Nonresident License Requirements
License Registration
Activities Requiring Licensure; Exemptions
License Renewals; Education; Status
Multiple and Group Licenses

KEY FLORIDA STATUTES AND RULES

The Florida legislature saw a need to protect consumers during real estate transactions from unethical and illegal practices such as fraud. Legislators also did not want to make it unreasonably difficult for an individual to enter into the real estate profession. Consequently, they established specific laws to meet these needs. The statutes are updated annually to create, amend, transfer, or repeal statutory material.

Chapter 20 of the Florida code covers the organizational structure of the Executive Branch of the state government. It is the statute that created the Department of Business and Professional Regulation and established the Divisions within the DBPR, such as the Division of Real Estate. This statute also established the organizational structure of the DBPR.

Chapter 475 is divided into four parts and provides regulations for brokers, sales associates, appraisers, and schools. Part I created the FREC and includes its organization, powers, and duties. It also covers regulations for licensure and brokerage practices, including violations and penalties.

Part II provides regulations for appraisers. Part III is known as the Commercial Real Estate Sales Commission Lien Act and provides regulations for a broker's lien for unpaid sales commission. Part IV is known as the Commercial Real Estate Leasing Commission Lien Act and provides regulations for a broker's lien for unpaid commission earned by a lease of commercial real estate.

Chapter 455, or the Business and Professional Regulation: General Provisions, is the law used by the DBPR in regulating the professions under the Department's auspices. It outlines the legislative intent in regulating these professions and includes restrictions on deterring qualified individuals from entering any of the chosen professions. It specifically holds that non-U.S. citizens may not be disqualified from practicing any of the professions regulated by the DBPR and covers the required qualifications to do so.

Chapter 455 also includes the powers and duties of the DBPR and the organizational and operational requirements of the boards under the DBPR. This chapter covers general licensing provisions; education requirements; licensure examinations and testing services; disciplinary grounds, actions, procedures, and penalties; and legal and investigative services. Section 455.02 provides guidelines for licensure of members of the armed forces and their spouses.

Chapter 61J2 contains the Florida Real Estate Commission's (FREC) rules. These rules cover licensure and education requirements, non-resident licensure, brokerage operation and business practices, trust fund handling, and disciplinary matters and procedures.

Chapter 83. also known as the Florida Residential Landlord and Tenant Act, covers both residential and nonresidential tenancies. It provides regulations for rental agreements, deposits, landlord and tenant obligations, tenancy terminations, and enforcement of rights and duties.

Chapter 718 regulates condominiums and includes rights and obligations of the developers and owners' association. It establishes procedures for creating, selling, and operating condominiums.

Chapter 719 recognizes cooperatives as a form of property ownership and regulates the creation, sale, lease, and operation of cooperatives.

Chapter 760 is the Florida Civil Rights Act, which created the Florida Commission on Human Relations with the intent of protecting all individuals within Florida from discrimination based on race, color, religion, sex, pregnancy, national origin, age, handicap, or marital status.

Other state statutes regulate taxation and collections, construction standards, lien foreclosures, and tax breaks for undeveloped land used for agricultural purposes (Florida Greenbelt Law of 1959). The Online Sunshine website provides access to these and other applicable Florida statutes.

GENERAL LICENSURE PROVISIONS

General qualifications
Required disclosures

General qualifications

To qualify for a real estate license in Florida, an individual must be at least 18 years old; hold a high school diploma or its equivalent; and be honest, truthful, trustworthy, and of good character. He or she must have a good reputation for fair dealing and be competent to handle real estate transactions. Being a U.S. citizen is not a requirement for licensure as long as the individual. meets all other requirements of licensure. However, applicants must have a Social Security number.

Required disclosures

An applicant must disclose any alias or also-known-as (aka) name. The applicant must also disclose whether he or she

> ▸ is under investigation for any crime or violation
> ▸ has been convicted or entered a plea of nolo contendere, no contest, or guilty for any crime
> ▸ has been denied licensure or registration for a regulated profession
> ▸ has been disciplined or is pending discipline in any jurisdiction
> ▸ has surrendered a license or had a license suspended or revoked
> ▸ has been guilty of any conduct that would be grounds for license suspension or revocation.

APPLICATION REQUIREMENTS

Background checks
Application approval
Application validity period
Nonresident applications
Course requirements
Education exemptions

Background checks

Applicants for a real estate license in Florida must submit to a background check and provide their fingerprints to the DBPR.

Fingerprints. Applicants may use any approved Level 2 FDLE fingerprinting Livescan vendor to submit their fingerprints. When submitting fingerprints, the applicant must also submit the Originating Agency Identification (ORI) number (which can be found on the www.myfloridalicense.com website).

Background check. On receiving the applicant's fingerprints, the Department will forward them to the Florida Department of Law Enforcement and the FBI for use in conducting a criminal history check on the applicant. Both agencies will send their background reports to the DBPR, usually within 3-5 days. To allow for adequate processing time, applicants should submit their fingerprints at least 5 days prior to submitting the license application. The DBPR will use these reports to determine if the applicant is qualified for examination and licensure based on the presence or lack of a criminal history.

Criminal history. If the background report indicates a criminal history, it is best if the applicant has already provided all associated information to the Department along with the application. This is accomplished by answering all application background questions completely and honestly and including documentation that provides details of any investigations, convictions, guilty pleas, or nolo contendere pleas with dates, findings, and penalties.

If the penalties have already been satisfied, the applicant should include documentation proving the satisfaction for each conviction.

Any applicant currently on probation as a result of a conviction should also include an official letter from the probation officer regarding the status of the current probation. The applicant may also want to include at least three character references with the application and other documentation. One reference letter may be from a family member, but all others must be from other people who know the applicant and can attest to his or her character.

Summary of applicants. If an applicant's background check indicates a criminal history, the application is placed on a Summary of Applicants list and submitted to the FREC for review in its monthly meeting. During the review, the FREC will determine if the applicant is approvable for examination and licensure or if the application requires additional consideration and information.

Additional information on digital fingerprinting and the approved vendors can be found on the DBPR's website at www.myfloridalicense.com. An applicant may order a criminal background report on him or herself on the Florida Department of Law Enforcement's website at www.fdle.state.fl.us.

Application approval

The Department must approve or deny a license application within 90 days of receiving it. If the Department fails to meet that deadline, the application is considered approved by default. Applicants who are approved by default are to notify the Department in writing of their intent to rely on the default approval. If the Commission denies the application, it must notify the applicant in writing of the denial and reasons for denial. The notice must inform the applicant of his or her appeal rights.

Application
validity period
    Initial application. The initial license application remains valid for two years after the date it was received by the DBPR.

    Exam eligible. The applicant has two years after completing the prelicense course work to pass the licensure examination. If the applicant fails to pass the examination within those two years, the completed course work becomes invalid.

Course
requirements
    The FREC requires applicants for licensure to complete prelicense real estate educational courses. These can be taken at an accredited college or university, a career center, or registered real estate school.

    A 4-year degree in real estate from an accredited school of higher education, with the coursework covering the same subject matter as required by the FREC, may be substituted for the required prelicense courses.

    A prelicense student may demonstrate FREC-approved minimal competencies that show the student is qualified for licensure as a substitute for taking specific classroom hours.

Education
exemptions
    Persons seeking licensure who are exempt from the requirement to complete prelicense education include the following.

> ▶ An active attorney in good standing with the Florida Bar who is qualified under real estate license law may obtain a real estate sales associate license without completing prelicense education courses. However, attorneys must pass the licensure examination.
>
> ▶ Anyone who has earned a 4-year degree or higher in real estate from a school of higher education may obtain a real estate license without completing prelicense education courses. However, individuals with this degree must pass the licensure examination.
>
> ▶ A nonresident licensed in a state that has a mutual recognition agreement with Florida may obtain a real estate license without completing prelicense education courses. However, these nonresidents must pass a 40-question licensure examination.

SALES ASSOCIATE LICENSE REQUIREMENTS

General license requirements
Prelicense course
State license examination

General license
requirements
    To qualify for a Florida sales associate license, the applicant must

- ▶ have a Social Security number
- ▶ receive approval of the license application
- ▶ pay all required fees
- ▶ meet all general licensure provisions including age, education, character, competency, submission of associated background history and fingerprints.

Prelicense course

Applicants for a sales associate license must complete 63 classroom hours of an FREC-approved prelicense course, referred to as Course I, to be taken at an accredited college, career center, or registered real estate school. The course includes the fundamentals of real estate principles and practices, real estate law and license law, and associated mathematics. The required hours consist of 60 hours of instruction, either in the classroom or by way of distance learning, and three hours allowed for the end-of-course examination.

State license examination

After completing the prelicense coursework and passing the end-of-course examination, an applicant has 2 years to take and pass the state licensure examination. If the applicant waits longer than the 2 years, he or she must retake the prelicense course to be eligible to take the licensure examination.

Failing the examination. An applicant who fails the examination may request a review of the questions answered incorrectly. The request must be made within 21 days of taking the exam and may be performed only for the applicant's most recent exam. The applicant must pay a fee for the review and is given half of the exam administration time for the review. During the review process, the applicant may challenge the incorrect answer to have it reviewed by a subject matter expert.

Whether or not the applicant challenges the results of the failed exam, he or she may pay a fee and retake the exam as many times as necessary within 2 years. There is no waiting period to retake the examination.

License issuance. The license is issued in an inactive status. To activate the license, the sales associate must establish an association with a broker and then either activate his or her own license by printing the DBPR RE 11 Sales Associate or Broker Sales Associate – Become Active form and having the broker sign it or by having the broker add the sales associate to the broker's online account.

The sales associate must be licensed, associated with a broker, and activated prior to performing any real estate services which require a license.

The RE 11 form can be found online at http://www.myfloridalicense.com/dbpr/re/documents/DBPR_RE_11_Change_of_Status_Associates.pdf.

BROKER LICENSE REQUIREMENTS

General license requirements
Experience requirement
Prelicense course
State license examination

General license requirements

Just as with a sales associate license, an applicant for a Florida broker license must meet certain general licensure requirements. To qualify for a broker license, the applicant must

▸ have a Social Security number
▸ submit and receive approval of the DBPR RE-2 license application
▸ pay all required fees
▸ meet all general licensure provisions including age, education, character, competency, submission of all associated background history and fingerprints

An applicant who has been licensed as a sales associate in Florida during the preceding 5 years must complete the sales associate post license education requirements, prior to applying for the broker license. This post license education requirement does not apply to applicants who hold an out-of-state sales associate license.

Experience requirement

In addition to meeting the general licensure requirements, the applicant must have held an active real estate sales associate license for at least 2 years during the 5 years prior to applying for a broker license. The applicant must also have

▸ worked under one or more real estate brokers who are licensed in Florida or any other U.S. state, territory, or jurisdiction or in any foreign national jurisdiction
▸ performed real estate services as a salaried employee of a governmental agency, or
▸ been licensed in any other U.S. state, territory, or jurisdiction or in any foreign national jurisdiction

Applicants who have gained their required experience from a jurisdiction outside of Florida need to submit a current certification of real estate license history from the licensing agency of that jurisdiction. The certificate must not be more than 30 days old and should be attached to the broker license application.

Prelicense course

A licensed sales associate who is applying for a broker license must complete the required prelicense Course II. The course includes 69 classroom hours and 3 end-of-course examination hours. The course covers the fundamentals of real estate appraising, investment, financing, and brokerage and management operations.

**State license
examination**

After successfully completing the broker prelicense coursework and passing the end-of-course exam, the applicant must take and pass the state licensure examination within 2 years of completing the course. If the applicant waits longer than the 2 years, he or she must retake the prelicense course to be eligible to take the licensure examination.

NONRESIDENT LICENSE REQUIREMENTS

Florida resident defined
Nonresident application requirements
Mutual recognition
The Occupational Opportunity Act

**Florida resident
defined**

Florida statutes define a resident as

1) a person who has resided in Florida, continuously for a period of 4 calendar months or more, within the preceding one year; or

2) a person who presently resides in Florida with the intention to reside continuously in Florida for a period of 4 months or more, commencing on the date that the person began the current period of residence in Florida.

**Nonresident
application
requirements**

Nonresident applicants must hold a license in their state of residency. To apply for licensure in Florida, an applicant must submit the appropriate DBPR application form for a sales associate or broker license along with the required fee, fingerprints, and any required supporting documentation, including a certification of license history issued by the state from which the applicant is claiming mutual recognition.

Mutual recognition

Mutual recognition agreements allow Florida to recognize and accept the prelicense education and experience obtained in the other state as a substitute for the requirements in the state where the nonresident is applying for a license.

The nonresident applicant must pass a written examination on general real estate law and codes with emphasis on Chapters 455 and 475 and Chapter 61J2. The Laws and Rules examination contains 40 questions and requires the applicant to correctly answer at least 30 of those questions. Only after passing the examination will the applicant be issued a Florida license. The nonresident licensee is then responsible for completing all post-license and continuing education that is required of a Florida licensee.

Florida licensees may seek licensure in any state that has a mutual recognition agreement with Florida, keeping in mind that each state may have different requirements for nonresident licensure. To apply for a nonresident license, the Florida licensee should contact the other state's real estate commission.

The Occupational Opportunity Act

Although Florida does not have reciprocity agreements with other states, the Occupational Opportunity Act (FL House Bill 615, as amended in Chapter 2017-135) mandates that Florida provide reciprocal licensure for military members, their spouses, their surviving spouses, and low-income individuals. The Act covers all professions regulated by the DBPR, including real estate. The purpose of the Act is to make transfers to Florida easier for military members and spouses who hold licenses in the same profession in another state.

To qualify under the Act, military members must either be currently on active duty or have been honorably discharged. Surviving spouses qualify if the military member was on active duty at the time of death. Proof of the member's active duty must be submitted at the time of application. Applicants must be licensed in good standing in another state and must submit fingerprints for a background check at the time of application.

LICENSE REGISTRATION

Registration

Registration

Every person or entity who is licensed is required to register with the FREC, pay a registration fee, and submit all required information: name and address of the licensee, name and business address of the sales associate licensee's employing broker, license status of the sales associate and his or her employing broker, and whether or not the licensee is an officer, director, or partner of a real estate brokerage. Registrations must be renewed when the license is renewed.

Florida sales associates and broker associates are required to register under the employing broker and can only register under one broker at a time.

Partnerships, limited liability partnerships, limited liability companies, and corporations that act as brokers must register. Partnerships are required to license and register at least one partner as an active broker. Real estate brokerage corporations must license and register their officers and directors. Brokers must also register all branch offices.

If a licensee changes names or trade names, the license must be reissued in the new name and re-registered. Trade names are to be shown on both the license and the registration.

ACTIVITIES REQUIRING LICENSURE; EXEMPTIONS

Individuals required to be licensed
Individuals exempt from licensure

Individuals required to be licensed

Individuals who perform real estate services for compensation or the expectation of compensation must be licensed as real estate sales associates or brokers. As noted earlier, real estate services that require licensure include the sale, exchange, purchase, rental, appraisal, auction, and advertising of real property, business enterprises, and business opportunities, and the offer to perform any of these services. Services include procuring sellers, buyers, lessors, and lessees.

Individuals exempt from licensure

The following individuals are not required to hold a Florida real estate license:

- owners who sell, exchange, or lease their own properties
- corporations, partnerships, trusts, joint ventures, or other entities or officers, partners, or directors of entities that sell, exchange, or lease their own properties, unless an agent, employee, or independent contractor is employed and paid by the entity on a transactional basis to sell, exchange, or lease property; however, partners must be licensed if their percent of sale profits are higher than their individual percent of ownership in the business
- any person acting as an attorney in fact who is authorized to act in another person's place to execute contracts or conveyances
- any attorney at law performing his or her duties without being compensated for performing real estate services
- any certified public accountant performing his or her duties
- any personal representative, receiver, trustee, or general or special magistrate appointed by a will or court order
- any trustee acting under a deed of trust or trust agreement
- any salaried employee of an apartment community who works in an onsite rental office to lease apartments for any time period and who is not paid on a transactional basis
- any apartment community tenant who receives a referral fee of $50 or less for referring a new tenant to the community
- any salaried manager of a condominium or cooperative apartment complex who handles individual unit rentals for periods of 1 year or less, not paid per transaction
- any owner occupant of a timeshare period selling the period
- any licensed or certified appraiser performing appraisal duties
- any person or entity who is paid to rent or advertise for rent transient lodgings, such as hotels or motels

- any dealer registered under the securities and exchange act who sells, buys, exchanges, or rents business enterprises to accredited investors
- any employee of a real estate developer who is paid a salary but not paid on a transactional basis
- any individual who rents lots in mobile home parks or recreational travel parks
- any individual who sells cemetery plots

LICENSE RENEWAL

Issue and expiration. Licenses are issued for 2-year licensure periods, at the end of which the license needs to be renewed to prevent it from expiring. All licenses expire on and must be renewed by either March 31 or September 30, depending on when they are issued. Consequently, the initial licensure period will be no less than 18 months and no greater than 24 months depending on when the license was initially received. To calculate when the initial license expires, the licensee would go back to the last expiration date, March 31st or September 30th and add 2 years.

Postlicense education. The licensee must complete the required post-license course prior to renewing his or her initial license. After the initial license period, the licensee must complete continuing education each license period prior to renewing the license.

License renewal and status. The DBPR sends a license renewal notice to the licensee at least 90 days before the license expiration date. The notice is sent to both active and inactive licensees at the last known address or e-mail address.

The licensee then must submit a completed renewal application, renewal fee, and proof of completing either the post-license or the continuing education courses. The licensee is to indicate whether he or she wants to renew in active or inactive status. Once the licensee has met all renewal requirements, the DBPR will issue a renewed license with the appropriate expiration date.

If the licensee does not renew by the expiration date, the license automatically becomes involuntarily inactive and may only be renewed when applicable requirements are met. The license is deemed delinquent for the following license period. The licensee is not allowed to practice real estate while on inactive status. If the licensee was on active status at the license expiration date, he or she may renew the license within 24 months by meeting renewal requirements and paying a late fee. If the licensee fails to renew within that time period, the license is rendered void.

Members of armed forces. Active-duty members of the U.S. armed forces who are in good standing with the FREC are exempt from license renewal requirements. This exemption is extended to 2 years after the member is discharged from active duty. However, if the member is engaged in real estate for profit in the private sector within Florida while on active duty and for 2 years after discharge from active duty, he or she must meet all renewal requirements but is exempt from paying the renewal fee.

The military member's spouse or the surviving spouse of a member who died while on active duty is also exempt from license renewal requirements if the member's active duty is outside of Florida. The spouse must be in good standing with the FREC and not be practicing in the private sector for profit. This exemption is in effect while the member is on active duty and for 6 months after the member's discharge.

LICENSE RENEWAL EDUCATION

Post license requirement
Continuing education
Reactivation education

**Post license
requirement**

Postlicense requirement. All *sales associate* licensees are required to complete a post-licensing course before the first license renewal, even if the license is inactive. The course is 45 classroom hours and includes an end-of-course examination. The course emphasizes development of skills for licensees to operate effectively and to increase public protection. Any sales associate licensee who applies for broker licensure must have completed all sales associate post-license requirements.

All *broker* licensees are required to complete post-license education which includes either one 60-hour course or two 30-hour courses and the related exams. All post-license requirements must be met prior to their first broker license renewal date.

Exam failure. On failing the course exam, a licensee may retake the exam after failing. However, the licensee may retake the exam only one time during the year after failing. A licensee who does not pass the exam within that year must then repeat the post-license course. If the licensee does not complete the post-license course and pass the exam prior to the first license renewal date, his or her license will be deemed null and void.

To re-qualify for licensure, the individual must retake the entire prelicense course, pass that end-of-course exam, and again pass the state licensure exam. However, a broker who does not meet the broker post-license requirements may be issued a sales associate license by completing a 14-hour continuing education course within 6 months of the expiration of the broker license.

Exemption. Licensees who hold a four-year degree in real estate from an accredited institute of higher learning are exempt from post-license education requirements.

Hardship cases. The FREC may allow a six-month extension past the first license renewal date for a licensee to complete post-license requirements if the licensee cannot meet the education completion deadline due to a personal hardship. The FREC administrative code qualifies the following as hardships:

▸ the long-term illness of the licensee or a close relative or person for whom the licensee has care-giving responsibilities

▸ the lack of reasonable availability of the required course

▸ the licensee's economic or technological hardship that substantially interferes with the ability to complete education requirements

▸ the licensee's economic inability to meet reasonable basic living expenses

Continuing education

Course completion. Florida real estate licenses are issued for 2-year periods, requiring renewal every 2 years. During the initial licensing period, licensees are required to complete post-licensing education based on the type of license held. During that same initial period, licensees are not required to complete continuing education, but continuing education is required for every 2-year licensing period thereafter.

During each licensing period, both active and inactive sales associates and brokers are required to complete 14 classroom hours of continuing education that must include at least 3 hours of Core Law education.

Continuing education courses may be taken in the classroom, through distance learning, or by correspondence (if the licensee qualifies for a hardship). The licensee must attend at least 90% of each of the classroom hours to receive the notice of completion. The DBPR may deny license renewal for any licensee who fails to complete continuing education requirements. Failure to provide proof of continuing education or providing false proof are grounds for disciplinary action

Course credits. Because Core Law covers Florida real estate license law, Commission rules, and agency law and provides an introduction to other state laws, federal laws, and taxes affecting real estate, it is advisable for the licensee to take a 3-hour Core Law course every year to stay up to date on the laws and rules.

Any licensee who does take the course each year will be awarded 3 hours of Core Law education and 3 hours of specialty education. Licensees whose licenses expire after September 30, 2018, are also required to take a 3-hour Business Ethics course every license period. Licensees who take the Business Ethics course each year will be awarded 3 hours of Business Ethics education and 3 hours of specialty education. The remaining hours required towards the total 14 hours may be taken in specialty education courses, also known as electives.

One time during each license period, the licensee may be awarded 3 classroom hours for attending an FREC legal agenda session. To receive the credit, the licensee needs to notify the Division of Real Estate of the intent to attend the session. No credit will be awarded if the licensee attends the session as a party to a disciplinary action.

The courses must be completed by either March 31 or September 30 based on the license expiration date. A 6-month extension past the renewal date may be available if the licensee cannot meet the education completion deadline due to a personal hardship.

Exemption. These continuing education requirements do not apply to attorneys in good standing with the Florida Bar.

Reactivation education

A licensee who has been on involuntary inactive status for 12 to 24 months may complete an FREC-prescribed 28-hour education course towards reactivating the license. The course covers material from the sales associate prelicense course. The course may be taken in the classroom, through distance learning, or by correspondence if the licensee qualifies for a hardship. Completion of the course does not entitle the licensee to reactivate the license until he or she has met all other requirements.

The licensee must also pass the end-of-course exam with a score of 70% or higher. Licensees must attend a minimum of 90% of the instruction hours to be eligible to take the exam. Licensees who fail the exam may retake it one time within a year of failure. If the licensee fails the retake exam, he or she must retake the reactivation course and the end-of-course exam.

Licensees who meet the qualifications of a hardship may request a 6-month extension after license expiration by submitting the hardship basis to the FREC.

LICENSE STATUS

Active status. Sales associate or broker licenses are initially issued on inactive status. Since licensees are allowed to practice real estate only if their licenses are on active status, they must activate their licenses before they offer or provide real estate services. Their licenses must also be on active status before the licensee can accept commission or other fees for a real estate service.

A sales associate can activate the license by registering under an employing broker or by having the employing broker activate the license through the broker's online account. Anyone who practices without an active status license is violating license law and may be disciplined. At any time after a license is issued, the licensee may decide to place the active license on inactive status. During the license renewal process, the licensee may choose to renew in either active or inactive status. Again, while on inactive status, the licensee may not practice real estate activities.

Voluntary inactive status. There are multiple ways a license may become voluntarily inactive: the licensee does not activate the license when it is initially issued; the licensee chooses to renew an active license on inactive status; or a licensee requests the DBPR place the license on inactive status. Most often, licensees choose voluntary inactive status because they have decided not to practice real estate for a period of time.

When a license is in voluntary inactive status, the licensee may reactivate the license at any time by applying to the DBPR, paying a reactivation fee, and meeting all post-license or continuing education requirements.

Just as with active licenses, voluntarily inactive licenses must be renewed every 2 years to remain valid. The inactive licensee needs to apply for renewal on inactive status, complete 12 hours of continuing education for each year the license was inactive, and pay the renewal fee.

Involuntary inactive status. If the licensee does not renew the active or voluntarily inactive license by the expiration date, the license status automatically becomes involuntarily inactive. The license is also deemed delinquent.

The DBPR will send a notice of involuntary inactive status at least 90 days prior to the license expiration date. If a broker's license is suspended or revoked, all sales associates and broker associates registered under that broker will automatically become involuntarily inactive. Their licenses will remain in that status until the broker is again reinstated or until they register under a new broker.

If these licensees decide not to practice real estate, they may change their licenses' involuntarily inactive status to voluntarily inactive through their online DBPR account.

Once in involuntarily inactive status for nonrenewal, the license can be renewed if the licensee applies to the DBPR, pays the renewal fee for each year the license was involuntarily inactive plus any associated late fees, and completes the required continuing education based on the time frame of inactive status.

The licensee can renew as either active or voluntarily inactive but must do so within 2 years of becoming involuntarily inactive. If the licensee fails to renew during the 2 years, the license automatically expires and becomes null and void.

Null and void license status. A license may become null and void under any of the following conditions.

▸ The sales associate does not complete post-license education prior to the renewal date for the initial licensure period. To reengage in real estate activities, the individual must requalify for licensure by retaking the prelicensure education and exams and passing the state examination.

▸ A licensee on involuntary inactive status does not renew the license within 2 years of becoming involuntarily inactive. The FREC may reinstate this license if the individual applies to the Commission within 6 months of becoming null and void, shows proof of a physical or financial hardship, completes continuing education, and pays all required fees.

If the licensee receives the hardship extension, the license will remain null and void until the individual submits a reinstatement application, related fees, and proof of reactivation education completion.

▸ A license is revoked for disciplinary reasons. Revoked licenses may never be reinstated, and the individual may never reapply for licensure.

▸ A licensee relinquishes the license unrelated to any disciplinary actions or investigations. The licensee must notify the DBPR of the intent to relinquish the license.

Null and void licenses are those that no longer exist unless they are reactivated under the above allowable conditions.

Reporting address changes. A broker must notify the Commission within 10 days of any business address change. Until the Commission is notified of the address change, the broker's license ceases to be in force. While the license is in that status, the broker may not engage in real estate activities.

The notice of change of address must include the names of any associates who are no longer employed by the broker. The notice will also serve as change of address notification for associates still employed by the broker. These licensees can notify the Commission of the changes on a Commission-provided form or through their online portal.

All licensees must notify the DBPR in writing of their *current residential mailing addresses*. They must notify the Department within 10 days of any changes of residential mailing addresses. Failure to do so can result in a disciplinary fine.

Any Florida resident licensee who becomes a nonresident by moving out of the state is required to notify the Commission within 60 days of the change of residency. If the licensee wishes to continue practicing in Florida, he or she must comply with all nonresident requirements. Failure to notify the Commission and comply with the requirements is a violation of license law and can result in disciplinary penalties.

Multiple licenses. Brokers are required to hold a separate individual license for each entity or business they serve. A broker who serves multiple entities needs multiple licenses. The broker must show that the multiple licenses are necessary to conduct the brokerage business and that the licenses will not be harmful or prejudicial to anyone. Each license must be renewed separately.

The Commission may deny a multiple license for the same reasons it can deny individual licenses. Any discipline against the broker's primary license will apply equally to his or her multiple licenses. Multiple licenses are not transferable to new relationships unless the broker ends all current relationships at the same time and then moves only one license to a new relationship.

Sales associates and broker associates are not eligible for multiple licenses because they are only allowed to work for one broker or brokerage at a time.

Group licenses. Property owner/developers are exempt from licensure. Consequently, they employ licensed sales associates or broker associates to sell their properties. Sometimes, an owner/developer owns properties through multiple business entities with different names. When those entities are connected (for example, subsidiaries) so that they are owned or controlled by one individual or group of individuals, any licensee employed by the owner/developer may obtain a group license to be eligible to sell for all of the entities.

Remember that a sales associate or broker associate may only be employed by one broker or owner/developer at a time. The group license allows the licensee to be employed by the one owner/developer but still sell properties for multiple entities as long as they are all owned or controlled by the employing owner/developer.

2 Florida License Law Review
Snapshot Review

KEY FLORIDA STATUTES AND RULES

- several enacted to protect consumers and to allow qualified individuals to enter real estate profession

GENERAL LICENSURE PROVISIONS

General qualifications
- 18 years old, high school education, good character, competence, Social Security number; US citizenship not necessary

Required disclosures
- disciplinary or criminal history
- aliases

APPLICATION REQUIREMENTS

Background checks
- submit to background check, provide fingerprints; provide information about criminal history

Application approval
- DBPR to approve or deny application within 90 days of receipt; applicant has right to appeal denial

Application validity
- application valid for 2 years; prelicense course valid for 2 years for licensure exam

Education exemptions
- exempt: attorneys; those with 4-year real estate degrees; those with mutual recognition agreement

SALES ASSOCIATE LICENSE REQUIREMENTS

General requirements
- SS number, application approval, fees paid, meet age, education, character, competency, background requirements

Prelicense course
- 60-hour course, 3-hour exam with 70% pass score

State license examination
- within 2 years of course completion; pass with 75% score; print and activate license
- retake failed exam unlimited times; may review incorrect answers
- license issued in inactive status; licensee must associate with broker before performing services

BROKER LICENSE REQUIREMENTS

General requirements
- SS number, application approval, fees paid, meet age, education, character, competency, background requirements; complete sales associate post license education

Experience requirement
- active sales associate license for 2 years within past 5 years; worked under broker

State license examination

- within 2 years of course completion; pass with 75% score; print and activate license
- retake failed exam unlimited times; may review incorrect answers
- issued as inactive; activate by filing form

NONRESIDENT LICENSE REQUIREMENTS

Florida resident defined

- reside in FL for 4 months or intend to continue to reside for 4 months

Nonresident application requirements

- hold license in resident state; submit certificate of license history; meet FL application requirements

Mutual recognition

- agreement of FL and another state to recognize other state's prelicense education and require laws and rules exam

Occupational Opportunity Act

- reciprocal license for military, spouses, surviving spouses, low income licensed in another state; prelicense course and exam waived

LICENSE REGISTRATION

- all licensees to register with FREC; sales & broker associates to register under broker

LICENSE RENEWAL EDUCATION

Post licensure requirement

- sales associates – 45-hour course and end-of-course exam with 75% pass score
- brokers – 60-hour course and end-of-course exam with 75% pass score

Continuing education

- 14 hours every 2-year license period to include 3 hours of Core Law & 3 hours of Business Ethics

Reactivation education

- involuntary inactive status for 12-24 months can reactivate with 28-hour course and exam with 70% pass score

ACTIVITIES REQUIRING LICENSURE; EXEMPTIONS

Individuals required to be licensed

- anyone who performs real estate services for compensation

Individuals exempt from licensure

- owners selling own property; attorney in fact or at law; CPA, trustee; certain paid employees; timeshare owner occupant; transient lodging employee, cemetery sales

LICENSE RENEWAL

- renew for 2-year periods; initial period 18-24 months; renew March 31 or September 30; complete post-license or continuing education; involuntary inactive status for nonrenewal
- renewal provisions or fees waived for military members and spouses of out-of-state members or deceased members

LICENSE RENEWAL EDUCATION

- Postlicense: sales associates – 45-hour course and end-of-course exam with 75% pass score
- Postlicense: brokers – 60-hour course and end-of-course exam with 75% pass score

- Continuing education: 14 hours every 2-year license period to include 3 hours of Core Law & 3 hours of Business Ethics

- License reactivation: involuntary inactive status for 12-24 months can reactivate with 28-hour course and exam with 70% pass score

LICENSE STATUS

- active required for practicing
- voluntary inactive when initial license not activated, when licensee chooses status at renewal, when licensee requests; reactivate by applying, paying fee, completing CE; renew every 2 years
- involuntary inactive for nonrenewal; reactivate by applying, paying fee, completing CE, all within 2 years of involuntary inactive status
- null and void for not completing post-license course, for not renewing involuntary inactive license within 2 years, for revoked license, for voluntary license relinquish
- ceases to be in force when business address changes; must report within 10 days
- licensee to notify DBPR of current mailing address or change of address within 10 days
- FL resident licensee becoming nonresident to notify FREC within 60 days

MULTIPLE AND GROUP LICENSES

- multiple - brokers who serve multiple business entities need a license for each entity; sales associates and broker associates not eligible for multiple licenses
- group - for sales associates or broker associates working for owner/developer who owns properties through multiple business entities that are connected and controlled by owner

SECTION TWO QUIZ: Florida License Law Review

1. Which of the following is a general requirement to obtain real estate licensure in Florida?

   a. Must be at least 21 years old
   b. Must disclose any criminal history
   c. Must be a U.S. citizen
   d. Must have a 4-year college degree

2. Which of the following statements is true?

   a. An applicant with an expunged criminal conviction does not need to disclose that conviction.
   b. An applicant who is currently on probation for a criminal conviction will not be placed on the Summary of Applicants list.
   c. An applicant's fingerprints are sent to the FBI for a criminal background check.
   d. If an applicant has a criminal history, he or she will automatically be denied licensure.

3. An applicant must be approved or denied within _____ days of application receipt.

   a. 90
   b. 60
   c. 45
   d. 30

4. Attorneys in good standing with the Florida Bar

   a. must complete prelicense education and pass the state exam.
   b. must complete prelicense education but are exempt from the state exam.
   c. are exempt from prelicense education but must take the state exam.
   d. must complete prelicense education and pass the end-of-course exam.

5. Sales associate applicants must

   a. complete 72 hours of prelicense education.
   b. pass the end-of-course exam with a score of 70% or higher.
   c. pass the state license exam with a score of 75% or higher.
   d. pass the state license exam on the first attempt.

6. Which of the following statements is false?

   a. Applicants who fail the state license exam may retake it only once within a year of failing it.
   b. Applicants who fail the state license exam may retake it as many times as necessary to pass it within 2 years of failing it.
   c. Applicants who pass the state license exam are issued a license in inactive status.
   d. Sales associate applicants who pass the state exam must become associated with a specific broker.

7. Which of the following is a requirement for a broker license but not a requirement for a sales associate license?

   a. Prelicense coursework
   b. Post-license coursework
   c. 4-year college degree
   d. 2-year experience requirement

8. A Florida resident is someone who

   a. plans to move to Florida within the next year.
   b. was born in Florida regardless of where the person now resides.
   c. has resided in Florida continuously for 4 or more months within the previous year.
   d. owns property in Florida whether or not the person lives on the property.

9. Florida provides reciprocity licensure for

   a. nonresidents from states with whom Florida has a reciprocity agreement.
   b. active duty military personnel who are licensed in another state.
   c. any low-income individuals from another state.
   d. non U.S. citizens.

10. Who must register with the FREC?

   a. Corporations who wish to become licensed
   b. Only sales associates
   c. Only brokers
   d. Every licensed person or entity

11. Brokers must complete _____ hours of post-license education.

   a. 60
   b. 45
   c. 30
   d. 0

12. When must post-license education be completed?

   a. During each license period after the initial renewal
   b. During the first license period prior to license expiration
   c. Prior to the license expiration date of every license period
   d. Within 1 year of initial licensure

13. If a licensee completes 3 hours of Core Law education each year during a license period, how many additional continuing education hours must be completed for that period?

   a. 14 hours
   b. 11 hours
   c. 8 hours
   d. 6 hours

14. Which of the following is NOT a requirement of reactivating an involuntary inactive license?

    a. Completing a 28-hour education course
    b. Passing an end-of-course exam with a 70% score
    c. Having a hardship
    d. Attending at least 90% of the instructional hours

15. The DBPR is governed by

    a. F.S. Title IV, Section 20.
    b. F.S. Chapter 455.
    c. F.S. Chapter 120.
    d. F.S. Chapter 475.

16. All licenses expire

    a. on April 30 or October 31.
    b. on March 31 or September 30.
    c. 2 years after the date of license issuance.
    d. on January 1 every 2 years.

17. Sally's first sales associate license was issued on March 15, 2029. When will her license expire?

    a. September 30, 2031
    b. March 15, 2031
    c. September 30, 2030
    d. March 31, 2031

18. Sally's first sales associate license was issued on March 15, 2029. What happens if Sally does not complete her post-license education before her license expiration date?

    a. Sally has 2 additional years to complete the education and renew her license.
    b. She will be charged a late renewal fee.
    c. Her license will become involuntarily inactive until she completes the post-license education.
    d. Sally's license will become null and void.

19. Sally is a member of the U.S. Navy. What must she do to renew her real estate license?

    a. Complete continuing education and apply for renewal
    b. Apply for renewal and pay the renewal fee
    c. Complete continuing education, apply for renewal, and pay the renewal fee
    d. Sally is exempt from renewal requirements.

20. If a licensee does not renew an active license by the expiration date, what happens?

    a. The license becomes voluntarily inactive.
    b. The license becomes null and void.
    c. The license becomes involuntarily inactive.
    d. Nothing, the licensee is automatically given 2 years to renew the license.

21. If a licensee changes employing brokers, he or she must notify the FREC of the change

    a. immediately.
    b. within 30 days of the change.
    c. within 10 days after the change.
    d. There is no need to notify the FREC of an employing broker change.

3 Florida Brokerage Relationships Review

Fiduciary Duties
Brokerage Relationship Disclosure Act

FIDUCIARY DUTIES

Fiduciary duties to the client
Agent's duties to the customer
Principal's general duties

The agency relationship imposes fiduciary duties on the client and agent, but particularly on the agent. An agent must also observe certain standards of conduct in dealing with customers and other outside parties.

Fiduciary duties to the client

Skill, care, and diligence. The agent is hired to do a job, and is therefore expected to do it with diligence and reasonable competence. Competence is generally defined as a level of real estate marketing skills and knowledge comparable to those of other practitioners in the area.

The notion of care extends to observing the limited scope of authority granted to the agent. A conventional listing agreement does not authorize an agent to obligate the client to contracts, and it does not allow the agent to conceal offers to buy, sell, or lease coming from a customer or another agent. Further, since a client relies on a broker's representations, a broker must exercise care not to offer advice outside of his or her field of expertise. Violations of this standard may expose the agent to liability for the unlicensed practice of a profession such as law, engineering, or accounting.

Fiduciary Duties

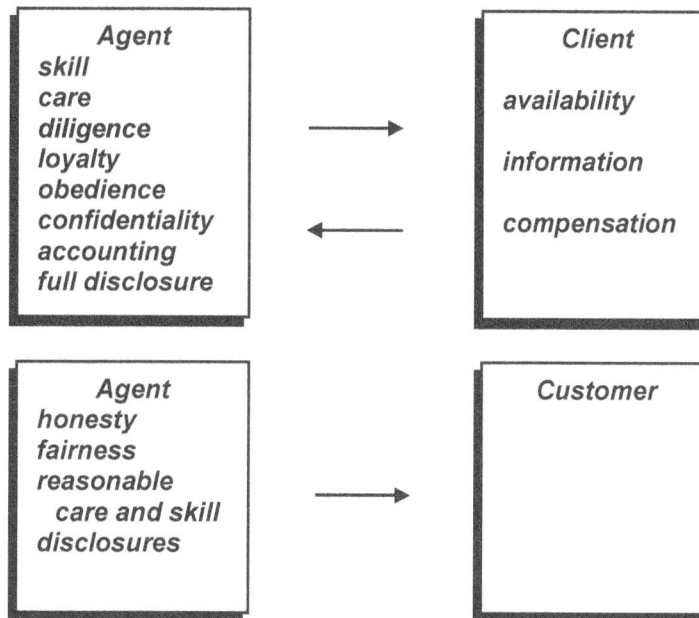

Agent	Client
skill care diligence loyalty obedience confidentiality accounting full disclosure	availability information compensation

→
←

Agent	Customer
honesty fairness reasonable care and skill disclosures	

→

Loyalty. The duty of loyalty requires the agent to place the interests of the client above those of all others, particularly the agent's own. This standard is particularly relevant whenever an agent discusses transaction terms with a prospect.

Obedience. An agent must comply with the client's directions and instructions, *provided they are legal*. An agent who cannot obey a legal directive, for whatever reason, must withdraw from the relationship. If the directive is illegal, the agent must also immediately withdraw.

Confidentiality. An agent must hold in confidence any personal or business information received from the client during the term of employment. An agent may not disclose any information that would harm the client's interests or bargaining position, or anything else the client wishes to keep secret.

The confidentiality standard is one of the duties that extends *beyond the termination of the listing*: at *no time* in the future may the agent disclose confidential information.

An agent must exercise care in fulfilling this duty: if confidentiality conflicts with the agent's legal requirements to disclose material facts, the agent must inform the client of this obligation and make the required disclosures. If such a conflict cannot be resolved, the agent must withdraw from the relationship.

Accounting. An agent must safeguard and account for all monies, documents, and other property received from a client or customer. Florida license law regulates the broker's accounting obligations and escrow practices.

Full disclosure. An agent has the duty to inform the client of all material facts, reports, and rumors that might affect the client's interests in the property transaction.

In recent years, the disclosure standard has been raised to require an agent to disclose items that a practicing agent *should know,* whether the agent actually had the knowledge or not, and regardless of whether the disclosure furthers or impedes the progress of the transaction.

The most obvious example of a "should have known" disclosure is a property defect, such as an inoperative central air conditioner, that the agent failed to notice. If the air conditioner becomes a problem, the agent may be held liable for failing to disclose a material fact if a court rules that the typical agent in that area would detect and recognize a faulty air conditioner.

There is no obligation to obtain or disclose information related to a customer's race, creed, color, religion, sex or national origin: anti-discrimination laws hold such information to be immaterial to the transaction.

Florida law requires a seller to make a written disclosure about property condition to a prospective buyer.

Disclosure of Material Facts

Critical material facts for disclosure include:

- the agent's opinion of the property's condition

- information about the buyer's motivations and financial qualifications

- discussions between agent and buyer regarding the possibility of the agent's representing the buyer in another transaction.

- adverse material facts, including property condition, title defects, environmental hazards, and property defects

Agent's duties to the customer

The traditional notion of *caveat emptor*-- let the buyer beware-- no longer applies unequivocally to real estate transactions. Agents *do* have certain obligations to customers, even though they do not represent them. In general, they owe a third party:

- ▶ honesty and fair dealing
- ▶ reasonable care and skill
- ▶ proper disclosure

An agent has a duty to deal fairly and honestly with a customer. Thus, an agent may not deceive, defraud, or otherwise take advantage of a customer.

"Reasonable care and skill" means that an agent will be held to the standards of knowledge, expertise, and ethics that are commonly maintained by other agents in the area.

Proper disclosure primarily concerns disclosure of agency, property condition, and environmental hazards.

An agent who fails to live up to prevailing standards may be held liable for negligence, fraud, or violation of state real estate license laws and regulations. Agents should be particularly careful about misrepresenting and offering inappropriate expert advice when working with customers.

Intentional misrepresentation. An agent may intentionally or unintentionally defraud a buyer by misrepresenting or concealing facts. While it is acceptable to promote the features of a property to a buyer or the virtues of a buyer to a seller, it is a fine line that divides promotion from misrepresentation. Silent misrepresentation, which is intentionally failing to reveal a material fact, is just as fraudulent as a false statement.

Negligent misrepresentation. An agent can be held liable for failure to disclose facts the agent was not aware of if it can be demonstrated that the agent *should have known* such facts. For example, if it is a common standard that agents inspect property, then an agent can be held liable for failing to disclose a leaky roof that was not inspected.

Misrepresentation of expertise. An agent should not act or speak outside the agent's area of expertise. A customer may rely on anything an agent says, and the agent will be held accountable. For example, an agent represents that a property will appreciate. The buyer interprets this as expert investment advice and buys the property. If the property does not appreciate, the buyer may hold the agent liable.

Principal's general duties

The obligations of a principal in an agency relationship concern the following:

Availability. In a special agency, the power and decision-making authority of the agent are limited. Therefore, the principal must be available for consultation, direction, and decision-making. Otherwise the agent cannot complete the job.

Information. The principal must provide the agent with a sufficient amount of information to complete the desired activity. This may include property data, financial data, and the client's timing requirements.

Compensation. If an agreement includes a provision for compensating the agent and the agent performs in accordance with the agreement, the client is obligated to compensate the agent. As indicated earlier, however, the agency relationship does not necessarily include compensation.

BROKERAGE RELATIONSHIP DISCLOSURE ACT

Residential transactions
Disclosure notices
Nonrepresentation relationships
Single agency relationships
Transaction broker relationships
Transitioning to transaction broker
Designated sales associate
Documentation

Residential transactions

Under the Brokerage Relationship Disclosure Act, all real estate transactions impose certain duties and obligations on licensees. Written disclosures, however, are required only when a brokerage is acting as a single agent or in a no-brokerage relationship in a residential sale transaction.

Residential sale transactions are those involving

- improved residential properties with four or fewer dwelling units
- unimproved residential properties zoned for four or fewer residential units
- agricultural properties of ten acres or less

The requirement for agency disclosures to be written thus excludes

- non-residential transactions
- rental or leasing transactions and sales of business opportunities unless they include an option to purchase a property with four or fewer residential units
- auctions
- appraisals

No written disclosure is needed when the brokerage is acting as a transaction broker, as this relationship is the default presumed under Florida law.

Disclosure notices

Under Florida's Brokerage Relationship Disclosure Act, licensees may establish a relationship with a buyer or seller as either a transaction broker or as a single agent. The licensee may also assist a buyer or seller with no brokerage relationship, known as nonrepresentation. The relationship established must be disclosed in writing to the involved parties. The licensee may transition from one type of relationship to the other type with the consent of the buyer and/or seller and with the disclosure of the duties owed to the client or customer under the new relationship.

The customer is not required to enter into any brokerage relationship with a licensee.

Nonrepresentation relationships

A licensee may enter into a listing agreement with a seller and be paid a commission or other compensation while having no brokerage relationship with buyer or seller. In this situation, the licensee owes no loyalty or other fiduciary duties to either party but still owes certain duties to the party or parties as customers. Those duties must be disclosed in writing before the licensee shows a property. F.S. Chapter 475.278(4)(c) mandates the following form and language for the disclosure:

NO BROKERAGE RELATIONSHIP NOTICE

FLORIDA LAW REQUIRES THAT REAL ESTATE LICENSEES WHO HAVE NO BROKERAGE RELATIONSHIP WITH A POTENTIAL SELLER OR BUYER DISCLOSE THEIR DUTIES TO SELLERS AND BUYERS.

As a real estate licensee who has no brokerage relationship with you, (insert name of Real Estate Entity and its Associates) owe to you the following duties:

1. *Dealing honestly and fairly.*
2. *Disclosing all known facts that materially affect the value of the residential property that are not readily observable to the buyer.*
3. *Accounting for all funds entrusted to the licensee.*

A buyer or seller who is looking for additional duties and a different level of assistance needs to enter into an agency relationship with the broker.

Single agency relationships

The agent represents one party in a transaction. The client may be either seller or buyer.

Seller agency. In the traditional situation, a seller or landlord is the agent's client. A buyer or tenant is the customer.

Buyer agency. Recently, it has become common for an agent to represent a buyer or tenant. In this relationship, the property buyer or tenant is the client and the property owner is the customer.

Dual agency. An agency relationship is established with a brokerage firm and not with any one agent within the firm. Therefore, a dual agency would exist if one agent within the firm represented the seller while another agent in the same firm represented the buyer. *Dual agency as a form of representation is prohibited in Florida whether it is disclosed or not disclosed.*

Subagency. In subagency, a broker associate or sales associate works as the agent of a broker who is the agent of a buyer or seller. In effect, the associate, as agent of the broker, is the subagent of the client. The subagent owes the same duties to the broker's client as the broker does.

The disclosure required for single agency is as follows. The disclosure must be made at the time of, entering into a listing agreement or an agreement for representation or before showing the property, whichever occurs first.

SINGLE AGENT NOTICE

FLORIDA LAW REQUIRES THAT REAL ESTATE LICENSEES OPERATING AS SINGLE AGENTS DISCLOSE TO BUYERS AND SELLERS THEIR DUTIES.

1. *As a single agent, (insert name of Real Estate Entity and its Associates) owe to you the following duties:*
2. *Dealing honestly and fairly;*
3. *Loyalty;*
4. *Confidentiality;*
5. *Obedience;*
6. *Full disclosure;*
7. *Accounting for all funds;*
8. *Skill, care, and diligence in the transaction;*
9. *Presenting all offers and counteroffers in a timely manner, unless a party has previously directed the licensee otherwise in writing; and*
10. *Disclosing all known facts that materially affect the value of residential real property and are not readily observable.*

Transaction broker relationships

Florida prohibits both parties to a transaction from being represented by the same brokerage in a dual agency relationship. Instead, the transaction broker relationship was created to allow a single brokerage to provide limited representation and duties to both the seller and the buyer in the same transaction. Limited representation means neither party is responsible for the licensee's actions.

In a transaction broker relationship, the broker does not represent either party in a fiduciary capacity or as a single agent. Neither party has the right of the licensee's undivided loyalty. Further, because the broker is not representing either one of the parties as a client, then all parties to the transaction are considered customers.

The transaction broker relationship is between the brokerage and the client. Consequently, one licensee within the brokerage may represent both the seller and the buyer, or one licensee may represent the seller while another licensee within the same brokerage represents the buyer. All licensees in the firm are providing the same limited representation to both parties. Neither the seller nor the buyer may be represented to the detriment of the other party.

Florida law makes the presumption that all licensees are operating as transaction brokers unless the broker and the customer have entered into a written single agent or nonrepresentation agreement. Consequently, transaction brokers are not required to provide customers with a transaction broker relationship notice or disclosure.

Duties of a transaction broker. As with any Florida agency relationship, the broker must disclose the duties owed to both parties.

- dealing honestly and fairly
- accounting for all funds
- using skill, care, and diligence in the transaction
- disclosing all known material facts that are not readily observable and that affect the property's value
- presenting all offers and counteroffers in a timely manner unless directed otherwise
- providing limited confidentiality unless either party waives in writing
- performing any additional duties agreed upon by both parties

The duty of limited confidentiality prevents the broker or licensee from disclosing any of the following information:

- the seller will accept a price less than the asking or listed price
- the buyer will pay a price greater than the price submitted in a written offer
- the motivation of any party for selling or buying property
- a seller or buyer will agree to financing terms other than those offered
- any other information requested by a party to remain confidential

Duties not imposed on the transaction broker. Since there are no fiduciary duties binding the transaction broker, the broker is held to standards for dealing with customers as opposed to clients. These include honesty, fair dealing, and reasonable care. The transaction broker is under no obligation to inspect the property for the benefit of a party or verify the accuracy of statements made by a party.

Transitioning to transaction broker

A single agency relationship may transition to a transaction broker relationship at any time the agent and principal wish to do so. With the transition, the licensee will now be providing limited representation and can assist both the buyer and the seller with no dedicated loyalty. The licensee must not represent one party to the detriment of the other party.

Consent. The licensee must obtain the principal's written consent to the single agency before or at the time of entering into a listing agreement, entering into an agreement for representation, or showing a property, whichever occurs first. Consent **to change the relationship from single agent to transaction representation must be obtained before the change occurs.**

CONSENT TO TRANSITION TO TRANSACTION BROKER

FLORIDA LAW ALLOWS REAL ESTATE LICENSEES WHO REPRESENT A BUYER OR SELLER AS A SINGLE AGENT TO CHANGE FROM A SINGLE AGENT RELATIONSHIP TO A TRANSACTION BROKERAGE RELATIONSHIP IN ORDER FOR THE LICENSEE TO ASSIST BOTH PARTIES IN A REAL ESTATE TRANSACTION BY PROVIDING A LIMITED FORM OF REPRESENTATION TO BOTH THE BUYER AND THE SELLER. THIS CHANGE IN RELATIONSHIP CANNOT OCCUR WITHOUT YOUR PRIOR WRITTEN CONSENT.

As a transaction broker, (insert name of Real Estate Firm and its Associates), provides to you a limited form of representation that includes the following duties:

1. *Dealing honestly and fairly;*
2. *Accounting for all funds;*
3. *Using skill, care, and diligence in the transaction;*
4. *Disclosing all known facts that materially affect the value of residential real property and are not readily observable to the buyer;*
5. *Presenting all offers and counteroffers in a timely manner, unless a party has previously directed the licensee otherwise in writing;*
6. *Limited confidentiality, unless waived in writing by a party. This limited confidentiality will prevent disclosure that the seller will accept a price less than the asking or listed price, that the buyer will pay a price greater than the price submitted in a written offer, of the motivation of any party for selling or buying property, that a seller or buyer will agree to financing terms other than those offered, or of any other information requested by a party to remain confidential; and*
7. *Any additional duties that are entered into by this or by separate written agreement.*

Limited representation means that a buyer or seller is not responsible for the acts of the licensee. Additionally, parties are giving up their rights to the undivided loyalty of the licensee. This aspect of limited representation allows a licensee to facilitate a real estate transaction by assisting both the buyer and the seller, but a licensee will not work to represent one party to the detriment of the other party when acting as a transaction broker to both parties.

I agree that my agent may assume the role and duties of a transaction broker. [must be initialed or signed]

_____

Designated sales associate

Non-residential transaction limitations. When a broker is dealing with a non-residential transaction where the buyer and seller have assets of $1 million or more, the customers may request that the broker designate sales associates to act as single agents for each customer in the same transaction. In other words, the broker may designate one sales associate to the buyer and another sales associate to the seller. Each of these sales associates has the same duties to the customer as a single agent does, including disclosures.

Disclosure requirements. While brokers who deal in residential sale transactions must comply with mandated disclosure requirements, those who deal in non-residential transactions do not have the same mandated disclosure requirements. The broker does not have to disclose duties to the customers, but the designated sales associates must disclose their single agent duties.

Additionally, the buyer and the seller must each sign disclosures stating that their assets meet the $1 million requirement and that they are requesting designated sales associates. The disclosure must include the following language:

FLORIDA LAW PROHIBITS A DESIGNATED SALES ASSOCIATE FROM DISCLOSING, EXCEPT TO THE BROKER OR PERSONS SPECIFIED BY THE BROKER, INFORMATION MADE CONFIDENTIAL BY REQUEST OR AT THE INSTRUCTION OF THE CUSTOMER THE DESIGNATED SALES ASSOCIATE IS REPRESENTING. HOWEVER, FLORIDA LAW ALLOWS A DESIGNATED SALES ASSOCIATE TO DISCLOSE INFORMATION ALLOWED TO BE DISCLOSED OR REQUIRED TO BE DISCLOSED BY LAW AND ALSO ALLOWS A DESIGNATED SALES ASSOCIATE TO DISCLOSE TO HIS OR HER BROKER, OR PERSONS SPECIFIED BY THE BROKER, CONFIDENTIAL INFORMATION OF A CUSTOMER FOR THE PURPOSE OF SEEKING ADVICE OR ASSISTANCE FOR THE BENEFIT OF THE CUSTOMER IN REGARD TO A TRANSACTION. FLORIDA LAW REQUIRES THAT THE BROKER MUST HOLD THIS INFORMATION CONFIDENTIAL AND MAY NOT USE SUCH INFORMATION TO THE DETRIMENT OF THE OTHER PARTY.

Designated single agent duties. As a designated single agent, the sales associate has the following duties to buyers and sellers:

1. dealing honestly and fairly
2. loyalty
3. confidentiality
4. obedience
5. full disclosure
6. accounting for all funds
7. skill, care, and diligence in the transaction
8. presenting all offers and counteroffers in a timely manner, unless a party has previously directed the licensee otherwise in writing
9. disclosing all known facts that materially affect the value of residential real property and are not readily observable

Documentation

Brokers are required to keep their business records for at least 5 years from the date of agreement execution. Disclosure documents related to transactions that resulted in a written contract to sell or purchase must be retained for 5 years.

Any document that has been the subject of or served as evidence in any civil action or appellate proceeding must be retained for at least 2 years after the conclusion of the action or proceeding, but no less than the required 5 years.

Even records related to transactions that did not close should be retained for 5 years.

3 Florida Brokerage Relationships Review
Snapshot Review

FIDUCIARY DUTIES

Fiduciary duties to the client
- skill, care, diligence; loyalty; obedience; confidentiality; disclosure; accounting

Agent's duties to the customer
- honesty and fair dealing; exercise of reasonable care and skill; proper disclosures; danger areas: misrepresentation; advising beyond expertise

Principal's general duties
- availability; provide information; compensation

Breach of duty
- liabilities: loss of listing, compensation, license; suit for damages

BROKERAGE RELATIONSHIP DISCLOSURE ACT

Transaction types
- written disclosure required for single agent or no-brokerage relationship in residential sale transaction
- residential sale: property with four or fewer dwelling units or zoned for four or fewer dwelling units

Disclosure notices
- duties, not representation choices
- separate forms for each representation type
- FL Brokerage Relationship Disclosure Act allows transaction broker, single agent, and nonrepresentation
- must disclose duties of each relationship

Nonrepresentation relationships
- no brokerage relationship with buyer or seller; still owe some duties

Single agency relationships
- seller agency; buyer agency; no dual agency in Florida
- broker's associates are agents of the broker, subagents of the broker's client; owe same duties to client as broker

Transaction broker relationships
- allows broker to represent both buyer and seller in same transaction; no fiduciary duties but limited duties still owed and must be disclosed
- relationship presumed unless another agency agreement is signed
- limited confidentiality – no disclosure that seller will lower price, buyer will raise offer, either will agree to other financing terms, either party's motivation, other information requested to remain confidential

Transitioning to transaction broker
- can transition from single agent to transaction broker with principal's written consent at any time
- disclosure requirements apply to residential and agricultural properties with exemptions
- disclosure provided prior to agreement execution or property showing; to meet type requirements and include signature line and duties

Designated sales associate
- nonresidential buyer and seller need assets in excess of $1 million; broker to designate separate sales associates to each as single agent

- standard disclosure requirements apply plus written assets disclosure and request for designated sales associates to follow required language
- must offer standard single agent duties

Documentation
- all records to be kept for 5 years, including disclosures related to written contracts; records related to legal proceedings to be kept for 2 years within the 5 or in addition to the 5 years

SECTION THREE QUIZ: Florida Brokerage Relationships Review

1. In an agency relationship, the principal is required to

   a. promote the agent's best interests.
   b. accept the advice of the agent.
   c. provide sufficient information for the agent to complete the agent's tasks.
   d. maintain confidentiality.

2. A principal discloses that she would sell a property for $375,000. During the listing period, the house is marketed for $425,000. No offers come in, and the listing expires. Two weeks later, the agent grumbles to a customer that the seller would have sold for less than the listed price. Which of the following is true?

   a. The agent has violated the duty of confidentiality.
   b. The agent has fulfilled all fiduciary duties, including confidentiality, since the listing had expired.
   c. The agent is violating the duties owed this customer.
   d. The agent has created a dual agency situation with the customer.

3. A principal instructs an agent to market a property only to families on the north side of town. The agent refuses to comply. In this case,

   a. the agent has violated fiduciary duty.
   b. the agent has not violated fiduciary duty.
   c. the agent is liable for breaching the listing terms.
   d. the agent should obey the instruction to salvage the listing.

4. An owner's agent is showing a buyer an apartment building. The buyer notices water stains on the ceiling, and informs the agent. The agent's best course of action is to

   a. immediately contract to paint the ceiling.
   b. immediately contract to repair the roof.
   c. suggest the buyer make a lower-price offer.
   d. inform the seller.

5. An agent owes customers several duties. These may be best described as

   a. fairness, care, and honesty.
   b. obedience, confidentiality, and accounting.
   c. diligence, care, and loyalty.
   d. honesty, diligence, and skill.

6. An agent fails to discover flood marks on the walls in the basement of a property. The agent sells the property, and the buyer later sues the agent for failing to mention the problem. In this case, the agent

   a. may be guilty of intentional misrepresentation.
   b. has an exposure to a charge of negligent misrepresentation.
   c. has little exposure, since the problem was not mentioned on the signed disclosure form.
   d. is not vulnerable, since the problem was not discovered.

7. An agent informs a buyer that a clause in a contract is standard language. After explaining the clause, the agent assures the buyer that the clause does not mean anything significant. If something goes wrong with the transaction, the agent could be liable for

   a. violating duties owed a customer.
   b. misinterpreting the clause.
   c. intentional misrepresentation.
   d. practicing law without a license.

8. Agent Bob, who works for Broker Bill, obtains an owner listing to lease a building. Bill's other agent, Sue, locates a tenant for Bob's listing. This situation is illegal in Florida unless

   a. Bob and Sue are implied agents.
   b. Bob and Sue are acting as transaction brokers.
   c. Bob and Sue are single agents.
   d. Sue is Bob's subagent.

9. A licensee acting as a transaction broker

   a. may not represent any party's interests to the detriment of the other party in the transaction.
   b. may not disclose material facts to any party in the transaction.
   c. must be obedient and loyal to both parties.
   d. must require that the principals share equally in paying the commission.

10. When may a licensee acting as a single agent transition to a transaction brokerage relationship with a principal?

   a. Only before an offer has been presented
   b. Only at the time of signing a listing agreement
   c. Whenever the licensee and principal agree to do so
   d. At no time; a single agent may not become a transaction broker..

11. What is a designated sales associate?

   a. A sales associate designated by a broker to represent one party in a transaction while another associate of the broker is designated to represent the other party
   b. A sales associate designated by a broker to manage a branch office for the broker.
   c. A sales associate who is a signatory on a broker's escrow account.
   d. An unlicensed person designated by a broker to perform a specific licensed task on a temporary basis.

12. For how long must a broker retain documents and records relating to a transaction?

   a. One year
   b. Three years
   c. Five years
   d. Permanently

13. A single agency disclosure must be made

   a. immediately prior to initial contact with a principal.
   b. at the time of signing a listing or representation agreement or before showing a property.
   c. immediately prior to substantive contact with any party.
   d. immediately following any offer executed by a buyer.

14. A licensee has a nonrepresentation relationship with a transaction principal. What fiduciary duties does the licensee owe to that person?

    a. None
    b. Confidentiality only
    c. Loyalty and confidentiality.
    d. Skill and care

15. Which type of brokerage relationship is illegal in Florida?

    a. Single agency
    b. Transaction broker
    c. Dual agency
    d. Nonrepresentation

16. Which duty is required in a nonrepresentation relationship?

    a. Disclosing facts that materially affect the property's value
    b. Using skill, care, and diligence in the transaction
    c. Limited confidentiality unless waived in writing
    d. Presenting all offers and counteroffers in a timely manner

17. Designated sales associates are used when

    a. the brokerage wants to represent both the residential buyer and the residential seller.
    b. the nonresidential buyer and seller have assets of $1 million or more.
    c. any client requests the designation.
    d. the broker is handling any nonresidential sale.

18. Which of the following statements is true?

    a. Transaction brokers owe fiduciary duties to their clients.
    b. The duty of limited confidentiality prevents the transaction broker from disclosing known material facts.
    c. Transaction brokers have no duty of undivided loyalty.
    d. Transaction brokers and single agents owe the same duties to their clients.

19. Brokerage relationship disclosure records must be retained

    a. until the transaction closes.
    b. for 2 years.
    c. for 5 years.
    d. only if related to a legal proceeding.

4 Property Disclosures and Professional Practices

Property Disclosures
Representing Licensee Expertise
Commission-related Practices
Ethical Practices

PROPERTY DISCLOSURES

Residential property condition
Environmental issues
Warranties
Inspections
Homeowners' associations

Residential property condition

Seller's disclosure form. Many states require sellers to make a written disclosure about property condition to a prospective buyer. This seller disclosure may or may not relieve the agent of some liabilities for disclosure. The residential property condition disclosure is the seller's written summary of the property's condition at the time of contracting for sale. The disclosure is entered on state-approved forms.

Flood disclosure. Sellers are required to disclose certain flood-related information to prospective buyers at or before executing a contract for the sale of residential property.

Owner's role. State legislation requires owners of previously occupied single-family homes and buildings containing 1-4 dwelling units to provide the disclosure to prospective buyers if they are selling, exchanging, or optioning their property. Some exceptions and exemptions apply. When required, the disclosure must be transmitted to the prospective buyer no later than when the buyer makes an offer.

A typical form requires the seller to affirm whether or not problems exist in any of the listed features and systems of the property. In denying that a problem exists, the seller claims to have no knowledge of a defect. If a defect does in fact exist, the seller can be held liable for intentional misrepresentation. A third possible response to a property condition question is that of "no representation." Here, the seller makes no claim of knowledge as to whether a problem exists. With this answer, the seller is no longer held liable for a disclosure of any kind relating to a particular feature, whether a defect is known or otherwise.

Once the seller has signed the form and delivered it to the buyer, the buyer must acknowledge receipt and knowledge of the property condition disclosures, along with other provisions set forth on the form.

Licensee's role. The residential property re-seller must comply with the property condition disclosure requirement whether an agent is employed in the transaction or not. If an agent is involved in the transaction, the agent must disclose any and all material facts he or she knows or should reasonably know about the property, regardless of what the seller may have disclosed on the form.

Right of rescission. Sellers who fail to complete and deliver the property condition disclosure statement to buyers in a timely fashion effectively give the buyer a subsequent right under certain conditions to rescind the sale contract and re-claim their deposits. The buyer must follow certain procedures and meet certain deadlines in order to legitimately effect the cancellation. The buyer's right to cancel persists until closing or occupancy, whichever comes first.

Property condition and material facts. An agent has the duty to inform the client of all material facts, reports, and rumors that might affect the client's interests in the property transaction. A material fact is one that might affect the value or desirability of the property to a buyer if the buyer knew it. Material facts include

- the agent's opinion of the property's condition
- adverse facts about property condition, title defects, environmental hazards, and property defects

In recent years, the disclosure standard has been raised to require an agent to disclose items that a practicing agent *should know,* whether the agent actually had the knowledge or not, and regardless of whether the disclosure furthers or impedes the progress of the transaction.

Facts not considered to be material, and therefore not usually subject to required disclosure, include such items as property stigmatization (e.g., that a crime or death occurred on the property) and the presence of registered sex offenders in the neighborhood (in accordance with Megan's Law, federal legislation that requires convicted offenders to register with the state of residence; in some states, agents must provide registry information to buyers).

The agent may be held liable for failing to disclose a material fact if a court rules that the typical agent in that area would detect and recognize the adverse condition. There is no obligation to obtain or disclose information that is immaterial to the transaction, such as property stigmas.

An agent who sees a "red flag" issue such as a potential structural or mechanical problem should advise the seller to seek expert advice. Red flags can seriously impact the value of the property and/or the cost of remediation. In addition to property condition per se, they may include such things as

- environmental concerns
- property anomalies, such as over-sized or peculiarly shaped lot
- neighborhood issues

> ▸ poor construction
> ▸ signs of flooding
> ▸ poor floorplan
> ▸ adjacent property features

The following exhibit is part of a typical property condition disclosure form showing the level of detail that is expected in a seller's disclosure.

Buyers and seller should be aware that any agreement executed between the parties will supercede this form as to any abligations on the part of the seller to repair items identified below and/or the obligation of the buyer to accept such items "as is".

INSTRUCTIONS TO THE SELLER

Complete this form yourself and answer each question to the best of your knowledge. If an answer is an estimate, clearly label it as such. The Seller hereby authorizes any agent(s) representing any party in this transaction to provide a copy of this statement to any person or entity in connection with any actual or anticipated sale of the subject property.

PROPERTY ADDRESS _____ CITY _____

SELLER'S NAMES(S) _____ PROPERTY AGE _____

DATE SELLER ACQUIRED THE PROPERTY_____ DO YOU OCCUPY THE PROPERTY? _____

IF NOT OWNER–OCCUPIED. HOW LONG HAS IT BEEN SINCE THE SELLER OCCUPIED THE PROPERTY? _____

(Check the one that applies) THIS PROPERTY IS A ☐ SITE BUILT HOME ☐ NONSITE BUILT HOME

☐ Range	☐ Central Air Conditioning	☐ Garage Door Opener(s)
☐ Oven	☐ Wall/Window Air Conditioning	☐ (Number of openers _____)
☐ Microwave	☐ Window Screens	☐ Intercom
☐ Dishwasher	☐ Rain Gutters	☐ TV Antenna/Satellite Dish
☐ Garbage Disposal	☐ Fireplace(s) (Number _____)	☐ Pool
☐ Trash Compactor	☐ Gas Starter for Fireplace	☐ Spa/Whirlpool Tub
☐ Water Softener Alarm	☐ Smoke Detector/Fire	☐ Hot Tub
☐ 220 Volt Wiring	☐ Burglar Alarm	☐ Sauna
☐ Washer/Dryer Hookups	☐ Patio/Decking/Gazebo	☐ Current Termite Contract
☐ Central Heating	☐ Irrigation System	☐ Access to Public Streets
☐ Heat Pump	☐ Sump Pump	☐ Other_____
		☐ Other_____

Garage:	☐ Attached	☐ Not Attached	☐ Carport	
Water Heater:	☐ Gas	☐ Solar	☐ Electric	
Water Supply:	☐ City	☐ Well	☐ Private Utility	Other_____
Waste Disposal:	☐ City Sewer	☐ Septic Tank	☐ Other _____	
Gas Supply:	☐ Utility	☐ Bottled	☐ Other _____	

Roof(s): Type _____ Age(approx) _____

Other Items: _____

To the best of your knowledge, are any of the above NOT in operating condition? ☐ YES ☐ NO

If YES, then describe (Attach additional sheets if necessary);

ARE YOU (SELLER) AWARE OF ANY DEFECTS/AMLFUNCTIONS IN ANY OF THE FOLLOWING?

	YES	NO	UNKNOWN		YES	NO	UNKNOWN
Interior Walls	☐	☐	☐	Central Heating	☐	☐	☐
Ceilings	☐	☐	☐	Central Air Conditioning	☐	☐	☐
Floors	☐	☐	☐	Electrical System	☐	☐	☐
Windows	☐	☐	☐	Exterior Walls	☐	☐	☐
Doors	☐	☐	☐	Roof	☐	☐	☐
Insulation	☐	☐	☐	Basement	☐	☐	☐
Plumbing	☐	☐	☐	Foundation	☐	☐	☐
Sewer/Septic	☐	☐	☐	Slab	☐	☐	☐
Heat Pump	☐	☐	☐	Driveway	☐	☐	☐
				Sidewalks	☐	☐	☐

If any of the above is/are marked YES, Please explain:

_____
_____
_____

This Form Compliments of Kirkland, Rothman-Branning & Associates, PLLC
901-758-558

ww. kr-ba.com
jtk10-02

C. ARE YOU (SELLER) AWARE OF ANY OF THE FOLLOWING?

	YES	NO	UNKNOWN
1. Substances, materials, or products which may be an environmental hazard such as, but not limited to: asbestos, radon gas, lead-based paint, fuel or chemical storage tanks, and/or contaminated water on the subject property	☐	☐	☐
2. Features shared in common with adjoining landowners, such as, but not limited to, walls, fences, and driveways, whose use or responsibility for maintenance may have an effect on the subject property	☐	☐	☐
3. Any authorized changes in roads, drainage, or utilities affecting the property, or contiguous to the property	☐	☐	☐
4. Any changes since the most recent survey of this property was done	☐	☐	☐
Most recent survey of the property: _____ [check here ☐ if unknown]			
5. Any encroachments, easements, or similar items that may affect your ownership interest in the property	☐	☐	☐
6. Room additions, structural modifications, or other alterations or repairs made without necessary permits	☐	☐	☐
7. Room additions, structural modifications, or other alterations or repairs not in compliance with building codes	☐	☐	☐
8. Is heating and air conditioning supplied to all finished rooms?	☐	☐	☐
If the same type of system is not used for all finished rooms, please explain _____			
9. Landfill (compacted or otherwise) on the property or any portion thereof	☐	☐	☐
10. Any settling from any cause, or slippage, sliding, or other soil problems	☐	☐	☐
11. Flooding, drainage, or grading problems	☐	☐	☐
12. Any requirement that flood insurance be maintained on the property	☐	☐	☐
13. Property or structural damage from fire, water, wind, storm, earthquake/tremor, landslide or wood destroying organisms	☐	☐	☐
14. Any zoning violations, nonconforming uses, and/or violations of "setback" requirements	☐	☐	☐
15. Neighborhood noise problems or other nuisances	☐	☐	☐
16. Subdivisions and/or deed restrictions or obligations	☐	☐	☐
17. A Homeowners Association (HOA) which has any authority over the subject property	☐	☐	☐
Name of HOA: _____			
HOA Address: _____			
Monthly Dues: _____ Special Assessments: _____			
18. Any "common area" (facilities such as, but not limited to, pools, tennis courts, walkways, or other areas co-owned in undivided interest with others)	☐	☐	☐
19. Any notices of abatement or citations against the property	☐	☐	☐
20. Any lawsuit(s) or proposed lawsuit(s) by or against the seller which affect or will affect the property	☐	☐	☐
21. Is any system, equipment or part of the property being leased	☐	☐	☐
If yes, please explain, and include a written statement regarding payment information.			
22. Any exterior wall covering of the structure covered with exterior insulation and finishing systems (EIFS), also known as "synthetic stucco"	☐	☐	☐
If yes, has there been a recent inspection to determine whether the structure has excessive moisture accumulation and/or moisture related damage? (The Tennessee Real Estate Commission urges any buyer or seller who encounters this product to have a qualified professional inspect the structure in question for the preceding concern and provide a written report of their finding.)	☐	☐	☐
If yes, please explain. If necessary, please attach an additional sheet.			

_____

_____

D. CERTIFICATION: I/we certify that the information herein, concerning the real property located at _____, is true and correct to the best of my/our knowledge as of the date signed. Should any of these conditions change prior to conveyance of title to this property, these changes will be disclosed in addendum(a) to this document.

_____	_____
Transferor (Seller)	Date

_____	_____
Transferor (Seller)	Date

> Parties may wish to obtain professional advice and/or inspections of the property and to negotiate appropriate provisions in the purchase agreement regarding advice, inspections, or defects.

TRANSFEREE/BUYER'S ACKNOWLEDGMENT: I/we understand that this disclosure statement is not intended as a substitute for any inspection, and that I/we have a responsibility to pay diligent attention to and inquire about those material defects which are evident by careful observation.

I/we acknowledge receipt of a copy of this disclosure.

_____	_____
Transferee (Buyer)	Date

_____	_____
Transferee (Buyer)	Date

Health hazards occur within structures, on real estate parcels, and in the area surrounding real estate. They may occur naturally or as a result of human activity. Environmental laws regulate some, but not all, health hazards that affect real estate. Real estate agents, owners, and sellers have various responsibilities for detecting, disclosing, and remediating regulated hazards. Some important issues are reviewed below.

Lead-based paint. This hazard cannot be absorbed through the skin, but it becomes dangerous when it is ingested or inhaled. It can be found in most homes built before 1978 and can be present in the air, drinking water, food, contaminated soil, deteriorating paint, and dust from the paint. Children are particularly susceptible because young children are known to eat chips of the paint, allowing the lead to enter their bloodstreams. Homebuyers and renters are required to be given the EPA-HUD-US Consumer Product Safety Commission's booklet, "Protect Your Family from Lead in Your Home" and must be informed if lead-based paint is present in the home. Buyers may have a risk assessment performed prior to purchasing the home.

Mold. This is a fungus that grows under moist conditions and causes allergic reaction for some people. The presence of mold in the home must be disclosed as a latent defect. Flooding and water damage must also be disclosed as both of those can lead to mold growth. Inspections do not always find mold because it often grows inside walls and ductwork. Most molds require removal by a professional.

Asbestos. While harmless in its original condition, it can cause lung cancer if its dust filters into the air. If it is found in a home during remodeling, it must be removed by professionals to prevent contamination. It can be found in roofing and siding, older insulation, textured paint, artificial ashes sold for gas fireplaces, some vinyl floor tiles, coatings for older hot water and steam pipes.

Air quality. The quality of air in a home can be adversely impacted by the presence of carbon monoxide, radon, deteriorating asbestos and lead-based paint, methamphetamine production, formaldehyde, and other toxic chemicals. Homes can and should be tested for many of these contaminants prior to purchase.

Water quality. Ground water is easily contaminated from septic tanks, agricultural runoff, highway de-icing, landfills, pesticides, animal waste, etc. Many people rely on ground water for drinking so must be aware that contaminated water can cause problems from mild stomach problems to cancer and death. The Environmental Protection Agency (EPA) sets standards for protecting ground water from contamination. It also offers advice and resources to facilitate the rehabilitation of contaminated ground water sources. One such means of protection is to advise private well users to have the water tested at least once a year.

Carbon monoxide. This is an odorless, colorless, toxic gas that can kill a person before its presence is known. It can be caused by unvented kerosene and gas space heaters; leaking chimneys; back-drafting from furnaces, gas water heaters, wood stoves, and fireplaces; gas stoves, gasoline powered equipment, vehicle exhaust in garages, tobacco smoke. Carbon monoxide can be detected in a structure by a unit similar to a smoke alarm which should be included in every home, especially those with gas equipment and fireplaces or furnaces.

Faulty septic systems. Inspections of septic systems are important because these systems take wastewater from the property, remove most of the contaminants, and then put the water into the soil. If the system is faulty, it can be releasing contaminated water into the soil, thereby contaminating the soil. Potential buyers and septic system users should have the county health department conduct an inspection of the system.

Illegal drug manufacturing. Manufacturing illegal drugs such as methamphetamine produces highly toxic fumes that last a long time. Continued exposure to the fumes can cause fatal burns to the lungs, can damage the liver and spleen, and can lead to learning disabilities. Any property suspected as having been a place for drug manufacturing should be investigated prior to being sold or leased, and the possible health hazards must be disclosed to the potential buyer or renter.

Radon. This is the easiest hazard to detect and mitigate. It is an odorless, colorless, tasteless, and radioactive gas that is created in the ground where uranium and radium exist. Prolonged exposure to radon can cause lung cancer. It can enter the home through any cracks, gaps, or cavities, including crawl spaces and openings around pipes. It can be easily detected by a radon test, so home inspections should include this test.

Urea formaldehyde. This type of hazard is found in foam thermal insulation in homes built before 1980. The formaldehyde gas emissions from the insulation decrease over time, so most homes with the insulation no longer pose a threat. The most common sources of formaldehyde in a home are pressed wood products such as particleboard, hardwood plywood paneling, and medium density fiberboard. Plastic furniture, new carpeting, and other vinyl materials also emit formaldehyde gases during the first few months after installation. Formaldehyde can cause eye problems, nausea, breathing problems, and allergic reactions.

Leaking underground storage tanks. USTs have at least 10 percent of their volume underground and are used to store fuel oil, gasoline, and other toxic fluids. Tanks made of steel can corrode over time and leak their contents into the surrounding soil, contaminating groundwater. They also provide a potential for fire and explosion. Tank removal is expensive, so removal is not common. Therefore, potential buyers must be informed of the presence of a UST on the property and of the health and financial risks of purchasing a property that contains a UST.

Clean Air and Clean Water Acts. The Clean Air Act of 1963, since amended a number of times, was designed to control air pollution on a national level. Among other things, the act authorizes the setting of standards for controlling the emission of pollutants and monitoring air quality. It identifies hazardous air pollutants such as formaldehyde and regulates their use. Importantly, the act allows private citizens to sue other citizens to enforce the law.

The Clean Water Act, officially known as the Federal Water Pollution Control Act Amendments of 1972, together with revisions contained in the Clean Water Act of 1977 and the Water Quality Act of 1987, is the primary federal law governing water pollution. It applies to all waters connected with navigable waters, but the interpretation of exactly which waters are covered remains open to dispute. The Clean Water Act does not directly deal with groundwater contamination, which is addressed in the Safe Drinking Water Act, Resource Conservation and Recovery Act, and the Superfund act.

Safe Drinking Water Act. Congress passed the Safe Drinking Water Act (SDWA) in 1974 (amended 1986 and 1996) to regulate and protect the public supply of drinking water. The act authorizes the setting of standards, protection of water sources, training of operators, funding of improvements, and dissemination of information. Under the act, water suppliers must report health risks to the EPA within 24 hours of discovery. Hydraulic fracturing (fracking) oil and gas production poses one of the greatest current threats to groundwater.

Property sellers generally must disclose the source of drinking water for the property and the presence, type and location of any septic system on the property. A water supply other than a municipal one and any septic system other than a standard one should be tested.

Brownfields Law. Brownfields are abandoned commercial or industrial sites that are likely to contain toxic material. The Small Business Liability Relief and Brownfields Revitalization Act (known as the Brownfields Law), passed in 2002 provides clean-up funds, liability protections, and tax incentives to reclaim contaminated properties. Under this law, owners who neither caused nor contributed to the contamination are released from liability for the clean up.

Environmental Protection Agency. The EPA was established on December 2, 1970 to bring together federal research, monitoring, standard-setting and enforcement activities into one agency dedicated to environmental protection. The EPA, working with state, local, and tribal governments, enforces the Clean Air and Clean Water Acts along with other environmental laws.

Disclosure obligations and liabilities. Licensees are expected to be aware of environmental issues and to know where to look for professional help. They are not expected to have expert knowledge of environmental law nor of physical conditions in a property. Rather, they must treat potential environmental hazards in the same way that they treat other material facts about a property: disclosure. It is advisable to have an attorney draft the appropriate disclosures to lessen the broker's liability should problems occur in the future.

The Lead-based Paint Act of 1992 requires a seller or seller's agent to disclose known lead problems in properties built before 1978. The licensee must give the buyer or lessee a copy of the EPA-HUD-US Consumer Product Safety Commission booklet, "Protect Your Family from Lead in your home."

Further, the 1996 lead-based paint regulation requires sellers or lessors of almost all residential properties built before 1978 to disclose known lead-based paint hazards and provide any relevant records available. The seller is not required to test for lead but must allow the buyer a ten-day period for lead inspection. Only a licensed lead professional is permitted to deal with testing, removal or encapsulation. It is the real estate practitioner's responsibility to ensure compliance.

Under CERCLA and the Superfund Amendment of 1986, current landowners as well as previous owners of a property may be held liable for environmental violations, even if "innocent" of a violation. Sellers often carry the greatest exposure, and real estate licensees may be held liable for improper disclosure.

In sum, for their own protection, licensees should be careful to:

> ▶ be aware of potential hazards
> ▶ disclose known material facts
> ▶ distribute the HUD booklet
> ▶ know where to seek professional help.

Warranties

Purpose and scope. Home warranties, or home service contracts, cover service, repair, or replacement of a home's major systems and appliances. Warranties are usually purchased for one year at a time with the annual cost determined by the following:

> ▶ the location of the property – prices vary from state to state due to cost of living and property regulations in the specific area
> ▶ the type of property – single family homes have different price points than mobile homes or multifamily properties
> ▶ the size of the property – smaller homes have cheaper coverage options than large homes. often, the home's square footage determines the cost of the warranty
> ▶ the amount of coverage – standard coverage plans may exclude certain parts of the property, resulting in a lower price for the plan. The excluded items can be covered with a more extensive plan at a higher cost

Home warranties are often included in the purchase price of a home or are purchased by the buyer at the time of the home purchase.

Limitations. Purchasers of home warranties need to fully understand their coverage limitations in order to have realistic expectations of the warranty. Similarly, it is important for a homeowner to understand what may not be covered in the warranty. These items may include

> ▶ conditions that existed prior to the effective coverage of the warranty
> ▶ failures caused by something other than normal wear and tear
> ▶ improperly installed or modified items
> ▶ damages caused by failure of another system or appliance, such as kitchen cabinets being damaged from a plumbing leak in the pipes under the sink, called consequential damages
> ▶ outdoor items such as sprinklers or swimming pool
> ▶ repairs to faucets
> ▶ refrigerators, washers and dryers, or garage door openers are often not covered

Basically, unless an item is specifically listed in the warranty contract, it will not be covered.

With a home warranty, the homeowner must go through the warranty company to have the service performed. The company usually has established relationships with specific service providers and may use only those providers for service under the warranty. The homeowner is typically charged a service fee on top of the annual fee for each repair job.

Inspections

Process. Property inspections may identify builder oversights or the need for major repairs. They may also identify the need for regular maintenance to keep the property in good condition. In addition to looking for structural issues, plumbing and electrical problems, and roof and foundation issues, inspections can uncover termites or other pests that are damaging the structure. Inspections can also uncover environmental issues that have a detrimental impact on the property.

Termite inspections. Termites are destructive pests that exist in all states except Alaska. They cause an estimated $50 billion in damage to buildings each year. They often cause extensive damage to the property before the owner even realizes there is a problem. Termites eat wood from the inside out, so they are not easily discovered except by professional inspectors. Having homes inspected annually for termites can prevent substantial damage and cost.

The most common type of termite is the subterranean termite. They are often confused with winged ants, but they are much more destructive. Termite inspectors look for the following indications that termites are present in the structure:

> ▶ swarms of termites inside the home
> ▶ termite excrement
> ▶ termite bodies found in spider webs near the structure
> ▶ the presence of termite mud tubes by which termites traverse open spaces between sources of wood; the tubes protect the termites from dehydration and predators; their diameter is similar to that of a drinking straws
> ▶ areas on the property that serve to harbor termites, such as wood fencing, mulch, piles of firewood, dead tree limbs, etc.
> ▶ a hollow sound when a wood beam is tapped
> ▶ long, deep grooves in wood

Because termites cause such extensive damage and can live inside the structure of a home for years, a termite inspection should be part of any home buying transaction as well as a periodic event.

U.S. Department of
Housing and Urban
Development
Federal Housing Administration (FHA)

OMB Approval No: 2502-
0538 (exp. 04/30/2018)

For Your Protection:
Get a Home Inspection

Why a Buyer Needs a Home Inspection

A home inspection gives the buyer more detailed information about the overall condition of the home prior to purchase. In a home inspection, a qualified inspector takes an in-depth, unbiased look at your potential new home to:

> Evaluate the physical condition: structure, construction, and mechanical systems; Identify items that need to be repaired or replaced; and
> Estimate the remaining useful life of the major systems, equipment, structure, and finishes.

You Must Ask for a Home Inspection

> A home inspection will only occur if you arrange for one. FHA does not perform a home inspection.

> Decide early. You may be able to make your contract contingent on the results of the inspection.

Appraisals are Different from Home Inspections

An appraisal is different from a home inspection and does not replace a home inspection. Appraisals estimate the value of the property for lenders. An appraisal is required to ensure the property is marketable. Home inspections evaluate the condition of the home for buyers.

FHA Does Not Guarantee the Value or Condition of your Potential New Home

If you find problems with your new home after closing, FHA cannot give or lend you money for repairs, and FHA cannot buy the home back from you. Ask a qualified home inspector to inspect your potential new home and give you the information you need to make a wise decision.

Radon Gas Testing and other safety/health issues

The United States Environmental Protection Agency and the Surgeon General of the United States have recommended that all houses should be tested for radon. For more information on radon testing, call the toll-free National Radon Information Line at 1-800-SOS-Radon or 1-800-767-7236.

Ask your home inspector about additional health and safety tests that may be relevant for your home.

Be an Informed Buyer

It is your responsibility to be an informed buyer. You have the right to carefully examine your potential new home with a qualified home inspector. To find a qualified home inspector ask for references from friends, realtors, local licensing authorities and organizations that qualify and test home inspectors.

HUD-92564-CN (6/14)

Environmental inspections. Home inspections should include looking for common environmental issues that can affect the property and the residents of the property. Environmental hazards can have a significant impact on the sale of a property. An environmental site assessment (ESA) may be conducted to identify environmental impairments and protect parties against becoming involved in contamination issues. Such assessments are performed in three phases. A Phase 1 ESA identifies potential problems on or near the subject property. A Phase 2 ESA involves active testing of soil, water, and other components of the subject property.

Environmental impact statements. When a project is federally funded, the responsible parties must provide an environmental impact statement (EIS) detailing how the project will affect the environment. Privately funded projects are also often required to prepare an EIS before any permits are issued. An EIS is expected to address air and water quality issues, noise, health and safety, wildlife, vegetation, water and sewer requirements, traffic, population density, and other issues as appropriate.

Agent disclosure duties. Most states require disclosure of known material facts regarding residential properties of one to four units. If a licensee knows the result of an inspection, this is a material fact to be disclosed. Disclosure of environmental issues on commercial and industrial properties is often not mandated. Where disclosure is not required, real estate licensees should suggest the use of a professional environmental audit.

Homeowners' associations

States have various requirements for a seller's property condition disclosure statement to be completed by the seller and furnished to the buyer. Any such disclosure is likely to include whether the property is subject to a common interest property plan (e.g. condominium), whether the plan imposes any restrictions, whether membership in a Homeowners' Association (HOA) is obligatory, and the identity of the HOA, if any.

State law will typically require the association or management company to provide association documents to the buyer to satisfy the seller disclosure requirements. These documents may be attached to or delivered in conjunction with the sale contract. The contract itself usually specifies the timing of the disclosures. There may be a place on the contract for the buyer to acknowledge receipt and knowledge of the HOA disclosures. In some states, the seller's agent gathers and provides the documents to a buyer or buyer's agent before the writing of an offer.

Florida state requirements. The state of Florida requires that homeowners' associations with management responsibility for properties containing 100 or more parcels deliver physical or digital copies of their rules and covenants to all members and new members.

Condominium associations of 25 or more units are required to post digital copies of official condominium documents on their websites. These documents must include bylaws and rules, articles of incorporation, declarations, annual financial statements and budgets, FAQ sheets, building inspection reports and reserve studies.

A typical HOA disclosure package includes

- declarations
- articles of incorporation
- bylaws
- articles of organization
- operating agreements
- rules and regulations
- party wall agreements
- minutes of annual owners' meeting
- minutes of directors' or managers' meetings
- financial documents: balance sheet, income and expenditures, budget, reserve study, unpaid assessments, audit report, list of fees and charges
- list of insurance policies
- list of assessments by unit type

The seller is responsible for making the disclosures, but the buyer must exercise due diligence in the reading and understanding of them. The agent's responsibility is to make sure the disclosures are made.

HOA Bill of Rights. The HOA Bill of Rights establishes fundamental rights for homeowners to protect them against unfair practices. This includes stringent measures against kickbacks, fraudulent activities, and conflicts of interest in homeowners' associations. The HOA Bill of Rights also outlines conditions for removing HOA officers and directors and restricts HOAs from converting fines into liens against homeowners' property.

REPRESENTING LICENSEE EXPERTISE

Offering an opinion of title
Offering a representation of value
Misrepresentation of value
Unauthorized practice of law

**Offering
an opinion of title**

In Florida, real estate licensees are seen as experts in the field of real estate. Consequently, their clients rely on them to provide expert opinions. However, there are some opinions that licensees are not qualified or permitted to provide. For example, an opinion of title is to be provided by an attorney and not by a real estate licensee. The attorney will use the abstract of title to give an opinion of the condition and marketability of the property's title. It is indeed an opinion and not a guarantee or proof of a clear title.

Under Florida law, no one with a real estate license is allowed to give any opinion on the title to real estate. Instead, a Florida licensee is required to advise the property buyer to consult with an attorney or a title company for an opinion of title and/or to purchase title insurance. Licensees may obtain the opinion from an attorney and then provide information on the title to the buyer.

Offering a representation of value

There are several ways to derive an opinion of a property's value. Real estate licensees are qualified and permitted to perform comparative market analyses, broker price opinions, and opinions of value and then provide the resulting information to their buyers and sellers. They may not represent any of these methods as an appraisal, which is performed only by a licensed or certified appraiser.

Opinions of value ae not subject to regulation nor required to follow any specific professional standards. As a result, licensees who are motivated to obtain a listing may be led to distort the estimated value or price of the property. However, licensees must comply with their duty of honest and fair dealings with their customers and represent the value as accurately as possible with no exaggerations or misrepresentations.

Misrepresentation of value

Again, licensees have a duty to deal honestly and fairly with their customers and clients. They are required to disclose all known facts that materially affect the value of property even when the facts are not readily observable. Omitting a material fact may result in the value of the property being misrepresented. Other ways the value may be misrepresented include the following:

- listing a lower value for the property so as to obtain a quick sale
- overvaluing the property resulting in the buyer paying too much
- misrepresenting the comparable properties to induce a buyer to offer higher than is justified
- misrepresenting the square footage of the property

Misrepresenting the property's value can constitute fraud, breach of contract, or breach of trust and can result in lawsuits and disciplinary action against the licensee. When a buyer or seller is harmed because of the misrepresentation of value, his or her only real remedy is to file a lawsuit to either rescind the transaction or to seek financial recovery of damages.

The injured party can sue the other party, the licensee, and the brokerage that employs the licensee. Even if the misrepresentation was a mistake, Florida law allows the offending party(ies) to be held liable for negligent misrepresentation.

Unauthorized practice of law

The Supreme Court of Florida established the Unlicensed Practice of Law (UPL) program to protect the public against harm caused by individuals practicing law without a law degree and license. The Florida Bar will investigate and take legal action against anyone practicing law without a license to do so. The unlicensed practice of law is a third-degree felony in Florida, punishable by up to 5 years of probation, up to 5 years in prison, up to $5,000 in fines, and restitution paid to the victim(s).

Practicing law in Florida involves giving advice that requires the legal knowledge of someone who is licensed to practice law. Real estate law is complex, making it easy for innocent people to get hurt by licensees who give advice when they are not educated and licensed to do so.

While licensees need to be familiar with real estate laws, at no time is the licensee allowed to give legal advice. It is common for clients to ask licensees legal questions, but answering those questions could result in the licensee being held liable if the answers are incorrect.

Further, when completing contracts, such as a purchase contract, licensees must not make additions or modifications to the contract itself. To do so is considered the unlicensed practice of law.

COMMISSION-RELATED PRACTICES

Prohibitions
Kickbacks
Procuring cause

Prohibitions

Price fixing. When two or more brokers get together and agree to charge the same set commission percentage or fee for their services, this is called price fixing. Price fixing is against the law and leads to monopolies wherein competition is restricted. Antitrust laws encourage and protect competition and can impose criminal penalties on the price fixers. Each broker must establish his or her own commission rate separately from other brokers.

Sales associate contracting directly with principal. Sales associates work under the employment and supervision of a broker. They are prohibited from contracting directly with the principal or being paid directly by the principal. Any commission the sales associate receives must come directly from the employing broker based on the commission agreement the associate has with the broker and not directly from the principal.

Sales associate suing principal for commission. Because all contracts are between the principal and the broker, only the broker may sue a principal for unpaid commission. If the broker has been paid by the principal but does not pay the sales associate, the associate may sue the broker for the unpaid compensation but may not sue the principal directly.

Sharing a commission with an unlicensed person. Commissions are paid for services rendered in selling or purchasing property. Providing real estate services requires a real estate license. Therefore, only licensed real estate brokers and sales associates may provide such services. Consequently, sharing a commission with an unlicensed person is a violation of license law. The one exception allowed by the FREC is sharing the commission with a party to the transaction, such as the buyer or seller, as long as doing so is disclosed in writing to all parties to the transaction.

Paying an unlicensed person for performing real estate services. Again, providing real estate services requires a real estate license. Just as sharing a commission with an unlicensed person is prohibited, so is paying an unlicensed person to perform real estate services. Paying an unlicensed person for these services is a violation of license law.

New rules prohibit listing of commission on MLS. As a result of the National Association of Realtors (NAR) lawsuit, agent commission is no longer permitted to be listed on the Multiple Listing Service (MLS).

Buyer-Agent compensation must be negotiated. Buyer-Agent compensation must be negotiated between the Buyer-Agent and the Buyer. Buyer agents are required to have a Buyer-Agent Agreement signed by their Buyer prior to showing properties.

Kickbacks

Conditions. Under the Real Estate Settlement Procedures Act (RESPA), it is illegal for a real estate licensee to accept a kickback or rebate from any business providing a service used to close a real estate transaction, such as a surveyor, appraiser, property inspector, title company, mortgage lender, etc. A kickback may take the form of favors, advertising, money, gifts, or other items of value given to the licensee or broker in return for sending clients to the particular service provider.

The licensee may utilize these service providers and pay them for services they actually perform. However, the licensee must not accept anything in return from the service provider for utilizing a particular provider.

The licensee also may not give or accept any portion, split, or percentage of any fee the service provider is paid for the service. Brokers may have affiliated business arrangements with certain service providers but must be careful that the arrangement does not include any illegal kickback or rebate.

However, under certain conditions, kickbacks are legal:

▸ all parties to the transaction must be fully informed of the kickback
▸ the kickback must not be prohibited by any other law, such as RESPA
▸ a referral or finder's fee (no more than $50) may be paid to a tenant in an apartment complex for introducing a prospective tenant to the property management company or the complex owner for the purpose of renting or leasing an apartment
▸ as mentioned above, sharing a commission with an unlicensed buyer or seller as a rebate is allowed as long as all parties to the transaction are informed in writing
▸ a broker licensed in Florida may pay a referral fee or share a commission with a broker licensed or registered in a foreign state as long as the foreign broker does not violate any Florida law

Procuring cause

The main item of performance for the client is payment of compensation, if the agreement calls for it. A broker's compensation is earned and payable when the broker has performed according to the agreement. The amount and structure of the compensation, potential disputes over who has earned compensation, and the client's liability for multiple commissions are other matters that a listing agreement should address.

Disputes often arise as to whether an agent is owed a commission. Many such disputes involve open listings where numerous agents are working to find customers for the principal, and none has a clear claim on a commission. In other cases, a client may claim to have found the customer alone and therefore to have no responsibility for paying a commission. There are also situations where cooperating brokers and subagents working under an exclusive listing dispute about which one(s) deserve a share of the listing broker's commission.

The concept that decides such disputes is that the party who was the "procuring cause" in finding the customer is entitled to the commission or commission share. The two principal determinants of procuring cause are:

▸ being first to find the customer
▸ being the one who induces the customer to complete the transaction

For example, Broker A and Broker B each have an open listing with a property owner. Broker A shows Joe the property on Monday. Broker B shows Joe the same property on Friday, and then Joe buys the property. Broker A will probably be deemed to be the procuring cause by virtue of having first introduced Joe to the property.

ETHICAL PRACTICES

Codes of ethics
General disclosures
Fraud and negligence
Brokerage cooperation
Job performance
Duties to clients
Duties to customers
Professional relationships

Codes of ethics

The real estate industry has developed a code of professional standards and ethics as a guideline in serving the real estate needs of consumers. This professional code has emerged from three primary sources:

▸ federal and state legislation
▸ state real estate licensing regulation
▸ industry self-regulation through trade associations and institutes

Federal legislation focuses primarily on anti-discrimination laws and fair-trade practices. State laws and licensing regulations focus on agency and disclosure requirements and regulating certain brokerage practices within the state jurisdiction. Real estate trade groups focus on professional standards of conduct in every facet of the business.

By observing professional ethics and standards, licensees will serve clients and customers better, foster a professional image in the community, and avoid regulatory sanctions and lawsuits.

Today's professional ethics are not only important for one's career; they are also legal imperatives. Unethical practice, such as misrepresentation of material facts, fraud, and culpable negligence, is prohibited and punishable in all aspects of real estate practice.

General disclosures

Proper disclosures are an integral part of ethical behavior. In compliance with applicable laws and to promote respect for the real estate profession, licensees should be careful to disclose

- that the agent is going to receive compensation from more than one party in a transaction
- property defects if they are reasonably apparent; however there is no duty to disclose a defect which it would require technical expertise to discover
- any interest the agent has in a listed property if the agent is representing a party concerning the property
- any profits made on a client's money
- the agent's identity in advertisements
- the agent's representation of both parties in a transaction
- the existence of accepted offers
- identity of broker and firm in advertising as required by state law

Fraud and negligence

Fraud. Fraud is a misrepresentation of a material fact used to induce someone to do something, like sign a contract. *Actual fraud* occurs when one person intentionally deceives another person by misrepresenting a material fact that induces the person to rely upon the fact. *Negative fraud* is intentionally failing to disclose a material fact.

For a cause of action for fraud to be initiated, the following elements must exist:

- The licensee must have misrepresented a material fact or must have failed to disclose the material fact.
- The licensee must have known or should have known that he or she was misrepresenting the fact or that he or she should have disclosed the fact.
- The buyer or other party to whom the licensee misrepresented the fact relied on what the licensee said.
- The buyer or other party to whom the licensee misrepresented the fact or failed to disclose the fact was damaged as a result of the misrepresentation or omission.

Culpable negligence. Culpable negligence occurs when a person, such as a real estate broker, does not perform his or her required duties and responsibilities as the broker knows he or she should. The failure to perform need not be intentional to be considered negligent. It is more of a disregard of the duties and consequences of not performing them. Remember, one fiduciary duty of brokers is skill, care, and diligence. Failure to perform real estate activities with skill, care, and diligence may be ruled culpable negligence. In Florida, culpable negligence is not only unethical but is also a misdemeanor of the second degree.

Brokerage cooperation

Professional conduct excludes disparagement of competitors. Real estate professionals also

> ▶ forgo pursuit of unfair advantage
> ▶ arbitrate rather than litigate disputes
> ▶ respect the agency relationships of others
> ▶ conform to accepted standards of co-brokerage practices

Job performance

A professional real estate agent must understand the skills and knowledge the profession requires and make a commitment to maintain and improve expertise in these areas. Of particular importance are:

> ▶ market knowledge
> ▶ real estate laws
> ▶ evolving standards of practice

Other aspects of professional performance that are usually supported include:

> ▶ promoting exclusive listings
> ▶ promoting the professionalism of the real estate industry
> ▶ promoting arbitration of disagreements rather than litigation
> ▶ obtaining transactional agreements between parties in writing
> ▶ submitting offers and counteroffers in a timely and objective manner
> ▶ keeping the funds of others separate from broker and personal funds
> ▶ providing equal professional services to all persons
> ▶ providing services only within the agent's area of competence or with the assistance of a specialist
> ▶ observing the highest standards of truthfulness in advertising
> ▶ cooperating with real estate boards and commissions in their enforcement of standards

A real estate professional must recognize the limits of the agent's role and avoid practicing other professions beyond the agent's qualifications, such as law, investment counseling, securities brokerage, and tax advising.

Duties to clients

Most codes of ethics uphold the commitment to fulfill fiduciary duties. Specific applications include:

> ▶ honestly representing market value and property condition
> ▶ respecting rights and duties of other client-agent relationships
> ▶ submitting all offers

> ▸ avoiding commingling and conversion
> ▸ keeping transaction documents current
> ▸ maintaining confidentiality
> ▸ managing client property competently

Duties to customers   Some of the guidelines for working with customers are:

> ▸ honestly representing market value and property condition
> ▸ avoiding calling a service "free" that in fact is contingent on receiving a commission
> ▸ advertising truthfully

Professional relationships

Professional conduct excludes disparagement of competitors. Real estate professionals also

> ▸ forgo pursuit of unfair advantage
> ▸ arbitrate rather than litigate disputes
> ▸ respect the agency relationships of others
> ▸ conform to accepted standards of co-brokerage practices

4 Property Disclosures and Professional Practices
Snapshot Review

PROPERTY DISCLOSURES

Residential property condition
- written seller disclosure may be required; may or may not relieve agent of some liabilities
- seller discloses known problems including flooding issues; agent discloses known material facts known or should have known; failure to disclose grants right of rescission to buyer
- agent should advise seller of red flag issues detected; may include environmental concerns, property size and shape, neighborhood, construction quality, flooding, floorplan, adjacent property

Environmental issues
- duties of detecting, disclosing, remediating for owner and agent vary; typically include: lead-based paint, mold, asbestos, air quality, water quality, carbon monoxide, septic system, drug manufacturing, radon, formaldehyde, underground tanks
- agents need to be familiar with requirements of EPA, CERCLA/Superfund Act, Clean Air and Water Acts, Lead-based Paint Act, among others
- licensees must be aware of issues, know where to find professional help, disclose

Warranties
- agents should inform clients of limitations of home warranties; not a substitute for inspection

Inspections
- inspections can reveal structural, electrical, plumbing, roof, foundation, pest, environmental issues; agent must disclose inspection results if known

Homeowners' Associations
- agent must make sure existence, requirements, mandates, costs of homeowners' association are disclosed

REPRESENTING LICENSEE EXPERTISE

Opinion of title
- prohibited from offering opinion of title not written by attorney

Representation of value
- may offer value opinion derived from BPO or CMA; not to represent as appraisal

Misrepresentation of value
- constitutes fraud, breach of contract, or breach of trust, resulting in lawsuits and discipline

Unauthorized practice of law
- third degree felony punishable with probation, prison time, fines, and restitution

COMMISSION-RELATED PRACTICES

Prohibitions
- price fixing, sales associate contracting directly with principal, sales associate suing principal for commission, sharing commission with unlicensed person, paying unlicensed person for performing real estate services

Kickbacks
- prohibited acceptance of favors, advertising, money, gifts, etc. for referring clients to certain businesses unless all parties are informed, no other law prohibits it, paying referral fee to tenant for prospective other tenant, sharing commission with foreign broker

Procuring cause	• broker's compensation is earned and payable when the broker has performed according to the agreement; two determinants: first to find customer, inducing customer to complete transaction
ETHICAL PRACTICES	
Codes of ethics	
	• codes of ethics provide self-regulating standards of conduct covering all facets of the profession; serve clients, customers, and the public; avoid sanctions and liability; cover practices such as job performance, duties to clients and customers, disclosures, non-discrimination, professional relationships
General disclosures	• compensating parties; property defects; agent's interest in property; use of client funds; agent's identity in advertising
Fraud & negligence	• **fraud:** actual fraud when misrepresentation of material fact is intentional; negative fraud when failure to disclose material fact is intentional
	• **culpable negligence:** when duties are not performed as required, whether or not intentional
Brokerage cooperation	• **professional conduct:** no unfair advantage; arbitrate disputes; respect relationships; follow accepted practices
Job performance	• maintain knowledge of market, laws, practices; recognize limits of agent's role
Duties to clients	• fiduciary duties; truthful representation of facts; respect client relationships; submit offers; avoid illegal practices; document transaction
Duties to customers	• truthful representation of facts; truthful advertising
Professional relationships	• no disparagement of competitors; no unfair advantage; respect for others; arbitration of disputes

SECTION FOUR QUIZ: Property Disclosures and Professional Practices

1. If a licensee knows a negative material fact about a client's property that the client has not disclosed, the licensee must

   a. keep the fact confidential.
   b. report the seller to the local real estate board.
   c. disclose the information to others.
   d. change the seller's disclosure form.

2. How does CERCLA concern real estate agents?

   a. It may cause them to be held liable for improper disclosure of potential violations.
   b. It requires them to conduct Phase II Environmental Site Assessments.
   c. It makes them subject to Environmental Protection Agency orders.
   d. It absolves them of any responsibility for knowing about environmental hazards.

3. Which of the following is a fact about home warranties that an agent should be sure a client knows?

   a. If the homeowner has paid an annual fee for the warranty, there are no additional charges for service.
   b. Conditions that pre-existed the coverage date of the warranty will not be covered.
   c. Any item that is not specifically excluded in the warranty contract may be assumed to be covered.
   d. Warranties are usually purchased to cover the full term of the mortgage loan.

4. What is an agent's duty regarding inspections?

   a. Personally conduct a detailed inspection of all major structures and systems
   b. Accompany all inspectors as they inspect the agent's listed property
   c. Disclose the result of any inspection, if known to the agent
   d. Interview and hire inspectors for clients.

5. Under what circumstances may a licensee offer an opinion of title?

   a. When the licensee develops the opinion of title with assistance from his employing broker
   b. When the licensee obtains the opinion of title from an attorney and passes the information on to the client
   c. When the licensee uses the abstract of title completed by the title company to develop the opinion of title
   d. When the client does not wish to consult an attorney

6. In Florida, the unlicensed practice of law is a

   a. misdemeanor of the third degree.
   b. first-degree felony.
   c. civil violation.
   d. third-degree felony.

7. Sarah is a sales associate who handled the sale of John's property. John paid the commission to Sarah's employing broker, Stan, but Stan never paid Sarah her share of the commission. What can Sarah do?

    a. Sue John for not paying Sarah directly.
    b. Sue Stan for not paying Sarah her share of the commission.
    c. Report Stan to the FREC for a license law violation.
    d. Nothing, sales associates are not permitted to sue.

8. The listing agent knows that a home contains lead paint. What are they consequently required to do?

    a. They must disclose it because it is a title defect.
    b. They do not have to disclose it because they represent the seller.
    c. They have to disclose it because it is a property defect.
    d. The agent does not have to disclose it because it has been painted over.

9. What does the right of rescission allow the buyers to do?

    a. It allows them to cancel the contract and regain their deposit.
    b. It gives the buyers the right to extend their inspection period.
    c. It allows the buyers to renegotiate the purchase price.
    d. It gives buyers the option to withdraw their contract and lease the home instead.

10. What is negative fraud?

    a. Accidentally misrepresenting a material fact
    b. Intentionally failing to disclose a material fact
    c. When a real estate broker does not perform his or her required duties
    d. Writing a contract incorrectly

11. Which kickbacks are legal?

    a. All kickbacks are illegal.
    b. A finder's fee of $100
    c. Ones where all parties are verbally informed
    d. Ones that RESPA or any other law does not prohibit

12. What should licensees do if clients ask for an opinion of title?

    a. They should refer them to an attorney or title company.
    b. They should share what they find alarming.
    c. They should tell them to talk to their lender about it.
    d. They should advise them not to be worried and that everything will be okay.

13. Which of the following property valuation methods must follow specific professional standards and regulations?

    a. Sales associate's price opinion
    b. Comparative market analysis
    c. Appraisal
    d. Price-per-foot survey

14. What are the repercussions of the unlicensed practice of law?

    a. Up to $100,000 in fines
    b. Up to 5 years in prison
    c. No jail time, just a fine
    d. Nothing

15. In what situation can a licensee share his or her commission?

    a. Licensees can never share their commission.
    b. Licensees can share their commission with the mortgage lender.
    c. They can share it with their unlicensed assistant as a gratuity for showing a home.
    d. Licensees can share their commission with buyers or sellers as long as it is in writing and disclosed to everyone involved in the transaction.

5 Brokerage Practice Regulations

Brokerage Offices
Essential Advertising Rules
Handling Trust Funds
Trade Names

BROKERAGE OFFICES

Office requirements
Branch offices
Entrance sign requirements
Sales associate officing

Office requirements Florida statute mandates that each active broker maintain an office that is located in a building of "stationary construction." The law further mandates that only brokers can own and maintain an office. Sales associates and broker associates may not have their own offices.

Brokers' offices must be registered with the Department of Business and Professional Regulation (DBPR). The office must include at least one enclosed room and have space to conduct private transactions. Additionally, the broker is required to keep any real estate files and records (physical or electronic) in the office so they are immediately available for inspection by the FREC or other governing authority.

A broker may have an office that is located outside the state of Florida if the broker agrees in writing to cooperate with any investigation conducted in accordance with Florida statutes and rules. The broker must also register the out-of-state office with the DBPR.

If local zoning allows, the broker may set up the office in a residential location, such as the broker's home, as long as all office requirements are met, including display of the broker's sign.

Branch offices If a broker conducts business at a location other than the main office, the broker may be required to register the additional office as a branch office and pay the required registration fee for each such office. All branch offices must be registered.

Additionally, if the broker or brokerage's name or advertising is displayed on an office other than the main office in such a way as to lead the public to believe the office is owned or operated by that same broker, then that office must be registered as a branch office.

If a broker decides to close a branch office and open a new branch office at a different location, the broker must register the new office and pay the registration fee for that office. The registration for the closed branch office may not be transferred to the new branch office. If the broker decides to re-open the closed branch office within that office's license period, no additional fee will be required.

Entrance sign requirements

Every office, whether main or branch, is required to display a sign at the entrance which can be seen and read easily by anyone entering the office. The sign can be on the exterior or interior entrance of the office. Florida law requires the sign to contain the broker's name and any trade name. If the brokerage is a partnership or corporation, the sign must contain the partnership or corporation's name or trade name as well as at least one of the brokers. The words "Licensed Real Estate Broker" or "Lic. Real Estate Broker" must be included on the entrance sign of any real estate brokerage or business entity.

Sales associate officing

At initial licensure, a sales associate must be registered with an employing broker. The sales associate must work under the direction, control, and management of the specified broker or an owner-developer. The associate must work out of an office maintained by that same broker. The sales associate may be registered under only one broker at a time and may not operate as a broker or operate for any other broker who is not the associate's registered employing broker.

ESSENTIAL ADVERTISING RULES

Prohibitions
Wording of advertisements
Internet advertising

Prohibitions

False or misleading advertising. Florida law prohibits licensees from placing or causing to be placed any advertisement for property or services that is fraudulent, false, deceptive, misleading, or exaggerated. This includes written ads as well as ads on television or radio that are used to induce the sale, purchase, or rental of real property.

Penalties. False, deceptive, fraudulent, or misleading advertising can result in administrative fines and license suspension.

Blind advertising. Florida law requires that all advertisements include the brokerage's licensed name so any reasonable person would know the ad is from a real estate licensee. The broker's nickname may be included in the advertising as long as his or her legal registered name is also included. The broker's personal name may also be included in the ad as long as the broker's last name as it is registered with the DBPR is included. Ads that do not include the brokerage's name are considered blind advertising and are prohibited.

Sales associates advertising or conducting business in own name. Brokerage services include advertising. Consequently, anyone placing advertisements must be a broker. Sales associates may create or place advertisements only under the supervision and in the name of their employing broker. Sales associates may not advertise in their own names. Any form of advertising created by a sales associate must include the brokerage's licensed name.

Team advertising. Teams within a brokerage firm may advertise only under the supervision of the broker and in the name of the brokerage firm. Certain words, namely "brokerage," "realty," and the like, are not allowed as potentially creating confusion for the public. The name of the team must be in a font that is no larger than that used for the name or logo of the registered broker.

Wording of advertisements

In addition to including the brokerage's name, real estate advertisements must be worded so that any reasonable person knows that the advertiser is a real estate licensee. They may not be worded in a way that makes the public believe the ad is from someone other than a real estate licensee.

Internet advertising

Just as with any other form of advertising, the brokerage's name must appear within an internet advertisement. Florida administrative rule requires the name to be placed adjacent to, immediately above, or immediately below the point of contact information. Again, this prevents blind advertising and any related penalties.

Point of contact information. Information on how to contact the brokerage firm or the individual licensee is referred to as "point of contact information." Such contact information includes mailing address, physical street address, e-mail address, telephone number, and facsimile (fax) telephone number.

Telephone solicitation laws

Telephone Consumer Protection Act. The TCPA (Telephone Consumer Protection Act) addresses the regulation of unsolicited telemarketing phone calls. Rules include the following:

- Telephone solicitors are banned from using an artificial or a pre-recorded voice to a residential line without prior express consent.
- Robocalls (prerecorded calls) from telemarketers or debt collectors without prior express consumer consent are banned.
- Solicitors are banned from using an auto dialer to send text messages to cell phones without prior express consumer consent.
- Calls after 9 p.m. and before 8 a.m. in the consumer's time zone are banned.
- telephone solicitors must identify themselves, on whose behalf they are calling, and how they can be contacted

- telemarketers must comply with any do-not-call request made during the solicitation call
- consumers can place their home and wireless phone numbers on a national Do-Not-Call list which is maintained by the Federal Trade Commission and which prohibits future solicitations from telemarketers.
- Information on the national registry can be found online at https://www.consumer.ftc.gov/articles/0108-national-do-not-call-registry or https://www.donotcall.gov/.
- Robocalls must provide an automated opt-out function during the call.

Exemptions from the Act.

- A real estate licensee who has an actual buyer for an advertised "for sale by owner" property only to negotiate a sale.
- A real estate licensee with an established business relationship with a customer even if the customer's number is on the national do not call list.
- A real estate licensee who has accepted a business inquiry or application from a customer within the last 3 months.

CAN-SPAM Act. The CAN-SPAM Act (Controlling the Assault of Non-Solicited Pornography and Marketing Act of 2003) supplements the Telephone Consumer Protection Act (TCPA) by covering solicitations through email. It

- bans sending unwanted email 'commercial messages' to wireless devices
- requires express prior authorization
- requires giving an 'opt out' choice to terminate the sender's messages

Florida telemarketing laws

Florida state telemarketing laws apply to businesses located within Florida and those outside the state who call Florida residents. The laws include the Florida Telemarketing Act and the Florida Telephonic Sales law. The laws include the following:

- Telephone solicitors must obtain a license from the Florida Division of Consumer Services before operating in Florida.
- Solicitors must restrict their calls to 8 a.m. to 9 p.m.
- Solicitors may not block caller ID.
- Solicitors may not accept only credit card payments.
- The solicitor has 30 seconds to state his or her true name, the name of the company the telemarketer represents, and the goods or services being sold.

> ▸ Solicitors must tell consumers about their right to cancel any agreement to purchase the goods or services being offered.

Florida has its own do not call list that prohibits telemarketers from calling residential phones, cell phones, or paging devices.

Real estate licensees are exempt when they are calling a property seller in response to a yard sign or other advertisement placed by the seller. However, a licensee is not exempt if the seller is a "for sale by owner" advertiser who has placed his or her telephone number on the national do-not-call list.

Brokers are required to develop written procedures for solicitation calling policies. They must obtain the do-not-call lists and train their employees and independent contractors on using and maintaining the lists. The lists should be reviewed periodically for new additions so the licensees can remove those additions from their own solicitation call lists. Reviewing the national list is critical since federal law does not exempt real estate licensees. If a number is on the national list, whether or not it is on the state list, real estate licensees must not call that number.

HANDLING TRUST FUNDS

Trust fund deposit requirements

Trust fund deposit requirements

Trust accounts. A trust account, also known as an escrow account, is an account in a bank, credit union, or savings and loan association within Florida that is established to hold funds until the time comes to disburse them for a particular purpose. The account is held by a third party to a transaction and holds money, such as earnest money from a property buyer, until the property ownership is transferred at closing. Title companies with trust powers and attorneys may also be used to hold funds in escrow.

Escrow accounts may be used to hold rental property deposits and rent payments; however, while not required, sales funds and rental funds should be kept in separate escrow accounts. The funds deposited into the escrow account include cash, checks, money orders, drafts, personal property, or item of value.

Florida law mandates that the account is to hold only third-party funds with no licensee personal funds intermingled. However, the law also allows the broker to deposit personal or brokerage funds into each escrow account to be used for account maintenance fees.

Sales associate trust funds delivery requirements. If a property buyer gives earnest money or any other deposit to a sales associate in relation to a real estate transaction, the sales associate is required to turn the money over to his or her employing broker no later than the end of the next business day, not counting

Saturdays, Sundays, or legal holidays. The same timing is required for rental deposits.

Definition of "immediately" for a broker. Florida administrative rules state that brokers who receive any form of funds from their sales associates related to a real estate transaction must immediately deposit those funds into an escrow account. The rule defines "immediately" as no later than the end of the third business day following receipt of the item to be deposited, with Saturdays, Sundays, and legal holidays not considered business days. The three business days begin when the sales associate receives the funds, not when the broker receives them from the sales associate.

If the funds have been placed in escrow with a title company or attorney, there is no Florida statute regulating those accounts. Consequently, the FREC will not step in to resolve any conflict over disbursement of the funds if the transaction does not close. To settle the dispute, the parties will need to rely on the appropriate court and bear the expense of doing so.

Escrow account maintenance. The broker is responsible for reconciling the accounts each month and for ensuring the accounts comply with Florida laws. The broker also must make a monthly written statement that compares the broker's total liability with the bank balances of all escrow accounts.

The broker must keep records of all deposits, the source of the funds, and each account and provide those records and transaction-related agreements to the DBPR when requested. The records must be kept for at least 5 years.

Requirements for conflicting demands for escrow funds. When a real estate transaction does not close, the earnest money and any other related funds must be disbursed to the appropriate party. If the parties to the transaction do not agree on who should receive the funds and both parties make demands for the funds, the broker must notify the FREC of the conflict within 15 business days of the last demand received for the funds. The broker should use the Notice of Escrow Dispute/Good Faith Doubt form found online at

http://www.myfloridalicense.com/dbpr/re/documents/EDO_Notice.pdf.

The broker must also proceed with a settlement procedure (see below) within 30 business days after the last demand and notify the FREC of the procedure being used to resolve the conflict. The notification timing requirements for both the conflict and the settlement procedure start on the same day.

Settlement procedures. When the need arises to settle an escrow conflict or a good-faith doubt, the broker may use any of four settlement procedures:

> ▶ *mediation* – an informal conflict settlement procedure that is conducted by a qualified third party

The intention is to bring the parties together and with the guidance of the mediator have the parties come to a mutually agreeable resolution. Mediation may be used to settle the conflict if all of the associated parties give written consent. Once an agreement is reached, it is put into writing and signed by both parties. It then becomes a binding contract.

If the parties do not all consent to mediation or if the conflict is not settled in mediation within 90 days of the last demand, the broker must employ one of the other settlement procedures. All statements made during mediation are confidential and may not be used in any other proceeding.

▶   *arbitration* – a process conducted by one or more (usually three) third party arbitrators acting as judges

Typically, each side chooses one arbitrator, and then those two select a third. The arbitrators hear evidence, make decisions, and give written opinions. The arbitrators' decisions are binding. The conflicting parties must agree in writing to go to arbitration and must agree to comply with the arbitrators' final decision.

▶   *litigation* – a legal procedure either party may use if parties do not agree to mediation or arbitration

In this case, one party would file a lawsuit for the conflict to be heard in court to reach a resolution. However, because mediation is so successful and cost effective, Florida courts require most lawsuits to be mediated before a court will hear the case. Litigation can involve either of the following procedures:

▪   *interpleader action* – a means for the broker holding the escrow funds to be removed from the dispute over the disbursement of the funds

The funds are placed in the court depository, and it is left up to the court to determine who is to receive the funds. This also removes the broker from any potential liability as a result of the final disbursement. Contracts often include provisions for the interpleader action costs to be paid with the escrow funds or for the loser of the case to pay the other party's attorney fees.

▪   *declaratory judgment* – requested when the broker claims part of the escrow funds

The broker would file for a declaratory relief or judgment to have the appropriate trial court decide each party's rights to the escrow funds.

▸ ***Escrow Disbursement Order (EDO)*** – a determination made by the FREC as to who is entitled to the escrow funds

If the funds are held by the broker, he or she can request the FREC issue an EDO. If the EDO is denied, then the broker must employ one of the other settlement procedures and notify the FREC of which procedure will be used. If the funds are held by an attorney or title company, the FREC will not issue an EDO.

Even though the broker is employing one of the settlement procedures, either party may still choose to file a civil lawsuit to settle the matter. If the broker has requested an EDO but the parties settle the matter by another means before the EDO is issued, the broker must notify the FREC of the settlement within 10 business days.

TRADE NAMES

Brokers register their brokerages under the broker's legal name or the business's legal name. They may also register under a trade name, a fictitious name other than their own name that the broker would like to use for the brokerage. The trade name must appear on the broker's license and registration and must be unique from any other business or trade name.

The broker may only register under one trade name and must have a new license issued if he or she changes the trade name. The registered trade name must appear on all brokerage signage and advertising.

Sales associates are not permitted to use a trade name or fictitious name. They must register under their real names and have only the real name show on the license.

Display of names. FREC administrative rules prohibit licensees from using or displaying any name, insignia, or designation of a real estate association or organization unless they are authorized to do so.

5 Brokerage Practice Regulations
Snapshot Review

BROKERAGE OFFICES

Office requirements

- per Florida, each broker to have an office in building with stationary construction; office to be registered with DBPR; to include enclosed room and space for private meetings; records to be kept in office; only brokers may have offices; may have office outside of Florida or at broker's residence; must comply with ADA

Branch offices

- any office in addition to main office; must be registered; new offices to be registered

Entrance sign requirements

- sign to be displayed at office entrance; must contain broker's name and trade name with "Licensed Real Estate Broker" included; sales associates' names not required but must be below broker's name

Temporary shelters

- to protect associates and customers; cannot be permanent assignment; no transaction closings

Sales associate officing

- sales associates to be registered under a broker and work out of broker's office; registered under one broker at a time

ESSENTIAL ADVERTISING RULES

Prohibitions

- false or misleading advertising; blind advertising; sales associate advertising or conducting business under own name
- licensees selling their own property outside brokerage may advertise but must disclose ownership and licensure
- team advertising to be done under employing broker's supervision and name
- must be clear the advertiser is a real estate licensee

Wording of advertisements

- must be clear the advertiser is a real estate licensee

Internet advertising

- broker's name to be included with point of contact information

Telephone solicitation laws

- Telephone Consumer Protection Act – no unsolicited calls, no robocalls, do not call compliance; opt-out option required; time of day restrictions
- exemptions include nonprofits, political organizations, federal debt collectors, real estate licensee with buyer for "for sale by owner", with established business relationship, with business inquiry within last 3 months
- CAN-SPAM Act – no unsolicited email with commercial message and without prior consent
- Junk Fax Prevention Act – no unsolicited faxes; all faxes to include date and time, company's name and phone number; unsolicited faxes to include opt-out option

Florida telemarketing laws

- Florida Telemarketing Act and Florida Telephonic Sales law – solicitors need license; time of day restrictions; no blocking caller ID; payments not limited to credit cards; caller has 30 seconds to identify him/herself; provide right to cancel info
- Florida do not call list to be merged with national list; exemptions include nonprofit, political, and religious organizations and licensed insurance professionals; also includes real estate licensees calling about yard sign placed by seller unless seller is on national do not call list

HANDLING TRUST FUNDS

Trust fund deposit requirements

- bank account used to hold funds belonging to third party until time to disburse; no comingling of broker funds with third party funds
- funds to be delivered to broker by end of next business day; broker to deposit funds immediately – by end of the third business day following receipt of funds
- attorney or title company escrow - same deposit requirements as for broker; licensee to note name, address, and phone on sales contract; broker to request proof of deposit within 10 business days of due date and provide seller proof within 10 business days of request
- broker to be signatory on escrow account; broker to reconcile account monthly and keep records; account may be interest bearing with parties agreeing on receiver of interest
- conflicting demands for escrow funds to be reported to FREC within 15 business days; broker to initiate settlement procedure within 30 business days; broker's good faith doubt results in notifying FREC and initiating settlement procedure
- settlement procedures include mediation, arbitration, litigation with interpleader action or declaratory judgment, escrow disbursement order; 3 exceptions to settlement procedures

TRADE NAMES

- fictitious name used as business name; must be registered and appear on license, signage and advertising
- sales associates prohibited from using trade name
- licensee must be authorized to display name, insignia, or designation of an association

SECTION FIVE QUIZ: Brokerage Practice Regulations

1. Real estate advertising is a regulated activity. One important restriction in placing ads is

   a. a broker may only place blind ads in approved publications.
   b. a broker must have all advertising approved by the proper state regulatory agency.
   c. the advertising must not be misleading.
   d. sales agents may only advertise in their own name.

2. Which of the following is NOT a state mandated requirement for a broker's office?

   a. Located in a building with stationary construction
   b. Separate enclosed offices for each broker and associate
   c. Located within State of Florida
   d. Accessible to handicapped individuals

3. Which of the following statements is true?

   a. Only the broker's main office must be registered.
   b. Closed branch offices may not be reopened.
   c. Sales associates' names must be shown on all office signage.
   d. The registration for a closed branch office may not be transferred to a new branch office.

4. Advertising that does not include the broker's licensed name is

   a. appropriate for signage.
   b. considered fraud.
   c. considered blind advertising.
   d. appropriate for internet advertising.

5. If a sales associate accepts as earnest money payment from a property buyer, what must the associate do with the check?

   a. Cash it and wait for it to clear the bank before depositing the funds into an escrow account.
   b. Deposit the check into the brokerage's escrow account within 48 hours.
   c. Turn the check over to the employing broker by end of the next business day.
   d. Give the check to the employing broker by end of the third business day following receipt of the check.

6. Brokers are required to deposit third party funds immediately. How does Florida define "immediately"?

   a. The same day the broker received the funds
   b. No later than the end of the third business day following receipt of the funds
   c. No later than the end of the next business day following receipt of the funds
   d. Within 24 hours of receipt of the funds

7. If the parties to a transaction do not agree on the disbursement of escrow funds, the broker must notify the FREC

   a. within 15 business days of the last demand.
   b. within 30 business days of the last demand.
   c. by end of the next business day.
   d. no later than the end of the third business day following the last demand.

8. An escrow conflict resolution procedure that places the funds into a court's depository and removes the broker from the dispute is called

   a. arbitration.
   b. escrow disbursement order.
   c. interpleader action.
   d. mediation.

9. Which of the following statements is true?

   a. Sales associates are not permitted to use a trade name.
   b. Trade names are not included on the broker's license.
   c. A broker need not have a new license issued if his trade name changes.
   d. Once registered, a broker is prohibited from changing trade names.

10. Licenses changing employing brokers are prohibited from

    a. listing the former broker's trade name on a resume.
    b. acting as a cooperating broker with the former broker.
    c. performing any licensed acts under the new broker for six months.
    d. removing records from the previous broker's office

11. Which of the following must be included in a brokerage office's signage?

    a. The words "licensed real estate broker'
    b. The company logo
    c. Every real estate organization they are a part of
    d. What real estate board the brokerage participates in

12. What should a licensee be aware of if they are conducting cold calls?

    a. That they are exempt from complying with the Do-Not-Call list
    b. Phone calls before 8 a.m. and after 9 p.m. are prohibited.
    c. That cold calls by two or more licensees are illegal.
    d. That auto-dialers are only allowed if they are used for text messages.

13. What is mediation?

    a. A legal procedure used if parties do not agree to arbitration.
    b. An informal conflict settlement procedure that is conducted by a qualified third party.
    c. A process conducted by one or more third party judges.
    d. A way for the broker to be removed from the dispute.

14. When can a licensee call a "for sale by owner"?

    a. When they drive by the yard sign but do not have time to check the do-not-call list
    b. If they see the advertisement online but do not check the do-not-call list
    c. When they pretend to have a buyer in hopes of winning the listing
    d. Only if the seller has a yard sign up and they are not on the do-not-call list

15. Within a given brokerage, which of the following is an appropriate real estate team name?

    a. Anderson Realty
    b. Tampa Bay Brokerage
    c. The Adams Team
    d. There are no rules about team names.

16. What does the TCPA stand for?

    a. Texting Customers Protection Act
    b. Telephone Consumer Protection Act
    c. Texting Clients Protection Act
    d. Telephone Clients Protection Act

17. Which of the following supplements the TCPA in regards to e-mails?

    a. CAN-SPAM Act
    b. Do-Not-Email Act
    c. Email Clients Protection Act
    d. Email Solicitation Act

6 Fair Housing and Landlord-Tenant Laws

Fair Housing Laws
Florida Fair Housing Laws
Florida Landlord Tenant Laws

FAIR HOUSING LAWS

Civil Rights Act of 1866
Civil Rights Act of 1968
Forms of illegal discrimination
Title VIII exemptions
Jones v. Mayer
Equal Opportunity in Housing poster
Fair Housing Amendments Act of 1988
Discrimination by the client
Fair financing laws
Americans with Disabilities Act
Interstate Land Sales Full Disclosure Act

Federal and state governments have enacted laws prohibiting discrimination in the national housing market. The aim of these **fair housing laws,** or **equal opportunity housing laws,** is to give all people in the country an equal opportunity to live wherever they wish, provided they can afford to do so, without impediments of discrimination in the purchase, sale, rental, or financing of property.

State Fair Housing Laws. While states have enacted fair housing laws that generally reflect the provisions of national law, each state may have slight modifications of national law. For that reason, it is incumbent upon real estate students to learn their state laws and, in particular, note where these laws differ from national fair housing laws.

Fair Housing and Local Zoning. The Fair Housing Act prohibits a broad range of practices that discriminate against individuals on the basis of race, color, religion, sex, national origin, familial status, and disability. The Act does not pre-empt local zoning laws. However, the Act applies to municipalities and other local government entities and prohibits them from making zoning or land use decisions or implementing land use policies that exclude or otherwise discriminate against protected persons, including individuals with disabilities.

Civil Rights Act of 1866

The original fair housing statute, the Civil Rights Act of 1866, prohibits discrimination in housing *based on race*. The prohibition relates to selling, renting, inheriting, and conveying real estate.

Executive Order 11063. While the Civil Rights Act of 1866 prohibited discrimination, it was only marginally enforced. In 1962, the President issued Executive Order 11063 to *prevent discrimination in residential properties financed by FHA and VA loans*. The order facilitated enforcement of fair housing where federal funding was involved.

Civil Rights Act of 1968

Title VIII (Fair Housing Act). Title VIII of the Civil Rights Act of 1968, known today as the Fair Housing Act, prohibits discrimination in housing *based on race, color, religion, or national origin*. The Office of Fair Housing and Equal Opportunity (FHEO) administers and enforces Title VIII under the supervision of the Department of Housing and Urban Development (HUD).

Forms of illegal discrimination

The Fair Housing Act specifically prohibits such activities in residential brokerage and financing as the following.

Discriminatory misrepresentation. An agent may not conceal available properties, represent that they are not for sale or rent, or change the sale terms for the purpose of discriminating. For example, an agent may not inform a minority buyer that the seller has recently decided not to carry back second mortgage financing when in fact the owner has made no such decision.

Discriminatory advertising. An agent may not advertise residential properties in such a way as to restrict their availability to any prospective buyer or tenant.

Providing unequal services. An agent may not alter the nature or quality of brokerage services to any party based on race, color, sex, national origin, or religion. For example, if it is customary for an agent to show a customer the latest MLS publication, the agent may not refuse to show it to any party. Similarly, if it is customary to show qualified buyers prospective properties immediately, an agent may not alter that practice for purposes of discrimination.

Steering. Steering is the practice of directly or indirectly channeling customers toward or away from homes and neighborhoods. Broadly interpreted, steering occurs if an agent describes an area in a subjective way for the purpose of encouraging or discouraging a buyer about the suitability of the area.

Blockbusting. Blockbusting is the practice of inducing owners in an area to sell or rent to avoid an impending change in the ethnic or social makeup of the neighborhood that will cause values to go down.

Restricting MLS participation. It is discriminatory to restrict participation in any multiple listing service based on one's race, religion, national origin, color, or sex.

Redlining. Redlining is the residential financing practice of refusing to make loans on properties in a certain neighborhood regardless of a mortgagor's qualifications. In effect, the lender draws a red line around an area on the map and denies all financing to applicants within the encircled area.

Title VIII exemptions   The Fair Housing Act allows for exemptions under a few specific circumstances. These are:

> ▶ a privately owned single-family home where no broker is used and no discriminatory advertising is used, with certain additional conditions
> ▶ rental of an apartment in a 1-4 unit building where the owner is also an occupant, provided the advertising is not discriminatory
> ▶ facilities owned by private clubs and leased non-commercially to members
> ▶ facilities owned by religious organizations and leased non-commercially to members, provided membership requirements are not discriminatory

Jones v. Mayer   In 1968, the Supreme Court ruled in *Jones v. Mayer* that all discrimination in selling or renting residential property based on race is prohibited under the provisions of the Civil Rights Act of 1866. Thus, while the Federal Fair Housing Act exempts certain kinds of discrimination, anyone who feels victimized by discrimination *based on race* may seek legal recourse under the 1866 law.

Equal Opportunity in Housing poster   In 1972, HUD instituted a requirement that brokers display a standard HUD poster. The poster affirms the broker's compliance with fair housing laws in selling, renting, advertising, and financing residential properties. Failure to display the poster may be construed as discrimination.

Fair Housing Amendments Act of 1988   Amendments to federal fair housing laws prohibit discrimination based on sex and discrimination against handicapped persons and families with children.

Exemptions. Federal fair housing laws do not prohibit age and family status discrimination under the following circumstances:

> ▶ in government-designated retirement housing
> ▶ in a retirement community if all residents are 62 years of age or older
> ▶ in a retirement community if 80 % of the dwellings have one person who is 55 years of age or older, provided there are amenities for elderly residents
> ▶ in residential dwellings of four units or less, and single family houses if sold or rented by owners who have no more than three houses

Discrimination by the client   Fair housing laws apply to home sellers as well as to agents, with the exception of the exemptions previously cited. If an agent goes along with a client's discriminatory act, the agent is equally liable for violation of fair housing laws. It is thus imperative to avoid complicity with client discrimination. Further, an agent should withdraw from any relationship where client discrimination occurs.

Examples of potential client discrimination are:

> - refusing a full-price offer from a party
> - removing the property from the market to sidestep a potential purchase by a party
> - accepting an offer from one party that is lower than one from another party

Fair financing laws   Parallel anti-discrimination and consumer protection laws have been enacted in the mortgage financing field to promote equal opportunity in housing.

Equal Credit Opportunity Act (ECOA). Enacted in 1974, the Equal Credit Opportunity Act requires lenders to be fair and impartial in determining who qualifies for a loan. A lender may not discriminate on the basis of race, color, religion, national origin, sex, marital status, or age. The act also requires lenders to inform prospective borrowers who are being denied credit of the reasons for the denial.

Home Mortgage Disclosure Act. This statute requires lenders involved with federally guaranteed or insured loans to exercise impartiality and non-discrimination in the geographical distribution of their loan portfolio. In other words, the act is designed to prohibit redlining. It is enforced in part by requiring lenders to report to authorities where they have placed their loans.

U. S. Department of Housing and Urban Development

**EQUAL HOUSING
OPPORTUNITY**

We Do Business in Accordance With the Federal Fair
Housing Law

(The Fair Housing Amendments Act of 1988)

It is illegal to Discriminate Against Any Person
Because of Race, Color, Religion, Sex,
Handicap, Familial Status, or National Origin

- In the sale or rental of housing or residential lots
- In advertising the sale or rental of housing
- In the financing of housing
- In the provision of real estate brokerage services
- In the appraisal of housing
- Blockbusting is also illegal

Anyone who feels he or she has been discriminated against may file a complaint of housing discrimination:
1-800-669-9777 (Toll Free)
1-800-927-9275 (TTY)
www.hud.gov/fairhousing

U.S. Department of Housing and
Urban Development
Assistant Secretary for Fair Housing and
Equal Opportunity
Washington, D.C. 20410

Previous editions are obsolete   form HUD-928.1 (6.2011)

Americans with Disabilities Act (ADA)

Purpose. The ADA, which became law in 1990, is a civil rights law that prohibits discrimination against individuals with disabilities in all areas of public life, including employment, education, transportation, and facilities that are open to the general public. The purpose of the law is to make sure that people with disabilities have the same rights and opportunities as everyone else.

The Americans with Disabilities Act Amendments Act (ADAAA) became effective on January 1, 2009. Among other things, the ADAAA clarified that a disability is "a physical or mental impairment that substantially limits one or more major life activities." This definition applies to all titles of the ADA and covers private employers with 15 or more employees, state and local governments, employment agencies, labor unions, agents of the employer, joint management labor committees, and private entities considered places of public accommodation. Examples of the latter include hotels, restaurants, retail stores, doctor's offices, golf courses, private schools, day care centers, health clubs, sports stadiums, and movie theaters.

Real estate practitioners are most likely to encounter Titles I and III and should acquire familiarity with these. In advising clients, licensees are well-advised to seek qualified legal counsel.

Requirements. The ADA requires landlords in certain circumstances to modify housing and facilities so that disabled persons can access them without hindrance.

The ADA also requires that disabled employees and members of the public be provided access that is equivalent to that provided to those who are not disabled.

> ▶ Employers with at least fifteen employees must follow nondiscriminatory employment and hiring practices.

> ▶ Reasonable accommodations must be made to enable disabled employees to perform essential functions of their jobs.

> ▶ Modifications to the physical components of a building may be necessary to provide the required access to tenants and their customers, such as widening doorways, changing door hardware, changing how doors open, installing ramps, lowering wall-mounted telephones and keypads, supplying Braille signage, and providing auditory signals.

> ▶ Existing barriers must be removed when the removal is "readily achievable," that is, when cost is not prohibitive. New construction and remodeling must meet a higher standard.

> ▶ If a building or facility does not meet requirements, the landlord must determine whether restructuring or retrofitting or some other kind of accommodation is most practical.

Interstate Land Sales Full Disclosure Act

The Interstate Land Sales Full Disclosure Act (ILSA) is a federal law passed by Congress in 1968. The purpose of the Act is to protect consumers from a developer's misrepresentation of material facts about a property being purchased sight unseen through means of interstate commerce or the mail.

The Act prohibits fraud and misrepresentation. It also requires specific provisions in purchase and lease agreements. One such provision is the buyer's right to cancel. Further, it requires the developer of a subdivision containing 100 or more lots to register the property by submitting a Statement of Record with HUD and to provide a property disclosure report to a buyer prior to the contract being signed. The Statement and the disclosure report include the state of the property's title, physical characteristics of the property, availability of roads and utilities, and current ownership information.

The Act specifically prohibits a developer or agent from using interstate commerce or mail to lease or sell any lot without meeting these requirements. Antifraud provisions applicable to subdivisions with 25 or more lots are included in the Act.

Once the buyer receives the report, he or she may cancel the contract any time before midnight on the seventh day after signing the contract. If the buyer does not receive the report prior to signing the contract, he or she may bring legal action within 2 years of contract signing to have the contract revoked.

If the subdivision contains fewer than 25 lots, it is exempt from provisions of the Act. If the land is already developed, it is exempt from the Act. Transactions that do not involve a developer or agent in the sale or lease of a lot in a subdivision are also exempt.

Other exemptions include cemetery lots, sales to builders, land being sold by any government agency, and land zoned for industrial or commercial development.

ILSA is administered by the Consumer Financial Protection Bureau and enforced by HUD. Violations of ILSA are subject to criminal penalties, civil damages and monetary penalties, and/or suspension of the developer's registration.

FLORIDA FAIR HOUSING LAWS

Florida Fair Housing Act
Service Dogs versus
    Emotional Support Animals (ESAs)
Florida Americans with Disabilities
    Accessibility Implementation Act

Florida Fair Housing Act

As discussed earlier, the Fair Housing Act is a federal law that prohibits housing discrimination based on seven protected classes. In conjunction with that federal law, Florida Statute Title XLIV, Chapter 760, Section 20, known as the Florida Fair Housing Act, protects those same seven classes: race, color, religion, sex, national origin, disability, and familial status. Marital status, age, and occupation are not covered.

The following acts are discriminatory and prohibited by the Florida Fair Housing Act:

▶ A prospective tenant is told on the telephone that an apartment rents for a certain price and is currently available but then, when meeting the landlord face to face, is told the rental price is higher or the apartment is no longer available when it is still available.

▶ A condominium association refuses to provide handicapped parking for a person with a disability.

- A landlord enforces a no pets policy when the prospective tenant has a service dog.
- A homeowner refuses to sell property to a member of any of the protected classes.
- A real estate licensee encourages a buyer to purchase a particular house because it is located in a specific religious community.
- A landlord refuses to rent to a single woman who is pregnant.

In Florida, someone who believes he or she has been the victim of housing discrimination may file a complaint with the Florida Commission on Human Relations and/or HUD within 1 year of the alleged discrimination. Further, he or she may file a civil lawsuit within 2 years of the alleged discrimination. If the court finds in favor of the complainant, a fine up to $10,000 may be imposed on a first-time violator or up to $25,000 on a repeat violator within the previous 5 years.

Service Dogs versus Emotional Support Animals (ESAs)

There is a difference between a service dog and an emotional support animal (ESA). Service dogs are specifically trained to perform a given job for their handler. ESAs are not trained to perform particular tasks. They provide comfort and companionship to someone suffering from a psychiatric or emotional condition.

The Department of Justice recognizes service dogs as essential to their handlers; therefore, they are not considered pets and are allowed access anywhere their handlers are permitted. ESAs do not have the same legal protection as service dogs.

Florida law requires ESA dog handlers to provide their landlord or property manager with a letter from a mental health professional. Research may be conducted to ensure the letter is from a licensed mental health professional.

Claiming a pet as a service dog when it is not is a second-degree misdemeanor in the state of Florida. Violations are punishable by up to 60 days in jail and/or a fine of up to $500.

Florida Americans with Disabilities Accessibility Implementation Act

The Florida **Americans with Disabilities Accessibility Implementation Act** was established to incorporate the accessibility requirements of the Americans with Disabilities Act (ADA) into Florida law. The statute adopts the ADA Standards for Accessible Design and incorporates the standards into the Florida Accessibility Code for Building Construction.

The Act also mandates that all new residential buildings, structures, and facilities in the state must provide at least one bathroom on grade level with a door opening of at least 29 inches and with wheelchair-accessible sinks and that any barriers at common or emergency doors must be removed.

The Act covers several other accessibility issues such as parking, building remodeling and conversions, grab-rail requirements in hotel and motel bathrooms, and accessibility to levels above the ground floor.

FLORIDA LANDLORD-TENANT LAWS

Florida Residential Landlord and Tenant Act

Florida Residential Landlord and Tenant Act

Overview. The Florida Residential Landlord and Tenant Act applies to the rental of a residential unit and provides regulations for all aspects of rental occupancies. It does not apply to rent-to-own contracts where required funds have been paid. Nor does it apply to transient occupancy in public lodging or occupancy in a cooperative unit or condominium unit.

Under the Act, unconscionable provisions within a rental agreement are not enforceable. If a rental agreement does not specify the duration of the tenancy, then the duration is determined to be the length of residency between rental payments. For example, if the rent payment is due each month, then the tenancy is for one month at a time.

Deposits, advance rents and fees. Landlords may require a security deposit and advanced rent payments (typically the last month's rent). In Florida, there is no limit on the amount of deposit landlords can charge, but they must comply with the Act in how they handle deposits and advanced rent payments. Landlords can also accept a fee or monthly fees instead of security deposits for new lease agreements.

Either in the lease agreement or within 30 days of receiving the security deposit and advance rent, the landlord is required to give the tenant written notice of the advance rent or security deposit.

Landlord's obligation to maintain premises. Landlords are required to comply with building, housing, and health codes in maintaining the rental property. If none of these codes exist, the landlord is required to keep the premises in good repair and maintain systems such as plumbing and heating in working condition.

The Act specifically states that window screens must be installed and kept in good repair, pests must be exterminated, and garbage is to be removed with outside receptacles provided. The landlord must also install smoke detectors in single family or duplex rental homes.

The landlord may charge the tenant for garbage removal, water, fuel, or utilities if included in the lease. The landlord is not responsible for conditions caused by negligence or wrongful acts of the tenant, family members, or guests.

Tenant's obligations. The tenant is obligated to comply with applicable building, housing, and health codes. The tenant must keep the premises clean and sanitary, including removing garbage, cleaning plumbing fixtures, and operating the dwelling's systems in a reasonable manner. Tenants are also obligated to conduct themselves so as not to disturb neighbors and refrain from damaging or removing any part of the premises that belongs to the landlord.

Landlord's access to premises. The landlord is permitted by law to enter the rental unit from time to time for inspections, repairs, alterations, supplying services, or show the unit to prospective tenants or buyers. The landlord is required to give the tenant at least 12 hours' notice prior to entry for repairs and may only enter between 7:30 a.m. and 8:00 p.m. The landlord may enter the premises for any of the above reasons only with the tenant's consent, if the tenant unreasonably withholds consent, or in case of an emergency.

Vacating premises. A tenant planning to vacate the rental premises must give the landlord a 30-day written notice that includes an address where the tenant can be reached.

Termination notice requirements. Amendments to the Landlord and Tenant Act clarify lease termination requirements for tenancy without a specific term. A minimum of 30-day notice is required for tenancies with an undefined term.

A 30-60 day notice period is now required for tenancies with a specific term.

If the landlord imposes a claim on the deposit and complies with notice requirements, the landlord may deduct the amount of the claim from the total deposit and then return the balance to the tenant within 30 days of the intention notice. The tenant may file an objection to the claim within 15 days of receiving the intention notice. If the tenant does not meet the timeline for objection, he or she may still seek damages in a separate legal action.

Termination of rental agreements by the tenant. The tenant may terminate the rental agreement if the landlord fails to maintain the premises as required by law or fails to comply with the provisions in the rental agreement. To do so, the tenant needs to deliver a written 7-day notice to the landlord specifying the noncompliance and stating the intention to terminate. If the landlord does not correct the noncompliance within the 7 days, the tenant may terminate the rental agreement.

Termination of rental agreements by the landlord. The landlord may terminate the rental agreement if the tenant fails to comply with tenant obligations or fails to comply with the provisions of the agreement. Just as when the tenant terminates the agreement, the landlord must deliver a written 7-day notice to the tenant specifying the noncompliance and stating the intention to terminate. If the tenant does not correct the noncompliance within the 7 days, the landlord may terminate the rental agreement.

If the tenant's noncompliance is nonpayment of rent, the landlord must give the tenant written notice of the requirement to pay the rent or vacate the premises within 3 business days. If the tenant still does not pay the rent after the 3 days, the landlord may terminate the rental agreement.

Florida State law pre-empts local rental rules. Florida state law overrides local regulations on residential tenant-landlord relationships. This applies to screening processes, security deposits, rental agreements, landlord and tenant rights, and fee regulations.

Protecting Private Property Rights. Florida law addresses squatters who occupy private property by allowing property owners or their agents to request the immediate removal of unlawfully occupying persons from a residential dwelling.

6 Fair Housing and Landlord Tenant Laws
Snapshot Review

FAIR HOUSING LAWS
- enacted to create equal opportunity and access to housing and housing finance
- state laws generally reflect federal fair housing laws; federal laws do not pre-empt local zoning laws but prohibit them from discriminating

Civil Rights Act of 1866
- no discrimination in selling or leasing housing *based on race*
- Executive Order 11063: no race discrimination involving FHA- or VA-backed loans

Civil Rights Act of 1968
- Title VIII (Fair Housing Act): no housing discrimination *based on race, color, religion, national origin*
- certain exceptions permitted

Forms of illegal discrimination
- discriminatory misrepresentation, advertising, and financing; unequal services; steering; blockbusting; restricting access to market; redlining

Title VIII exemptions
- privately-owned single-family with no broker and no discriminatory advertising; 1-4 unit apartment building where owner is resident and no discriminatory advertising; private club facilities leased to members; religious organization-owned facilities for members and no discrimination

Jones v. Mayer
- no race discrimination, without exception

Equal Opportunity in Housing Poster
- must be displayed by brokers

Fair Housing Amendments Act of 1988
- no discrimination *based on sex or against the handicapped or families with children*

Discrimination by the client
- agent liable for complying with client's discriminatory acts

Violations and enforcement
- file HUD complaint, sue in court, or both; may obtain injunction, damages; violators subject to prosecution

Fair financing laws
- Equal Credit Opportunity Act: no discrimination in housing finance based on race, color, religion, sex, marital status, age; Home Mortgage Disclosure Act: no redlining

Americans with Disabilities Act
- no discrimination against those with disabilities; applies to employment, education, transportation, public facilities; equivalent access

Interstate Land Sales Full Disclosure Act
- protects consumers when purchasing property sight unseen through interstate commerce
- requires subdivision of 100 or more lots to be registered and buyers to be given a property report; fewer than 25 lots are exempt

FLORIDA FAIR HOUSING AND LANDLORD-TENANT LAWS

Florida Fair Housing Act
- prohibits housing discrimination based on seven protected classes
- victims of discrimination may file complaint within 1 year or civil lawsuit within 2 years with fines imposed against violators

Florida Americans with Disabilities Accessibility Implementation Act
- incorporates federal accessibility standards into FL code with requirements for new residential buildings

Florida Residential Landlord and Tenant Act
- applies to residential rental units, not rent-to-own units or public lodging
- provides requirements for collecting and holding security deposits and advanced rent
- includes landlord's obligations to maintain the premises in good repair
- includes tenant's obligations to comply with applicable codes and keep unit clean
- designates when landlords may enter the premises for repairs and emergencies, etc.
- provides mandates for notices regarding the tenant vacating the unit and how to handle the security deposit and claims against it
- includes processes for termination of rental agreement by tenant or landlord
- provides procedures for collecting past due rent and evicting noncomplying tenants

SECTION SIX QUIZ: Fair Housing and Landlord-Tenant Laws

1. The principal theme of federal fair housing laws is to

   a. ensure all Americans a fair chance to own a home.
   b. prohibit discrimination in housing transactions.
   c. ensure that housing transactions are negotiated fairly.
   d. prohibit agents from dealing unfairly with clients and customers.

2. It is illegal to discriminate in selling a house based on race, color, religion, or national origin. This is provided for through

   a. the Civil Rights Act of 1866.
   b. Executive Order 11063.
   c. the Civil Rights Act of 1968.
   d. the Fair Housing Amendments Act of 1988.

3. Which of the following laws or rulings extended discrimination to include gender, handicapped status, and family status?

   a. Executive Order 11063
   b. the Civil Rights Act of 1968
   c. the Fair Housing Amendments Act of 1988
   d. Jones v Mayer

4. An agent informs numerous families in a neighborhood that several minority families are planning to move into the immediate area, and that the trend could have adverse effects on property values. This activity is

   a. blockbusting.
   b. legal but unprofessional redlining.
   c. discriminatory misrepresentation.
   d. negligent misrepresentation.

5. A minority family would like to buy a home in a certain price range. The agent shows the family all available properties in a neighborhood of families with similar backgrounds. The agent did not mention a number of homes in the family's price range in other neighborhoods. This agent could be liable for

   a. blockbusting.
   b. providing unequal services.
   c. steering.
   d. nothing; his services were legal and acceptable.

6. An agent does not like a particular minority buyer, and is very short with the person, refusing to engage in lengthy conversation or show him any properties. A second minority party visits the office the next day. The agent is very forthcoming, and shows the person five prospective properties. This agent could be liable for

   a. providing unequal services.
   b. steering.
   c. misrepresentation.
   d. nothing; both parties were minorities, and therefore no discrimination occurred.

7. Following the client's recommendation, an agent conceals the availability of a property from an employed but pregnant and unmarried minority woman. This agent could be liable for

   a. discriminatory misrepresentation.
   b. steering.
   c. violating fiduciary duty.
   d. nothing: an agent may show or not show any property at his or her discretion.

8. A condominium complex prohibits ownership of any unit by persons under 55 years of age. The association claims it has made the prohibition properly. Which of the following is true?

   a. They are violating the Civil Rights Act of 1866.
   b. They are violating the Fair Housing Amendments Act of 1988.
   c. They are guilty of age discrimination.
   d. The prohibition may be legal.

9. An owner suddenly pulls a property off the market after hearing from the agent on the phone that the agent had received a full-price offer from a minority party. The agent then informs the offeror that the home has been removed from the market and is unavailable. Which party or parties, if any, have violated fair housing laws?

   a. The agent only
   b. The owner only
   c. The agent and the owner
   d. Neither agent nor owner

10. The parts of the Americans with Disabilities Act that most concern real estate agents are those that deal with

    a. telecommunications and insurance.
    b. public accommodations and employment.
    c. state and local government.
    d. agency and public service.

11. The Interstate Land Sales Full Disclosure Act requires developers to provide land buyers with a property disclosure report. Once the buyer receives the report, he may cancel the purchase contract

    a. by end of business on the third day after receipt of the report.
    b. within 5 days of signing the contract.
    c. any time before midnight on the seventh day after signing the contract.
    d. by end of business on the fifth business day after receiving the report.

12. Which of the following acts is considered discriminatory?

    a. Licensee Lou shows a family with children a home in close proximity to a school.
    b. Joe owns an apartment building and has just interviewed a prospective tenant on the phone. When the tenant arrived to sign the lease, Joe realized the individual is Hispanic. Consequently, Joe refused to rent to this individual.
    c. A condominium association moves designated parking spaces for some residents to make room to designate handicapped parking for a disabled resident.
    d. Lou is showing a home to a Jewish family and points out the synagogue down the street.

13. Which of the following is not a requirement of the Florida Americans with Disabilities Accessibility Implementation Act?

    a. Allowing a service dog to live in a no-pet apartment building
    b. Installing a ramp at the entrance to an apartment building where a wheel-chair-bound tenant lives
    c. Widening the bathroom doorways to 29 inches in a new apartment building
    d. Providing handicapped parking in an apartment building's parking lot

14. If a lease agreement does not indicate where a security deposit is to be held, the landlord must provide that information to the tenant

    a. prior to signing the lease.
    b. within 15 business days of signing the lease.
    c. within 30 days of receiving the deposit.
    d. That information must be in the lease.

15. A landlord has _____ to notify a vacated tenant of a claim against the tenant's security deposit.

    a. 7 days
    b. 15 days
    c. 30 days
    d. 45 days

16. Which of the following is a protected class by the Florida Fair Housing Act?

    a. Race
    b. Marital status
    c. Age
    d. Occupation

17. In Florida, what is the maximum the landlord can require for an apartment deposit?

    a. First month's rent
    b. There is no maximum.
    c. The first and last month's rent
    d. Three month's rent

18. Residential tenants are subject to which of the following requirements?

    a. Exterminating pests
    b. Installing smoke detectors
    c. Maintaining the heating system
    d. Removing garbage and cleaning plumbing fixtures

19. If a landlord does not maintain the premises as required by law, how can the tenant terminate the rental agreement?

    a. By providing a written 7-day notice specifying the noncompliance and intention to terminate
    b. The tenant will have to remain until the end of the lease
    c. By providing a written 3-day notice with the intention to terminate
    d. By calling the landlord with witnesses nearby

20. What can a landlord charge the tenant for?

    a. Smoke detectors
    b. Broken plumbing
    c. Garbage removal
    d. Inoperable AC

7 Co-ops, Condos, Timeshares, HOAs & CDDs

Cooperatives
Condominiums
Time-shares
Homeowners' Associations
Community Development Districts

COOPERATIVES

Interests, rights, and obligations
Organization and management
Cooperative disclosures

In a cooperative, or co-op, one owns **shares** in a non-profit corporation or cooperative association, which in turn acquires and owns an apartment building as its principal asset. Along with this stock, the shareholder acquires a **proprietary lease** to occupy one of the apartment units.

The number of shares purchased reflects the value of the apartment unit in relation to the property's total value. The ratio of the unit's value to total value also establishes what portions of the property's expenses the owner must pay.

The Cooperative

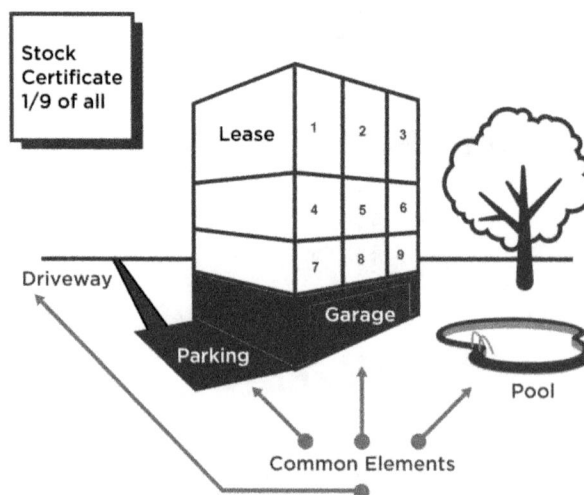

The exhibit shows a nine-unit apartment building. A cooperative corporation buys the building for $9,000,000. All nine units are of equal size, so the corporation decides that each apartment represents a value of $1,000,000, or 1/9 of the total. The co-op buyer pays the corporation $1,000,000 and receives 1/9 of the corporation's stock. The shareholder also receives a proprietary lease for apartment 1. The shareholder is now responsible for the apartment unit's pro rata share of the corporation's expenses, or 11.11%.

Interests, rights and obligations

Cooperative association's interest. The corporate entity of the cooperative association is the only party in the cooperative with a real property interest. The association's interest is an undivided interest in the entire property. There is no ownership interest in individual units, as with a condominium.

Shareholder's interest. In owning stock and a lease, a co-op unit owner's interest is *personal property* that is subject to control by the corporation. Unlike condominium ownership, the co-op owner owns neither a unit nor an undivided interest in the common elements.

Proprietary lease. The co-op lease is called a proprietary lease because the tenant is an owner (proprietor) of the corporation that owns the property. The lease has no stated or fixed rent. Instead, the proprietor-tenant is responsible for the unit's pro rata share of the corporation's expenses in supporting the cooperative. Unit owners pay monthly assessments. The proprietary lease has no stated term and remains in effect over the owner's period of ownership. When the unit is sold, the lease is assigned to the new owner.

Expense liability. The failure of individual shareholders to pay monthly expense assessments can destroy the investment of all the other co-op owners if the co-op cannot pay the bills by other means.

Since the corporation owns an undivided interest in the property, debts and financial obligations apply to the property as a whole, not to individual units. Should the corporation fail to meet its obligations, creditors and mortgagees may foreclose *on the entire property.* A completed foreclosure would terminate the shareholders' proprietary lease, and bankrupt the owning corporation. Compare this situation with that of a condominium, in which an individual's failure to pay endangers only that individual's unit, not the entire property.

Transfers. The co-op interest is transferred by assigning both the stock certificates and lease to the buyer.

Organization and management

A developer creates a cooperative by forming the cooperative association, which subsequently buys the cooperative property. The association's articles of incorporation, bylaws, and other legal documents establish operating policies, rules, and restrictions.

The shareholders elect a board of directors. The board assumes the responsibility for maintaining and operating the cooperative, much like a condominium board. Cooperative associations, however, also control the use and ownership of individual apartment units, since they are the legal owners. A shareholder's voting power is proportional to the number of shares owned.

Structural Integrity. All condos and co-ops over 3 stories that are 30 years or older, or buildings that are 25 years or older located within 3 miles of the coastline, are required to have an initial milestone structural inspection performed by a licensed architect or engineer. Thereafter, both condos and co-ops meeting this criteria are required to be reinspected every 10 years.

Associations must maintain a Structural Integrity Study Reserve (SISR). They must also maintain the Milestone Structural Inspection Report and the Structural Integrity Reserve Study for 15 years. Both must be available for review by owners and potential owners.

Cooperative disclosures

The Cooperative Act. F.S. Chapter 719 (the Cooperative Act) requires developers to disclose to prospective cooperative buyers within the sale or lease contract the right to cancel the contract. The disclosure must be made in "conspicuous" type and include language providing the buyer the right to cancel the contract in writing within 15 days after the buyer signed the contract. The buyer may also cancel the contract within 15 days if the contract has been amended in such a way that the offering is materially altered or modified in an adverse way to the buyer. This right to cancel may not be waived. The disclosure must also include language that the budget provided to the buyer contains estimates which, if they do not match actual costs, do not constitute adverse changes to the offering.

The Act requires non-developers selling their shares in the association to disclose the buyer's right to cancel in writing within 3 business days of signing the contract. This disclosure also is to include language that the buyer has been provided current copies of the associations governing documents: the Articles of Incorporation, Bylaws, Rules of the Association, and a Question and Answer sheet prior to signing the contract.

If the cooperative parcels are being sold or leased prior to construction completion, the developer must disclose a copy of the plans and specifications for the completion of the unit and common areas. All contracts and disclosures must contain language that oral representations cannot be relied upon.

CONDOMINIUMS

Airspace and common elements
Interests and rights
Organization and management
Owner responsibilities
Condominium disclosures

A condominium is a hybrid form of ownership of multi-unit residential or commercial properties. It combines ownership of a fee simple interest in the **airspace** within a unit with ownership of an undivided share, as a tenant in common, of the entire property's **common elements,** such as lobbies, swimming pools, and hallways.

A condominium **unit** is one airspace unit together with the associated interest in the common elements.

Airspace and common elements

The unique aspect of the condominium is its fee simple interest in the airspace contained within the outer walls, floors, and ceiling of the building unit. This airspace may include internal walls which are not essential to the structural support of the building.

Common elements are all portions of the property that are necessary for the existence, operation, and maintenance of the condominium units. Common elements include:

▶   the land (if not leased)

▶   structural components of the building, such as exterior windows, roof, and foundation

▶   physical operating systems supporting all units, such as plumbing, power, communications installations, and central air conditioning

▶   recreational facilities

▶   building and ground areas used non-exclusively, such as stairways, elevators, hallways, and laundry rooms

The Condominium

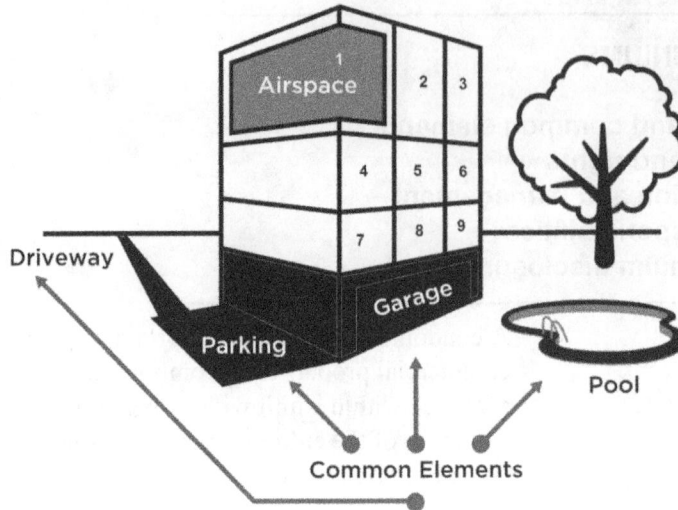

A buyer who purchases Unit #1 of the condominium illustrated obtains a fee simple interest in the airspace of apartment 1 and a tenancy in common interest in her pro rata share of the common elements. If all units in the building have the same ownership interest, the buyer would own an indivisible one-ninth interest in the common elements-- pool, parking lot, garage, pool, building structure, tree, etc.

Interests and rights

The condominium unit can be owned jointly, in severalty, in trust, or in any other manner allowed by state law. Unit owners hold an exclusive interest in their individual apartments, and co-own common elements with other unit owners as tenants in common.

Possession, use, and exclusion. Unit owners exclusively possess their apartment space, but must share common areas with other owners. The property's legal documents may create exceptions. For example, unit owners may be required to join and pay fees for use of a health club.

Unit owners as a group may exclude non-owners from portions of the common area, for instance, excluding uninvited parties from entering the building itself.

Transfer and encumbrance. Condominium units can be individually sold, mortgaged, or otherwise encumbered without interference from other unit owners. As a distinct entity, the condominium unit may also be foreclosed and liquidated. An owner may not sell interests in the apartment separately from the interest in the common elements.

Resale of a unit interest may entail limitations, such as the condominium association's prior approval of a buyer.

Condominium units are individually assessed and taxed. The assessment pertains to the value of the exclusive interest in the apartment as well as the unit's pro rata share of common elements.

Organization and management

Organization. Condominium declarations typically provide for the creation of an **owner's association** to enforce the bylaws and manage the overall property. The association is often headed by a board of directors. The association board organizes how the property will be managed and by whom. It may appoint management agents, hire resident managers, and create supervisory committees. The board also oversees the property's finances and policy administration.

Management. Condominium properties have extensive management requirements, including maintenance, sales and leasing, accounting, owner services, sanitation, security, trash removal, etc. The association engages professional management companies, resident managers, sales and rental agents, specialized maintenance personnel, and outside service contractors to fulfill these functions.

Owner responsibilities

Individual units. Owner responsibilities relating to the apartment include:

- ▶ maintaining internal systems
- ▶ maintaining the property condition
- ▶ insuring contents of the unit

Common area assessments. Unit owners bear the costs of all other property expenses, such as maintenance, insurance, management fees, supplies, legal fees, and repairs. An annual operating budget totals these expenses and passes them through as **assessments** to unit owners, usually on a monthly basis.

Should an owner fail to pay periodic assessments, the condominium board can initiate court action to foreclose the property to pay the amounts owed.

The unit's pro rata share of the property's ownership as defined in the declaration determines the amount of a unit owner's assessment. For example, if a unit represents a 2% share of the property value, that unit owner's assessment will be 2% of the property's common area expenses.

Condominium disclosures

The Condominium Act. F.S. Chapter 718 (the Condominium Act) requires developers selling condominium units to provide the buyer with copies of the governing documents (Declaration, Articles of Incorporation, Bylaws, Rules of the Association, and Frequently Asked Questions sheet) and have the buyer sign a receipt for the documents. The developer must also include a disclosure with the sales contract that provides the buyer with 15 days after signing the contract and receiving the required materials to submit a written cancellation notice. The buyer may also cancel within 15 days of receiving a contract amendment that is adverse to the buyer. The disclosure must also include language that the budget provided to the buyer contains estimates which, if they do not match actual costs, do not constitute adverse changes to the offering.

The Act requires condominium unit owners who are reselling their units to provide the buyer with copies of the governing documents, current year-end financial report, Frequently Asked Questions sheet, and a governance form. The Act also requires the seller to include a disclosure with the sales contract that provides the buyer with the right to cancel in writing within 3 business days of signing the contract.

TIME-SHARES

Time-share lease
Time-share freehold
Regulation
Time-share disclosures

Time-share ownership is a fee or leasehold interest in a property whose owners or tenants agree to use the property on a periodic, non-overlapping basis. This type of ownership commonly concerns vacation and resort properties. Time-share arrangements provide for equal sharing of the property's expenses among the owners.

Time-share lease

In a leasehold time-share, the tenant agrees to rent the property on a scheduled basis or under any pre-arranged system of reservation, according to the terms of the lease. Generally, the scheduled use is denominated in weeks or months over the duration of the lease, a specified number of years.

Time-share freehold

In a freehold time-share, or **interval ownership estate**, tenants in common own undivided interests in the property. Expense prorations and rules governing interval usage are established by separate agreement when the estate is acquired.

For instance, the Blackburns want a monthly vacation in Colorado once a year. They find a time-share condominium that needs a twelfth buyer. The available month is May, which suits the Blackburns. The total price of the condominium is $240,000, and annual expenses are estimated to be $9,600. The Blackburns buy a one-twelfth interest with the other tenants in common by paying their share of the price, $20,000. They are also obligated to pay one-twelfth of the expenses every year, or $800. They have use of the property for one-twelfth of the year, in the month of May.

Interval owners must usually waive the right of partition, which would enable an owner to force the sale of the entire property.

Regulation

The development and sale of time-share properties has come under increased regulation in recent years. Developers and brokers face stringent disclosure requirements regarding ownership costs and risks. Other laws provide for a cooling-off period after the signing of a time-share sales contract, and require registration of advertising.

In Florida, anyone selling time-share plans must hold a real estate license unless they are specifically exempted. Owners who occupy the timeshare for their own use are exempt from licensure. Owner/developers who sell timeshares may employ unlicensed individuals to sell the timeshares as long as those individuals are not paid commission on the sales and are not paid based on individual transactions.

If a timeshare plan is located in Florida but is being offered for sale outside of the state but within the United States, the offering or sale is not subject to the provisions of Florida time-share laws. If the timeshare plan is located in Florida but is being offered for sale outside of the United States, the offering is not subject to the provisions of Florida time-share laws as long as the developer files the timeshare plan with the Division of Florida Condominiums, Timeshares, and Mobile Homes for approval or the developer pays an exemption registration fee and files the required information to the Division for approval.

If a timeshare is located outside of Florida but is being offered for sale in Florida, the offering or sale is subject only to certain time-share laws, as specified in F.S. Chapter 721.03(1)(c).

Time-share disclosures

The Florida Vacation Plan and Timesharing Act and Rule 61J2-23.001, F.A.C. F.S. Chapter 721 (the Florida Vacation Plan and Timesharing Act) and Rule 61J2-23.001 0f the Florida Administrative Code require several disclosures to be included when timeshares are being sold.

Listing agreement disclosures. Listing agreements with brokers must be in writing and provided to the signing client at the time of signing. The agreement must include the following disclosures:

> ▶ *THERE IS NO GUARANTEE THAT YOUR TIME-SHARE PERIOD CAN BE SOLD AT ANY PARTICULAR PRICE OR WITHIN ANY PARTICULAR PERIOD OF TIME.*
>
> This disclosure must be included in conspicuous type and located directly above the signature line for the owner of the time-share period. The statement must also be included in any written advertising material used to solicit listing agreements.

> ▶ a complete and clear disclosure of fees, commissions, and other costs or compensation that will be paid to or received by the broker

> ▶ the term of the agreement with a statement regarding any party's ability to extend the agreement's term and a description of the conditions under which the agreement may be extended and at what cost

> ▶ a description of the services the broker will provide and the obligations of each party to the resale transaction, including costs and obligations in notifying the managing entity of the plan and any exchange company

- whether the broker has exclusive rights of obtaining a buyer during the agreement's term, to whom and when proceeds from the sale are to be disbursed, under what conditions any party may terminate the agreement, and the amount of commission or compensation owed to the broker at agreement termination prior to resale closing.

- whether the broker or anyone else may use the subject time-share period, a description of such use rights, and to whom rents or profits from the use will be paid

- the existence of any judgments or pending litigation against the broker due to or alleging a violation of Florida real estate statutes or consumer fraud

Resale contract disclosures. It is considered a violation of Florida real estate license laws if a licensee executes any contract or purchase agreement without complying with the required provisions. The contract or agreement must include the following disclosures, for which the broker may rely on written information provided by the managing entity:

- an explanation of the form of time-share ownership being purchased and a legally sufficient description of the time-share period being purchased

- the name and address of the plan's managing entity

- in conspicuous type and located directly above the signature line for the owner of the time-share period, the statement:

    THERE IS NO GUARANTEE THAT YOUR TIME-SHARE PERIOD CAN BE SOLD AT ANY PARTICULAR PRICE OR WITHIN ANY PARTICULAR PERIOD OF TIME.

- in at least 10-point type, all capitalized, and directly above the buyer's signature line, the statement:

    THE CURRENT YEAR'S ASSESSMENT FOR COMMON EXPENSES ALLOCABLE TO THE TIME-SHARE PERIOD YOU ARE PURCHASING IS ___. THIS ASSESSMENT, WHICH MAY BE INCREASED FROM TIME TO TIME BY THE MANAGING ENTITY OF THE TIME-SHARE PLAN, IS PAYABLE IN FULL EACH YEAR ON OR BEFORE ___. THIS ASSESSMENT (INCLUDES/DOES NOT INCLUDE) YEARLY AD VALOREM REAL ESTATE TAXES, WHICH (ARE/ARE NOT) BILLED AND COLLECTED SEPARATELY.

- if ad valorem real property taxes are not included in the current year's assessment for common expenses, the statement:

    THE MOST RECENT ANNUAL ASSESSMENT FOR AD VALOREM REAL ESTATE TAXES FOR THE TIME-SHARE PERIOD YOU ARE PURCHASING IS ___.) EACH OWNER IS PERSONALLY LIABLE FOR THE PAYMENT OF HIS ASSESSMENTS FOR COMMON EXPENSES, AND FAILURE TO TIMELY PAY THESE ASSESSMENTS MAY RESULT IN

RESTRICTION OR LOSS OF YOUR USE AND/OR OWNERSHIP RIGHTS.

▶ if a time-share estate is being conveyed, in conspicuous type, the statement:

> *For the purpose of ad valorem assessment, taxation and special assessments, the managing entity will be considered the taxpayer as your agent pursuant to section 192.037, Florida Statutes.*

▶ the terms and conditions of the purchase and closing, including the closing costs and title insurance obligations of the seller and/or the buyer

▶ the existence of any mandatory exchange program membership included in the plan

Disclosure for Florida timeshare being offered for sale outside of Florida. The following disclosure statement is required within the purchase contract in conspicuous type located directly above the buyer's signature line.

> *The offering of this timeshare plan outside the jurisdictional limits of the United States of America is exempt from regulation under Florida law, and any such purchase is not protected by the State of Florida. However, the management and operation of any accommodations or facilities located in Florida is subject to Florida law and may give rise to enforcement action regardless of the location of any offer.*

Disclosure of right to cancel. All time-share purchase agreements must include a disclosure that buyers have the right to cancel without penalty or obligation within 10 calendar days after the date of contract signing or the date the buyer received all of the required documents, whichever is later. The buyer must notify the seller of the cancellation in writing. The transaction closing may not take place before the expiration of the 10-day cancellation period. This right to cancel may not be waived.

HOMEOWNERS' ASSOCIATIONS (HOA)

Definition
Disclosures

Definition

F.S. Chapter 720, the Homeowners' Association Act, defines a homeowners' association as a Florida corporation responsible for the operation of a community or a mobile home subdivision in which the voting membership is made up of parcel owners or their agents, or a combination thereof, and in which membership is a mandatory condition of parcel ownership, and which is authorized to impose assessments that, if unpaid, may become a lien on the parcel. The term "homeowners' association" does not include a community development district or other similar special taxing district created pursuant to statute.

The association must be incorporated with the governing documents recorded in the local county's official records. The association includes officers and directors who have a fiduciary relationship to the members (owners). Owners of land parcels are required to become part of the community's membership and make up the voting membership. Any unpaid membership fee or assessment may result in a lien on the parcel.

Disclosures

Any developer or member who sells a parcel in a homeowner's association is required to provide the buyer with the following disclosure summary:

DISCLOSURE SUMMARY
FOR
(NAME OF COMMUNITY)

1. *As a purchaser of property in this community, you will be obligated to be a member of a homeowners' association.*
2. *There have been or will be recorded restrictive covenants governing the use and occupancy of properties in this community.*
3. *You will be obligated to pay assessments to the association. Assessments may be subject to periodic change. If applicable, the current amount is $___ per___. You will also be obligated to pay any special assessments imposed by the association. Such special assessments may be subject to change. If applicable, the current amount is $___ per___.*
4. *You may be obligated to pay special assessments to the respective municipality, county, or special district. All assessments are subject to periodic change.*
5. *Your failure to pay special assessments or assessments levied by a mandatory homeowners' association could result in a lien on your property.*
6. *There may be an obligation to pay rent or land use fees for recreational or other commonly used facilities as an obligation of membership in the homeowners' association. If applicable, the current amount is $___ per___.*
7. *The developer may have the right to amend the restrictive covenants without the approval of the association membership or the approval of the parcel owners.*
8. *The statements contained in this disclosure form are only summary in nature, and, as a prospective purchaser, you should refer to the covenants and the association governing documents before purchasing property.*
9. *These documents are either matters of public record and can be obtained from the record office in the county where the property is located, or are not recorded and can be obtained from the developer.*

DATE: *PURCHASER:*

The contract or agreement must also include in prominent language a statement that the buyer should not execute the contract until the disclosure summary has been received and read. The contract must also state that the buyer may cancel the contract with a written notice within 3 days after receiving the summary and prior to closing. This right applies when the disclosure summary was not provided prior to contract execution. This right to cancel may not be waived.

COMMUNITY DEVELOPMENT DISTRICTS (CDD)

Definition
Disclosures

Definition

F.S. Chapter 190 (the Community Development Districts Act of 1980) defines a Community Development District as a local unit of special-purpose government created to serve the long-term specific needs of its community. A CDD's purpose is the delivery of urban community development services.

CDDs have the authority to plan, finance, construct, operate, and maintain community-wide infrastructure and services specifically for the benefit of its residents. CDDs must comply with the Act in regard to the formation, powers, governing body, operation, duration, accountability, requirements for disclosure, and termination.

A CDD's responsibilities within a community may include such services as storm water management, potable and irrigation water supply, sewer and wastewater management, and street lights. Funding for these services is obtained through a CDD tax assessment on the homeowners used to refund bonds issued by the developer to finance construction of the infrastructure. The CDD tax assessments are separate to any city or county property taxes.

Disclosures

Contracts for the initial sale of a parcel of real property or a residential unit within the CDD must include the following disclosure:

THE *(Name of District)* COMMUNITY DEVELOPMENT DISTRICT MAY IMPOSE AND LEVY TAXES OR ASSESSMENTS, OR BOTH TAXES AND ASSESSMENTS, ON THIS PROPERTY. THESE TAXES AND ASSESSMENTS PAY THE CONSTRUCTION, OPERATION, AND MAINTENANCE COSTS OF CERTAIN PUBLIC FACILITIES AND SERVICES OF THE DISTRICT AND ARE SET ANNUALLY BY THE GOVERNING BOARD OF THE DISTRICT. THESE TAXES AND ASSESSMENTS ARE IN ADDITION TO COUNTY AND OTHER LOCAL GOVERNMENTAL TAXES AND ASSESSMENTS AND ALL OTHER TAXES AND ASSESSMENTS PROVIDED FOR BY LAW.

This disclosure must be printed in boldface and conspicuous type that is larger than the type for the remaining text within the contract.

7 Coops, Condos, Timeshares, HOAs & CDDs
Snapshot Review

COOPERATIVES

Interests, rights and obligations
- ownership of shares in owning corporation, plus proprietary lease in a unit; corporation has sole, undivided ownership

Organization and management
- developer forms association; buys property; incorporates; board of directors responsible for maintenance and operation

Cooperative disclosures
- 15-day and 3-day right to cancel with no waiver allowed
- plans and specifications for completing unfinished parcels

CONDOMINIUMS

Airspace and common elements
- freehold ownership of a unit of airspace plus an undivided interest in the common elements as tenant in common with other owners

Interests and rights
- may be sold, encumbered or foreclosed without affecting other unit owners

Organization and management
- owners' association and board of directors determine management, hires managers

Owner responsibilities
- maintain interior, insure contents, pay common area assessments

Condominium disclosures
- 15-day and 3-day right to cancel with no waiver allowed
- dollar amounts on budget are estimates
- plans and specifications for completing unfinished parcels
- oral representations cannot be relied upon
- provide required materials

TIME SHARES
- a lease or ownership interest in a property for the purpose of periodic use by the owners or tenants on a scheduled basis

Time-share regulation
- sellers of time-share plans must be real estate licensees unless exempted
- Some time-shares are not subject to Florida time-share laws

Time-share disclosures
- listing agreement disclosures: no guaranteed sell price; broker compensation, services, and rights; term and extension; broker use rights; existing judgments
- resale disclosures: form of ownership; no guaranteed sell price; current year's assessments; ad valorem tax assessment; terms of closing; exchange program
- sale offered outside of Florida exempt from FL law
- 10-day right to cancel with no waiver allowed

HOMEOWNER'S ASSOCIATIONS

- sales in Florida require licensure; occupying owners exempt; developer employees exempt if not paid on per transaction basis
- Florida timeshares offered outside of state not subject to Florida time-share laws
- out-of-state timeshares offered in Florida are subject to Florida time-share laws

- corporation responsible for operation of community or mobile home park with owner membership
- disclosure summary required
- 3-day right to cancel with no waiver allowed

COMMUNITY DEVELOPMENT DISTRICTS

- special purpose government created to provide urban community development services
- tax and assessment disclosure

SECTION SEVEN QUIZ: Condos, Co-ops, Timeshares, HOAs and CDDs

1. The distinguishing features of a condominium estate are

   a. ownership of a share in an association that owns one's apartment.
   b. tenancy in common interest in airspace and common areas of the property.
   c. fee simple ownership of the airspace in a unit and an undivided share of the entire property's common areas.
   d. fee simple ownership of a pro rata share of the entire property.

2. Who owns the property in a time-share estate?

   a. Ownership is shared by the developer and the broker.
   b. The property is owned by tenants in common or by a freehold owner who leases on a time-share basis.
   c. A real estate investment trust holds a fee simple estate.
   d. A general partner holds a fee simple interest and interval estates are owned by limited partners.

3. Which of the following is true of a cooperative?

   a. A cooperative may hold an owner liable for the unpaid operating expenses of other owners.
   b. The owners have a fee simple interest in the airspace of their respective apartments.
   c. Owners may retain their apartments even if they sell their stock in the cooperative.
   d. The proprietary lease is guaranteed to have a fixed rate of rent over the life of the lease term.

4. One difference between a cooperative estate and a condominium estate is that

   a. a default by a coop owner may cause a foreclosure on the entire property instead of just a single unit, as with a condominium.
   b. the condominium owner must pay expenses as well as rent.
   c. the coop owner owns stock and a freehold real estate interest whereas the condominium owner simply owns real estate.
   d. the condominium owner owns the common elements and the airspace whereas the coop owner only owns the apartment.

5. Which disclosure requirement is consistent for condominiums, cooperatives, and HOAs?

   a. Budget estimates
   b. Right to cancel
   c. Exchange program membership
   d. No guaranteed selling price

6. Which type of sale allows a 10-day right to cancel?

   a. Homeowners' Association
   b. Condominium
   c. Cooperative
   d. Timeshare

7. Which sale requires a Governance Form to be provided to buyers?

    a. Condominium resales
    b. Timeshare sales
    c. Cooperative initial sales
    d. HOA unit sales

8. Which sale requires a disclosure summary?

    a. CDD
    b. HOA
    c. Timeshare
    d. Cooperative

9. A _____ lease has no stated or fixed rent.

    a. quid-pro-quo
    b. gross
    c. proprietary
    d. modified gross

10. The Cooperative Act allows buyers to cancel the contract within ___ days of the buyer signing the contract.

    a. 10
    b. 12
    c. 5
    d. 15

11. What is the CDD responsible for?

    a. Pool maintenance
    b. Storm water management
    c. Maintaining the roof
    d. Lawn maintenance

12. Within how many days can buyers cancel a time share agreement without penalty?

    a. 10 days
    b. 15 days
    c. 5 days
    d. 20 days

13. What is the difference between condominium ownership and co-op ownership?

    a. The condominium owner uses a proprietary lease.
    b. A co-op owner owns a share of swimming pools, lobbies, and hallways.
    c. The co-op owner owns neither a unit nor an undivided interest in the common elements.
    d. A co-op owner owns an actual unit.

14. The scheduled use of a time-share is typically denominated in terms of _____.

    a.   weeks or months.
    b.   months or years.
    c.   days or weeks.
    d.   quarters or years.

15. Sellers of timeshare plans must hold a real estate license unless they are

    a.   paid a commission on the sale.
    b.   title company agents.
    c.   paid based on individual transactions.
    d.   owners who occupy the timeshare for their own use.

8 Foreclosures and Short Sales

Foreclosures
Short Sales

FORECLOSURES

Enforcement
Foreclosure
Deed in lieu of foreclosure

Enforcement

All liens can be enforced by the sale or other transfer of title of the secured property, whether by court action, operation of law, or through powers granted in the original loan agreement. The enforcement proceedings are referred to as foreclosure.

State law governs the foreclosure process. Broadly, a statutory or court-ordered sale enforces a general lien, including a judgment lien. A lawsuit or loan provision authorizing the sale or direct transfer of the attached property enforces a specific lien, such as a mortgage. Real estate tax liens are enforced through **tax foreclosure sales**, or **tax sales**.

The defaulting borrower may also offer the lender a **deed in lieu of foreclosure** to avoid the foreclosure process, but the lender does not have to accept it. Finally, there is the option of a **short sale**, which also avoids foreclosure but must be agreed to by the lender and borrower.

Foreclosure

Three types of foreclosure process enforce mortgage liens:

- ▶ judicial foreclosure
- ▶ non-judicial foreclosure
- ▶ strict foreclosure

Foreclosure Processes

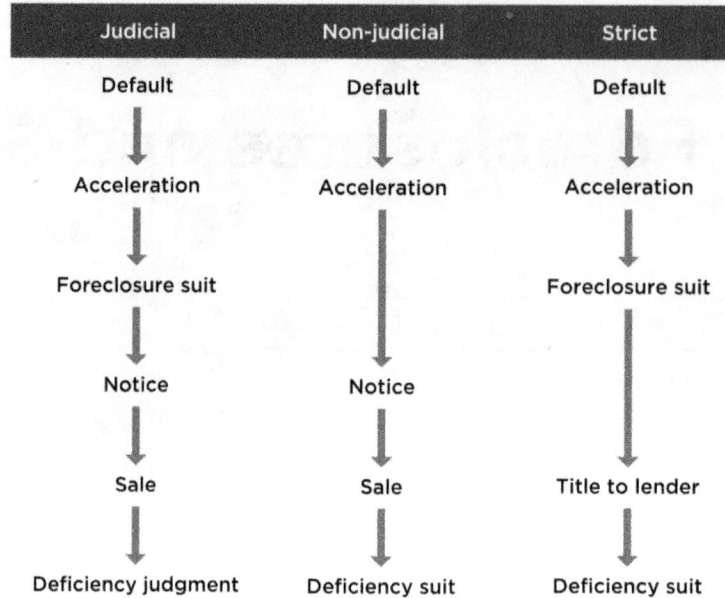

Judicial	Non-judicial	Strict
Default	Default	Default
↓	↓	↓
Acceleration	Acceleration	Acceleration
↓	↓	↓
Foreclosure suit		Foreclosure suit
↓	↓	↓
Notice	Notice	
↓	↓	↓
Sale	Sale	Title to lender
↓	↓	↓
Deficiency judgment	Deficiency suit	Deficiency suit

Judicial foreclosure. Judicial foreclosure occurs in states (such as Florida) that use a two-party mortgage document (borrower and lender) that does not contain a "power of sale" provision. Lacking this provision, a lender must file a **foreclosure suit** and undertake a court proceeding to enforce the lien.

▸ **acceleration and filing**

If a borrower has failed to meet loan obligations in spite of proper notice and applicable grace periods, the lender can **accelerate** the loan, or declare that the loan balance and all other sums due on the loan are payable immediately.

If the borrower does not pay off the loan in full, the lender then files a foreclosure suit, naming the borrower as defendant. The suit asks the court to:

- terminate the defendant's interests in the property
- order the property sold publicly to the highest bidder
- order the proceeds applied to the debt

▸ **lis pendens**

In the foreclosure suit, a **lis pendens** gives public notice that the mortgaged property may soon have a judgment issued against it. This notice enables other lienholders to join in the suit against the defendant.

▸ **writ of execution**

If the defendant fails to meet the demands of the suit during a prescribed period, the court orders the termination of interests of any and all parties in the property, and orders the property to be sold. The court's **writ of execution** authorizes an official, such as the county sheriff, to seize and sell the foreclosed property.

▶ **public sale and sale proceeds**

After public notice of the sale, the property is auctioned to the highest bidder. The new owner receives title free and clear of all previous liens, whether the lienholders have been paid or not. Proceeds of the sale are applied to payment of liens according to priority. After payment of real estate taxes, lienholders' claims and costs of the sale, any remaining funds go to the mortgagor (borrower).

▶ **deficiency judgment**

If the sale does not yield sufficient funds to cover the amounts owed, the mortgagee may ask the court for a deficiency judgment. This enables the lender to attach and foreclose a judgment lien on other real or personal property the borrower owns.

▶ **right of redemption**

The borrower's right of redemption, also called equity of redemption, is the right to *reclaim a property* that has been foreclosed by paying off amounts owed to creditors, including interest and costs. Redemption is possible within a **redemption period**. Florida allows redemption at any time until the foreclosure sale concludes.

Non-judicial foreclosure. When there is a "power of sale" provision in the mortgage or trust deed document, a non-judicial foreclosure can force the sale of the liened property *without a foreclosure suit*. The "power of sale" clause in effect enables the mortgagee to order a public sale without court decree.

▶ **foreclosure process**

On default, the foreclosing mortgagee records and delivers notice to the borrower and other lienholders. After the proper period, a "notice of sale" is published, the sale is conducted, and all liens are extinguished. The highest bidder then receives unencumbered title to the property.

▸ **deficiency suit**

The lender does not obtain a deficiency judgment or lien in a non-judicial foreclosure action. The lender instead must file a new deficiency suit against the borrower.

▸ **reinstatement and redemption**

During the notice of default and notice of sale periods, the borrower may pay the lender and terminate the proceedings. Reinstatement and redemption rights in Florida end with the conclusion of the foreclosure sale. There is no redemption right in non-judicial foreclosure.

Strict foreclosure. Strict foreclosure is a court proceeding that gives the lender title directly, by court order, instead of giving cash proceeds from a public sale.

On default, the lender gives the borrower official notice. After a prescribed period, the lender files suit in court, whereupon the court establishes a period within which the defaulting party must repay the amounts owed. If the defaulter does not repay the funds, the court orders transfer of full, legal title to the lender.

Deed in lieu of foreclosure

A defaulting borrower who faces foreclosure may avoid court actions and costs by voluntarily deeding the property to the mortgagee. This is accomplished with a deed in lieu of foreclosure which transfers legal title to the lienholder. The transfer, however, does not terminate any existing liens on the property.

SHORT SALES

Short sale transaction benchmarks
Seller's role
Buyer's role
Listing agent's role
Buyer agent's role
Lender's role
Short sale case illustration
Short sale case exercise

Short sale transaction benchmarks

A **short sale** is what must transpire whenever a property owner attempting to convey his or her property owes more than resale value and loan pay-off amount. In the short sale transaction, the seller agrees to let the lender dictate or approve the terms of the transaction in exchange for the lender's promise to release the owner from the mortgage lien and to convey marketable title to the buyer.

The lender, however, may or may not agree to accept the deficient price as a satisfactory loan payoff and may require the seller to make up deficient amounts by way of a deficiency judgment. In other instances, there may be tax consequences for the seller if the lender agrees to grant an increment of loan forgiveness – which can amount to taxable income for the seller. To avoid the deficiency charge in the short sale, the seller must make sure that the agreements include a full release of the underlying debt and a statement that it was fully satisfied.

The parties to a short sale are the buyer, the seller, their agents and the lender. The lender is a third-party contingency who must approve the sale. The process of a short sale generally unfolds as follows.

Short sale transaction benchmarks

1. The borrower-sellers or their agents contact the lender to discuss the short sale option.
2. If willing, the lender sets the required terms of the short sale.
3. For an updated valuation estimate, the real estate agent provides the lender with a Broker's Price Opinion (BPO).
4. Subsequently, the agent lists the property for sale at the highest possible price that the market will bear.
5. The agent places the listing into the MLS with a special note to the brokerage community stating that the lender will consider a short sale.
6. At some point, a buyer submits takes an interest in the property and submits an offer.
7. After negotiating price and terms, the owner and buyer agree to the terms of a contract
8. The lender is then brought into the proceedings to evaluate and (hopefully) approve the final terms of the short sale.
9. The closing date is established, the pre-closing period is completed, and ideally, the transaction closes.
10. The final terms may or may not include a deficiency proceeding to recover unacceptable shortfalls in the sales proceeds.

The success of a short sale transaction depends on the collaboration of the seller, buyer, agents, and all lenders involved (1st, 2nd, 3rd position lienholders). Each party has a specific role to ensure the transaction can go smoothly.

**Seller's role
in the short sale**

To get the transaction off to a good start, the seller must accurately identify exactly how much is owed on the property. The lenders can certainly provide this information. It is vital that the seller be upfront with all parties about every property-secured loan they have, as well as any equipment they are leasing (water softeners, solar panels, adjunct power systems, etc., all of which will have to be paid off with the sale of the home).

The seller should request payoff amounts from all lenders and provide this information to the listing agent so they can together create a net sheet. The net sheet will help the seller determine what they can afford to pay back to the various lenders once the closing costs are built in.

One common characteristic of a short sale is that the homeowner is experiencing some form of hardship that is putting pressure on the owners to sell in the short term as opposed to waiting until financial conditions improve. These circumstances should not be concealed. In order to get the short sale approved by the lender, the seller will need to provide documentation supporting the fact that they are experiencing financial hardship. Subsequently, to have a successful transaction under these adverse conditions, the seller's role will need to involve open and honest collaboration with the lender's representatives. In addition, the seller will need to understand that the short sale will require more time to complete than conventional conveyances.

Buyer's role in a short sale

Once the buyers decide to submit an offer for a short sale property, they can choose whether they would like to hire a short sale negotiator. Since short sales have become more commonplace in recent years, title companies and law firms have augmented their staffs with short sale specialists. These negotiators can be very beneficial to both principal parties – for the seller they can secure a top-dollar price, and for the buyer they can negotiate difficult agreements that might otherwise fail. The job of the short sale negotiator is to argue with the lenders and persuade them to approve the buyer's offer price.

Once a short sale is approved by all lenders, the buyer will go under contract. Since it is a short sale, the buyer should be prepared for a longer transaction and for additional paperwork. The buyer should also be aware that it is rare for any repairs or price accommodations for repairs to be accepted.

Above all, the buyer should be prepared for a very common outcome – that the short sale negotiations fail and the transaction falls apart. A consummated short sale is never a guaranteed proposition since the lenders can change their requirements at any point. Buyers (and sellers) must understand that the lender does not have to agree to lose money. While the risk of a defaulted loan is higher, lenders are under stockholder pressure to generate earnings, like everyone else. The lender can just wait it out until conditions improve. Such changes can result in lost time and not insignificant losses of money for the buyer.

Listing agent's role

One of the most important roles of a listing agent is to provide a net sheet for th sellers. They can either create their own net sheet or request one from a title company. When creating this net sheet, the listing agent should ask the seller to disclose all current mortgages. This net sheet will help the seller to better understand what position they are in.

The listing agent is responsible for generating a Broker's Price Opinion on the property. They do this by selecting the best comparable properties and adjusting them accordingly to determine an appropriate price. Once the agent completes the BPO, they will submit it, along with the seller's documentation of hardship, to the seller's lender. The lender will then review the information and either counter or accept the BPO. The review process could take weeks or months depending on the situation, the backlog in the market, and the number of lenders involved. Each lender will have to agree to collaborate with the short sale terms and parties. The more mortgagees involved, the longer it could take to approve the short sale.

Within the short sale transaction scenario, the seller can either wait for the official approval from the lender, or opt to list the property immediately. Here, the listing agent is responsible for submitting the listing into the MLS and marking it as a short sale. The listing agent should be upfront with all buyers whether the short sale is lender-approved or still under review. They must also be ready to explain the short sale process to all potential buyers as well as notify them that repair and price negotiations are unlikely.

It is also important to note that, as yet another negative characteristic of the short sale transaction, the real estate agent's commission might be lower than what practitioners typically charge for residential conveyances. Indeed, all parties must give and take in order to make short sales happen.

Buyer agent's role

The buyer's agent role in the short sale transaction – in addition to all the duties inherent in a conventional transaction -- is to inform the buyer of how the short sale process works and what they should expect. In particular, short sale properties are not always in the best condition, and most sellers cannot afford to make whatever repairs that might be identified as necessary by the inspection. Thus, the short sale is, in effect, an "as-is" conveyance, and buyers should be aware of the fact that the price may not be their last expense in completing their move.

The buyer's agent should also disclose to the buyer whether or not the listing already has an approved short sale price. If the price is not yet approved by the lender, then the process can take months of negotiating with the lender. The buyer should understand that this circumstance is much like a financing contingency that must be removed for the closing to take place.

Again, it is also important to note that a real estate agent's commission might be lower with the short sale compared to conventional transactions.

Lender's role

Each lender will have to collaborate with the sellers to agree on a short sale price. They will also typically discuss the listing agent's BPO. If necessary, the lender will generate its own BPO to validate the listing agent's value estimate.

As an interesting possibility in the short sale transaction, one should realize that the final price going onto the market may not be less than market value. If the lender does not agree to a certain price, the seller might have to list it at market value – then see what happens. But from the buyer's perspective, the short sale is not necessarily a below-market bargain or fire sale.

If there are multiple lenders who are owed money in the transaction, it can become difficult to have them all agree on their smaller payoff amounts. This negotiation process can significantly expand the time required to consummate the short sale transaction.

Another important consideration from the lender's perspective is that, in fact, the common alternative to a short sale is a default and foreclosure, both of which can cost more than loan forgiveness amounts lost in the short sale. Thus, the lender has no real win-win outcomes, and the ultimate decision to approve the upside-down short sale price must be measured against indeterminable losses incurred by a default.

Short sale exercise

The following is a short participation exercise for the student. Read the case scenario presented. Then, as the listing agent, develop a defensible answer to the question posed. Then review the response then follows.

Elijah just lost his job. He is struggling to keep up with his mortgage payments and realizes he is going to have to sell his home. He bought his house for $900,000 at the peak of the market. Now he fears that the values have declined significantly. Per his real estate agent friend, he is informed that the homes in his neighborhood are only selling for around $750,000. What should Elijah do to minimize the potential financial consequences of his predicament?

Answer: Elijah should first speak to a real estate agent who will help him determine an accurate market value for his home. The agent will do so by finding comparable homes and generating a BPO. Once the agent settles on a price, he can then create a net sheet for Elijah. In order to calculate the most accurate net profit for Elijah, the agent will need to know about every single mortgage and lien on the home. If Elijah ends up owing more than his home is worth, then he will need to consider pursuing a short sale. If his home is worth more than he owes, then he can move forward with a regular sale.

If Elijah needs to pursue a short sale, he will have to gather documents that prove he cannot afford to pay back the lenders what he owes them. If Elijah has a second home, he might need to sell it in order to pay the lender back. The lender will then review the BPO and the hardship documents and come to a decision on whether or not Elijah is eligible for a short sale. Not the prettiest picture, but it is worth a try.

8 Foreclosures and Short Sales
Snapshot Review

**FORECLOSURES
AND SHORT SALES**

Enforcement
- enforcement of mortgage lien by tax foreclosure sale, deed in lieu of foreclosure, or short sale

Foreclosure
- enforcement of liens through liquidation or transfer of encumbered property by judicial, non-judicial, or strict foreclosure
- judicial: lawsuit and court-ordered public sale; deficiency judgments, redemption rights; used in Florida
- non-judicial: "power of sale" granted to lender; no suit; no deficiency judgment; no redemption period after sale
- strict: court orders legal transfer of title directly to lender without public sale

**Deed in lieu of
foreclosure**
- defaulted borrower deeds property to lender to avoid foreclosure

SHORT SALES

Transaction benchmarks
- short sales necessary when seller owes more on mortgage than property is worth
- lender must agree to the short sale price and terms
- benchmarks: lender sets terms using BPOs; agent lists, markets; offers presented to lender for approval; lender decides; if positive, transaction is completed

**Roles of seller, buyer, agents
lender**
- seller typically enduring financial hardship; establishes relationship with listing agent; identifies all amounts owed; reviews net sheet to understand degree of deficiency
- buyer role is to appreciate difficulty of short sale; extended transaction time; limited negotiation flexibility; possibility of failure
- listing, buyer agent's roles are to facilitate communications with principals, MLS, and lenders; key action is to generate BPO to justify pricing; conduct negotiations for client
- lender's role is to approve the pricing package and the eventual buyer's offer

SECTION EIGHT QUIZ: Foreclosures and Short Sales

1. The process of enforcing a lien by forcing sale of the lienee's property is called

   a. execution.
   b. attachment.
   c. foreclosure.
   d. subordination.

2. An important difference between a judicial foreclosure and a non-judicial foreclosure is

   a. there is no right to redeem the property in a non-judicial foreclosure.
   b. a judicial foreclosure forces a sale of the property.
   c. a non-judicial foreclosure ensures that all liens are paid in order of priority.
   d. the lienor receives title directly in a non-judicial foreclosure.

3. A defaulting borrower may avoid foreclosure by giving the mortgagee

   a. a promissory note.
   b. a deed in lieu of foreclosure.
   c. a redemption notice.
   d. a lis pendens.

4. The person who executes a mortgage is called the

   a. executor.
   b. trustor.
   c. mortgagor.
   d. mortgagee.

5. Why is mortgage priority important to a mortgage lender?

   a. It establishes the level of lender risk.
   b. It determines the importance of the loan in the lender's portfolio.
   c. It reassures the borrower that the lender will give full attention to servicing of the loan.
   d. It makes recording of the loan unnecessary, thereby saving the lender money.

6. A _____ occurs when a property owner owes more than the resale value and loan pay-off.

   a. strict foreclosure
   b. short sale
   c. non-judicial foreclosure
   d. lis pendens

7. When can an equitable redemption occur?

   a. Any time before the foreclosure sale is concluded
   b. Within 15 days of filing for foreclosure
   c. After the property has been auctioned off
   d. Within 10 days of the foreclosure suit

8. In a strict foreclosure, what happens first?

    a. The lender files suit in court.
    b. The legal title gets transferred to the lender.
    c. The lender gives the borrower official notice.
    d. The owner is given a period of time to repay the amounts owed.

9. In a short sale, who determines the approved sale price?

    a. The lender determines the short sale price.
    b. The listing agent determines the short sale price.
    c. The broker determines the short sale price.
    d. The seller determines the short sale price.

10. Who submits the BPO in a short sale?

    a. The buyer's agent
    b. The listing agent
    c. The seller
    d. The appraiser

9 Real Estate Market Economics

The Market System
Real Estate Market Dynamics

Real estate is an economic product that is subject to economic laws and influences, much like all of the other goods and services in our economic system.

Real estate professionals do not have to be economists; in fact, they are better off leaving complex economic theories to those professing expertise in that often confusing field. However, brokers and agents do need a basic understanding of how our economy works, and particularly, how real estate as an economic product fits into the real estate marketplace.

Understanding the fundamentals of real estate economics enables one to:

▶ recognize the effect of current economic conditions in the real estate market on transactions, prices, and values
▶ apply economic principles to estimates of future conditions in the real estate market
▶ apply economic principles to specific geographical areas and property types in order to assess economic conditions for a particular property and site

These are abilities that will benefit the clients of any real estate professional.

THE MARKET SYSTEM

Supply and demand
Price and value
Productivity and costs
Market interaction
Market equilibrium

Supply and demand

The goal of an economic system is to produce and distribute a *supply* of goods and services to satisfy the *demand* of its constituents. Economic activity therefore centers on the production, distribution and sale of goods and services to meet consumer demand.

Supply is *the quantity of a product or service available for sale, lease, or trade at any given time.*

Demand is *the quantity of a product or service that is desired for purchase, lease, or trade at any given time.*

The interplay of supply and demand is what makes an economy work: consumers demand goods and services; suppliers and sellers produce and distribute the goods and services for a negotiated price.

Price and value

The price mechanism. In addition to supply and demand, the other critical component of an economic system is the price mechanism, or simply, price. A **price** is the amount of money or other asset that a buyer has agreed to pay and a seller has agreed to accept to complete the exchange of a good or service. It is a quantification of the value of an item traded.

Price in this context means the final trading price; it is not the preliminary asking price of the seller nor the initial bidding price of the purchaser. Asking and bidding prices are pricing positions in a negotiation between the parties prior to the exchange. The true price of an item or service is the final number the parties agree to.

Value and value determinants. Price is not something of value in itself. It is only a number that *quantifies value*. The economic issue underlying the interplay of supply and demand is, how do trading parties arrive at the value of a good or service as indicated by the price?

Consider consumer demand for air conditioners. Why do air conditioners have value? How do they command the price they do?

The value of something is based on the answers to four questions:

- ▶ How much do I desire it?
- ▶ How useful is it?
- ▶ How scarce is it?
- ▶ Am I able to pay for it?

Desire. One determinant of value is how dear the item is to the purchaser. Returning to the air conditioner example, the question becomes "how much do I desire to be cool, dry, and comfortable?" To a person who lives in the tropics, it is safe to say that air conditioning is *more valuable* than a heating system. It is also safe to say the opposite is true for residents of northern Alaska.

Utility. The second determinant of value is the product's *ability to do the job*. Can the air conditioner satisfy my need to stay cool? How cool does it make my house? Does it even work properly? Of course, I won't pay as much if it is old or ineffectual.

Scarcity. The third critical element of value is a product's *availability in relation to demand*. The air conditioner is quite valuable if there are only five units in the entire city and everyone is hot. On the other hand, the value of an air conditioner goes down if there are ten thousand units for sale in a 500-person market.

Purchasing power. A fourth component of value is the *consumer's ability to pay* for the item. If one cannot afford to buy the air conditioner, the value of the air conditioner is diminished, since it is financially out of reach. If all air conditioners are too expensive, consumers are forced to consider alternatives such as ceiling fans.

In the marketplace, the relative presence or absence of the four elements of value is constantly changing due to innumerable factors. Since price is a reflection of the total of all value factors at any time, changes in the underlying factors of value trigger changes in price.

Productivity and costs

To produce a good or service, a supplier incurs **costs**, or those expenses necessary to generate and deliver the item to the market. The essential production costs are the costs of capital, materials, and supplies; labor; management; and overhead.

Costs play an important role in the dynamics of supply, demand, and value. Since a producer has limited resources, it is imperative to maximize the efficiency of the production process and minimize its costs. Moreover, since consumers will pay the lowest possible price for comparable goods and services, the producer must be price-competitive to stay in business. A competitor who can produce an item of similar quality for less will eventually force higher-priced items out of the market.

Cost and price. Consider a producer who is efficient and produces the product or service in demand at the lowest possible cost. Adding to the cost a required profit margin, the producer establishes a minimum price for the item. In this scenario, cost essentially equals price. To the efficient producer, costs and sufficient profit are paramount, since a lower price puts the producer out of business. At that point, the elements of value-- desire, utility, scarcity, and purchasing power-- do not matter: if the consumer wants the item at all, he or she must cover the producer's costs and profit.

In summary, supply, demand, and price interact continuously in a market. Underlying and influencing these forces are the dynamics of value and the costs of producing goods and services.

Market interaction

What is a market? A market is a place where supply and demand encounter one another: suppliers sell or trade their goods and services to demanders, who are consumers and buyers. It is a *transaction arena* where the price mechanism is constantly defining and quantifying the value produced by the relative elements of supply and demand.

Supply, demand and price interrelationships. In a market economy, the primary interactions between supply, demand and price are:

> ▸ if supply increases relative to demand, price decreases
> ▸ if supply decreases relative to demand, price increases
> ▸ if demand increases relative to supply, price increases
> ▸ if demand decreases relative to supply, price decreases

These relationships reflect simple common sense: if a valued product becomes increasingly scarce, its value and price go up as consumers compete for the limited supply. If there is an overabundance of a product, the price falls, as demand is largely met. On the other side, if demand for a product or service increases in relation to supply, prices will go up as consumers compete for the popular item. If demand diminishes, the price drops with it.

The inverse of these principles also applies. By tracking a price trend, one can draw conclusions about supply and demand trends:

> ▸ if price decreases, demand is declining in relation to supply
> ▸ if price increases, demand is increasing in relation to supply

To assess price movements, the supply and demand of a product or service must always be considered together. It is always possible for demand and supply to rise and fall together at the same rate, with no detectable price change resulting.

For example, if demand for bicycles jumps a million units, and manufacturers easily produce the necessary new supply, there may be no increase in price. The price may even go down as manufacturers obtain better prices on the larger quantities of raw materials they now use.

Market equilibrium

Another significant principle of supply/demand/price interaction is **market equilibrium**:

> ▸ a market tends toward a state of equilibrium in which supply equals demand, and price, cost, and value are identical

According to this principle, market demand moves to meet supply, and supply moves to meet demand. If there is an extreme shortage of an item for which there is normally a strong demand, suppliers will rush to increase production to close the gap. If inventories of an item are very high, suppliers will stop production until the oversupply has been depleted.

Similarly, if the price of an item far exceeds its cost, new suppliers will enter the market with lower prices. If the price of an item is far less than its perceived value, either consumers will bid up the price or the perceived value will decline.

For example, a new convenience store opens on the edge of a rapidly growing town. The owners know demand will increase, so they anticipate the demand with their increment of supply. Initially, the store creates excess supply, so business is slow. However, as people move in, demand increases, and the store begins to make substantial profits. After some time, other retailers hear that the store is profitable: demand now significantly exceeds supply, and the operator's costs are out of line with values and prices. A second retailer opens a store to equalize the imbalance. The new competitor, an addition of supply, now forces prices, costs, and profits into closer proximity.

The equilibrium time lag. In theory, markets strive for equilibrium, but in reality there is always a time lag between a recognized imbalance and the completion of the market adjustment. Since the underlying determinants of supply and demand (scarcity, desire, utility, purchasing power and costs) are constantly changing, a market is usually in some condition of imbalance.

REAL ESTATE MARKET DYNAMICS

Economic characteristics of real estate
Real estate supply and demand
Market influences on supply and demand

As an economic commodity, real estate is bought, sold, traded, and leased as a product within a real estate market.

Economic characteristics of real estate

Real estate, like other products and services, is:

- subject to the laws of supply and demand
- governed in the market by the price mechanism
- influenced by the producer's costs to bring the product to market
- influenced by the determinants of value: utility, scarcity, desire, and purchasing power

Distinguishing features. In comparison with other economic products and services, real estate has certain unique traits. These include:

- **Inherent product value**

  Land is a scarce resource as well as a required factor of production. Like gold and silver, it has both inherent value and utility value.

- **Unique appeal of product**

  Since no two parcels of real estate can be alike (each has a different location), every parcel of real property has its own appeal. Likewise, no two parcels of real estate can have exactly the same value, except by coincidence.

- **Demand must come to the supply**

  Since real property cannot be moved, real property investors and users must come to the supply. This creates risk, because if demand drops, the supply cannot be transported to a higher demand market.

- **Illiquid**

  Real estate is a relatively illiquid economic product, meaning it cannot always be readily sold for cash. Since it is a large, long-term investment that has no exact duplicate, buyers must go through a complex process to evaluate and purchase the right parcel of real estate.

> ▸ **Slow to respond to changes**

Real estate is relatively slow to respond to market imbalances. Because new construction is a large-scale, time-consuming process, the market is slow to respond to increases in demand. The market is similarly slow to respond to sharp declines in demand, since the product cannot be moved and sold elsewhere. Instead, owners must wait out slow periods and simply hope for the best.

> ▸ **Decentralized, local market**

A real property cannot be shipped to a large, central real estate marketplace. Real estate markets are thus local in nature and highly susceptible to swings in the local economy.

Real estate supply and demand

Supply. In real estate, supply is the *amount of property available* for sale or lease at any given time. Note that supply is generally not the number of properties available, except in the case of residential real estate. The units of supply used to quantify the amount of property available differ for different categories of property. These supply units, by property type, are:

> ▸ residential: dwelling units
> ▸ commercial and industrial: square feet
> ▸ agricultural: acreage

Factors influencing supply. In addition to the influences of demand and the underlying determinants of value, real estate supply responds to

> ▸ development costs, particularly labor
> ▸ availability of financing
> ▸ investment returns
> ▸ a community's master plan
> ▸ government police powers and regulation

Demand. Real estate demand is the amount of property buyers and tenants wish to acquire by purchase, lease or trade at any given time. Units of demand, by property classification, are:

> ▸ residential: households
> ▸ commercial and industrial: square feet
> ▸ agricultural: acreage

The unit of residential demand is the household, which is an individual or family who would occupy a dwelling unit. Residential demand can be further broken down into demand to lease versus buy, and demand for single family homes versus apartments.

Residential demand can be very difficult to quantify. One measure is the number of buyers employing agents to locate property. Another measure is the net population change in an area, plus families that attempted to move in but could not.

The unit of commercial (retail and office) and industrial real estate demand is the square foot, further broken down into demand for leased space versus purchased space. In most instances, the area demanded refers to the improved area rather than the total lot area.

Demand for office and industrial real estate is calculated by identifying employment growth or shrinkage in a market, then multiplying the employment change times the average area of floor space a typical employee uses. For example, consider an office property market where employment in the community increases by 500 employees. If each employee uses an average of 120 square feet, the increased demand for space is 60,000 square feet.

Factors affecting demand. The demand for particular types of real estate relates to the specific concerns of users. These concerns revolve around the components of value: desire, utility, scarcity, and purchasing power.

Residential users are concerned with:

- quality of life
- neighborhood quality
- convenience and access to services and other facilities
- dwelling amenities in relation to household size, lifestyle, and costs

Retail users are concerned with:

- sufficient trade area population and income
- the level of trade area competition
- sales volume per square foot of rented area
- consumer spending patterns
- growth patterns in the trade area

Office users are concerned with:

- costs of occupancy to the business
- efficiency of the building and the suite in accommodating the business's functions
- accessibility by employees and suppliers
- matching building quality to the image and function of the business

Industrial users are concerned with:

- functionality
- the availability and proximity of the labor pool
- compliance with environmental regulations
- permissible zoning
- health and safety of the workers
- access to suppliers and distribution channels

Base employment and total employment. The engine that drives demand for real estate of all types in a market is employment-- *base* employment and *total* employment.

Exhibit Basis of Real Estate Demand

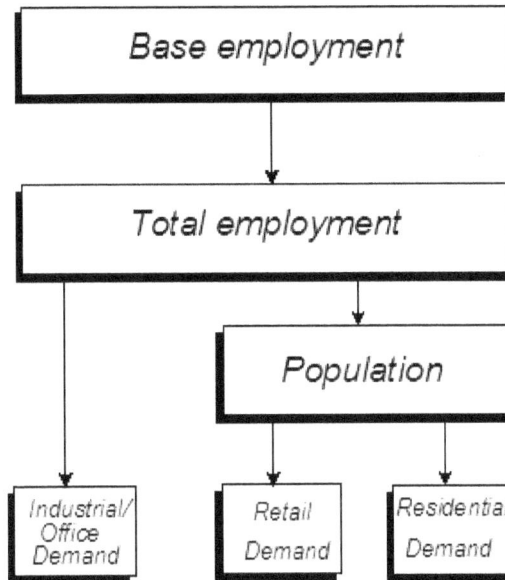

```
┌─────────────────────────────┐
│      Base employment        │
└─────────────────────────────┘
               │
               ▼
┌─────────────────────────────┐
│      Total employment       │
└─────────────────────────────┘
       │              │
       │              ▼
       │      ┌──────────────────┐
       │      │    Population     │
       │      └──────────────────┘
       │         │           │
       ▼         ▼           ▼
┌──────────┐ ┌────────┐ ┌─────────────┐
│Industrial/│ │ Retail │ │ Residential │
│  Office   │ │ Demand │ │   Demand    │
│  Demand   │ │        │ │             │
└──────────┘ └────────┘ └─────────────┘
```

Base employment is the number of persons employed in the businesses that represent the economic foundation of the area. For example, the auto industry has traditionally been the primary base employer of the Detroit metropolitan area.

Base industries lead to the rise of supporting and secondary industries in the market. If the auto industry is the base, auto parts manufacturers and assembly industries will develop to support the auto manufacturing plants. In addition, service businesses emerge to support the many needs of the local population engaged in primary and secondary employment.

Thus, base employment feeds total employment. Total employment in a market includes base, secondary, and support industries. Total employment creates a demand for a labor force. From total employment derives demand for industrial and office space on the one hand; on the other hand, as employment grows, so grows the population, leading to the demand for housing and for retail support. In addition to creating demand for real estate, employment creates the purchasing power necessary for households to acquire dwellings and retail products.

Without employment, a real estate market evaporates, as there is no demand for commercial or industrial facilities, nor is there demand for retail services or housing. The best example of this phenomenon is a gold rush boom town: as soon as the gold runs out, there is no more mining. Without mining employment, everyone moves away and the town becomes a ghost town.

Supply and demand interaction. Real estate supply and demand, like supply and demand for other economic products, interact in the marketplace to produce *price movements.*

Exhibit - Real Estate Supply-Demand Cycle

As the exhibit illustrates, prices, construction, and vacancy move up and down in the cycle. Construction represents the addition of new supply. **Vacancy** is the amount of total real estate inventory of a certain type that is unoccupied at a given time. **Absorption** is the amount of available property that becomes occupied over a period of time.

Taking the point of undersupply, or high demand, as a starting point in the cycle, vacancy is low and prices are high. This situation stimulates suppliers to construct additional housing or commercial space. New construction, by adding supply, causes vacancy to rise and prices to fall until supply-demand equilibrium results. As more new space is added, supply begins to outstrip demand, vacancy continues to rise, and prices continue to fall. At the bottom of the cycle, prices and vacancy are at unacceptable levels, and construction ceases. The market "dies" until excess supply can be absorbed. The absorption process continues through the equilibrium point until price and vacancy conditions are sufficiently attractive to encourage renewed construction. Then the cycle repeats.

Market influences on supply and demand

Numerous factors in a market influence the real estate cycle to speed up or slow down. These influences can be local or national, and from the public or private economic sector.

Local market influences. Since the real estate market is local by definition, local factors weigh heavily in local real estate market conditions. Among these are:

- ▶ cost of financing
- ▶ availability of developable land
- ▶ construction costs
- ▶ capacity of the municipality's infrastructure to handle growth

- ▸ governmental regulation and police powers
- ▸ changes in the economic base
- ▸ in- and out-migrations of major employers

National trends. Regional and national economic forces influence the local real estate market in the form of:

- ▸ changes in money supply
- ▸ inflation
- ▸ national economic cycles

In recent years international economic trends have increasingly influenced local real estate markets, particularly in border states, large metropolitan areas, and in markets where the economic base is tied to foreign trade. In these instances, currency fluctuations have significant impact on the local economy.

Governmental influences. Governments at every level exert significant influence over local real estate markets. The primary forms of government influence are:

- ▸ local zoning power
- ▸ local control and permitting of new development
- ▸ local taxing power
- ▸ federal influence on interest rates
- ▸ environmental legislation and regulations

A good example of government influence over the local real estate market is a city government's power to declare a moratorium on new construction, regardless of demand. Such officially declared stoppages may occur because of water or power shortages, insufficiency of thoroughfares, or incompatibility with the master plan.

THE MARKET SYSTEM

Supply and demand

- supply: goods or services available for sale, lease, or trade

- demand: goods or services desired for purchase, lease, or trade

Price and value

- price mechanism: quantified value of an exchange

- value components: desire; utility; scarcity; purchasing power

Productivity and costs

- cost plus profit equals minimum price; production cost possible component of value

Market interaction

- market: transaction arena where suppliers and demanders define value through the price mechanism

- if supply increases relative to demand, price decreases; if demand increases relative to supply, price increases

Market equilibrium

- supply and demand tend toward balance where they are equal

- market equilibrium: price, cost, value theoretically the same; market imbalances are caused by changes in supply or demand

REAL ESTATE MARKET DYNAMICS

Economic characteristics of real estate

- governed by supply, demand, price, costs, value components, government influence

- inherent value; unique appeal; immovable supply; illiquid; slow response to cycles; decentralized market

Real estate supply and demand

- supply: property available for sale or lease; measured in dwelling units, square feet, acres; influenced by costs, finance, returns, government regulation

- demand: property buyers and tenants wish to acquire; measured in households, square feet, acres; influences: residential-- quality, amenities, price convenience; retail-trade area, sales, competition, site access, visibility; growth patterns; office-efficiency, costs, functionality; industrial-- functionality, labor, regulatory compliance, access to labor, supplies, distribution channels

- base employment, total employment, population determine overall demand

- if employment and population increase, demand and prices increase; if they decrease, the opposite occurs

- supply-demand indicators are price, vacancy, and absorption; vacancy is existing, unoccupied supply; absorption is the "filling up" of vacancy

- real estate supply-demand cycle: undersupply > accelerated construction adds supply > equilibrium > construction adds more supply > oversupply > construction stops > equilibrium > demand absorbs supply

Market influences on supply and demand

- local economic factors; national economic trends in money supply, inflation; government regulation at all levels

SECTION NINE QUIZ: Real Estate Market Economics

1. Price is best described as

    a. what suppliers charge for goods and services.
    b. the amount of money consumers are willing to pay for a product or service.
    c. the amount of money a buyer and seller agree to exchange to complete a transaction.
    d. a control placed on prices by the federal government.

2. Four principal determinants of value underlying the price for a product are

    a. durability, quality, scarcity, and materials.
    b. desire, utility, scarcity, and purchasing power.
    c. popularity, utility, quality, and discount.
    d. desire, costs, convenience, and time.

3. A town has a rapidly growing population, but there are no longer any vacant lots around the lake to build more houses. In this case, it is likely that the price of existing homes on the lake

    a. will stabilize, since the population must stabilize.
    b. will increase.
    c. will decline, since no further building can take place.
    d. will not show any predictable movement.

4. If there is a significant undersupply of homes in a market, construction will tend to increase. This is an example of

    a. supply outstripping demand.
    b. overpricing products.
    c. the price mechanism.
    d. the market tending toward equilibrium.

5. If commercial real estate rental prices are falling in a market, it is likely that

    a. demand has outstripped supply of space.
    b. the market is in equilibrium.
    c. the market is over-supplied.
    d. employment is increasing.

6. Which of the following is an important economic characteristic of real estate?

    a. The demand must literally come to the supply.
    b. Real estate is a highly liquid product.
    c. The product is quick to adapt to market changes.
    d. The market is centralized.

7. The foremost factor contributing to commercial and residential demand in a market is

    a. marketing.
    b. base employment.
    c. existing supply of properties.
    d. household income.

8. A construction boom in a market is an indication that prices

   a. have been increasing.
   b. have been declining.
   c. have been in equilibrium.
   d. have exceeded supply.

9. A local government could stimulate the real estate market by

   a. increasing labor costs and curbing the money supply.
   b. increasing taxes and interest rates.
   c. declaring a moratorium on construction.
   d. expanding the sewer system.

10. Two important concerns of retail property users are

    a. trade area population and spending patterns.
    b. quality of life and dwelling amenities.
    c. costs of occupancy and building efficiency.
    d. environmental regulations and access by suppliers.

11. Two important concerns of office property users are

    a. trade area population and visibility.
    b. convenience and neighborhood make-up.
    c. costs of occupancy and building efficiency.
    d. environmental regulations and zoning.

12. What is a property's trading price?

    a. The final price both buyer and seller agree to
    b. The preliminary asking price
    c. The initial bidding price
    d. The amount a buyer offers

13. A market tends toward a state of _____ in which supply equals demand, and price, cost, and value are identical.

    a. tranquility
    b. equilibrium
    c. equality
    d. justness

14. What is a distinguishing feature of real estate?

    a. Real estate has no utility value.
    b. The demand does not come to supply.
    c. It is quick to respond to market imbalances.
    d. Real estate is illiquid.

15. If supply increases relative to demand, the price _____

    a. stays the same.
    b. increases.
    c. decreases.
    d. multiplies.

16. What drives demand for real estate of all types?

   a. Stock market
   b. Employment
   c. Tourism
   d. Neighborhood quality

17. Two similar parcels of real estate generally have _____ because of the uniqueness of real property.

   a. comparable
   b. increasing values
   c. differing values
   d. homogeneous values

10 Estimating Property Value

Concepts of Value
Defining Market Value
Estimating Residential Property Value
Estimating Income Property Value

CONCEPTS OF VALUE

Basic value determinants
Valuation principles

Basic value determinants

Price is not something of value in itself. It is only a number that *quantifies value*. The economic issue underlying the interplay of supply and demand is, how do trading parties arrive at the value of a good or service as indicated by the price?

Consider consumer demand for air conditioners. Why do air conditioners have value? How do they command the price they do?

The value of something is based on the answers to four questions:

▸ How much do I desire it?
▸ How useful is it?
▸ How scarce is it?
▸ Am I able to pay for it?

Desire. One determinant of value is how dear the item is to the purchaser. Returning to the air conditioner example, the question becomes "how much do I desire to be cool, dry, and comfortable?" To a person who lives in the tropics, it is safe to say that air conditioning is *more valuable* than a heating system. It is also safe to say the opposite is true for residents of northern Alaska.

Utility. The second determinant of value is the product's *ability to do the job*. Can the air conditioner satisfy my need to stay cool? How cool does it make my house? Does it even work properly? Of course, I won't pay as much if it is old or ineffectual.

Scarcity. The third critical element of value is a product's *availability in relation to demand*. The air conditioner is quite valuable if there are only five units in the entire city and everyone is hot. On the other hand, the value of an air conditioner goes down if there are ten thousand units for sale in a 500-person market.

Purchasing power. A fourth component of value is the *consumer's ability to pay* for the item. If one cannot afford to buy the air conditioner, the value of the air conditioner is diminished, since it is financially out of reach. If all air conditioners are too expensive, consumers are forced to consider alternatives such as ceiling fans.

In the marketplace, the relative presence or absence of the four elements of value is constantly changing due to innumerable factors. Since price is a reflection of the total of all value factors at any time, changes in the underlying factors of value trigger changes in price.

Valuation principles A number of economic forces interact in the marketplace to contribute to real estate value. Appraisers must consider these forces in estimating the value of a property. Among the most recognized of these principles are those listed below.

Economic Principles Underlying Real Estate Value

supply and demand	change
utility	highest and best use
transferability	conformity
anticipation	progression and regression
substitution	assemblage
contribution	subdivision

Supply and demand. The availability of certain properties interacts with the strength of the demand for those properties to establish prices. When demand for properties exceeds supply, a condition of scarcity exists, and real estate values rise. When supply exceeds demand, a condition of surplus exists, and real estate values decline. When supply and demand are generally equivalent, the market is considered to be in balance, and real estate values stabilize.

Utility. The fact that a property has a use in a certain marketplace contributes to the demand for it. Use is not the same as function. For instance, a swampy area may have an ecological function as a wetland, but it may have no economic utility if it cannot be put to some use that people in the marketplace are willing to pay for.

Transferability. How readily or easily title or rights to real estate can be transferred affects the property's value. Property that is encumbered has a value impairment since buyers do not want unmarketable title. Similarly, property that cannot be transferred due to disputes among owners may cause the value to decline, because the investment is wholly illiquid until the disputes are resolved.

Anticipation. The benefits a buyer *expects to derive from a property over a holding period* influence what the buyer is willing to pay for it. For example, if an investor anticipates an annual rental income from a leased property to be one million dollars, this expected sum has a direct bearing on what the investor will pay for the property.

Substitution. According to the principle of substitution, a buyer will *pay no more for a property than the buyer would have to pay for an equally desirable and available substitute property*. For example, if three houses for sale are essentially similar in size, quality and location, a potential buyer is unlikely to choose the one that is priced significantly higher than the other two.

Contribution. The principle of contribution focuses on the degree to which a particular improvement affects market value of the overall property. In essence, the contribution of the improvement is *equal to the change in market value that the addition of the improvement causes*. For example, adding a bathroom to a house may contribute an additional $15,000 to the appraised value. Thus the contribution of the bathroom is $15,000. Note that an improvement's contribution to value has little to do with the improvement's cost. The foregoing bathroom may have cost $5,000 or $20,000. Contribution is what the market recognizes as the change in value, not what an item cost. If continuous improvements are added to a property, it is possible that, at some point, the cost of adding improvements to a property no longer contributes a corresponding increase in the value of the property. When this occurs, the property suffers from *diminishing marginal return,* where the costs to improve exceed contribution.

Change. Market conditions are in a state of flux over time, just as the condition of a property itself changes. These fluctuations and changes will affect the benefits that can arise from the property, and should be reflected in an estimate of the property's value. For example, the construction of a neighborhood shopping center in the vicinity of a certain house may increase the desirability of the house's location, and hence, its value.

Highest and best use. This principle holds that there is, theoretically, a single use for a property that produces the greatest income and return. A property achieves its maximum value when it is put to this use. If the actual use is not the highest and best use, the value of the property is correspondingly less than optimal. Technically, highest and best use must be legally permissible, physically possible, financially feasible, and maximally productive.

For example, a property with an old house on it may not be in its highest and best use if it is surrounded by retail properties. If zoning permits the property to be converted to a retail use, its highest and best use may well be retail rather than residential.

Conformity. This principle holds that a property's maximal value is attained when its form and use are in tune with surrounding properties and uses. For example, a two-bedroom, one-bathroom house surrounded by four-bedroom, three-bathroom homes may derive maximal value from a room addition.

Progression and regression. The value of a property influences, and is influenced by, the values of neighboring properties. If a property is surrounded by properties with higher values, its value will tend to rise (progression); if it is surrounded by properties with lower values, its value will tend to fall (regression).

Assemblage. Assemblage, or the conjoining of adjacent properties, sometimes creates a combined value that is greater than the values of the unassembled properties. The excess value created by assemblage is called **plottage value.**

Subdivision. The division of a single property into smaller properties can also result in a higher total value. For instance, a one-acre suburban site appraised at $50,000 may be subdivided into four quarter-acre lots worth $30,000 each. This principle contributes significantly to the financial feasibility of subdivision development.

DEFINING MARKET VALUE

Market value is an opinion of the price that a willing seller and willing buyer would probably agree on for a property at a given time if:

▸ the transaction is a cash transaction

▸ the property is exposed on the open market for a reasonable period

▸ buyer and seller have full information about market conditions and about potential uses

▸ there is no abnormal pressure on either party to complete the transaction

▸ buyer and seller are not related (it is an "arm's length" transaction)

▸ title is marketable and conveyable by the seller

▸ the price is a "normal consideration," that is, it does not include hidden influences such as special financing deals, concessions, terms, services, fees, credits, costs, or other types of consideration.

Another way of describing market value is that it is the highest price that a buyer would pay and the lowest price that the seller would accept for the property.

The market price, as opposed to market value, is what a property actually sells for. Market price should theoretically be the same as market value if all the conditions essential for market value were present. Market price, however, may not reflect the analysis of comparables and of investment value that an estimate of market value includes.

Broker's opinion of value. A broker's opinion of value may resemble an appraisal, but it differs from an appraisal in that it is not necessarily performed by a disinterested third party or licensed professional and it generally uses only a limited form of one of the three appraisal approaches. In addition, the opinion is not subject to regulation, nor does it follow any particular professional standards.

ESTIMATING RESIDENTIAL PROPERTY VALUE

Steps in the approach
Identifying comparables
Adjusting comparables
Weighting comparables
Broker's comparative market analysis

The sales comparison approach, also known as the *market data approach*, is used for almost all properties. It also serves as the basis for a broker's opinion of value. It is based on the principle of substitution-- that a buyer will pay no more for the subject property than would be sufficient to purchase a comparable property-- and contribution-- that specific characteristics add value to a property.

The sales comparison approach is widely used because it takes into account the subject property's specific amenities in relation to competing properties. In addition, because of the currency of its data, the approach incorporates present market realities.

The sales comparison approach is limited in that every property is unique. As a result, it is difficult to find good comparables, especially for special-purpose properties. In addition, the market must be active; otherwise, sale prices lack currency and reliability.

Steps in the approach

The sales comparison approach consists of comparing sale prices of recently sold properties that are comparable with the subject, and making dollar adjustments to the price of each comparable to account for competitive differences with the subject. After identifying the adjusted value of each comparable, the appraiser weights the reliability of each comparable and the factors underlying how the adjustments were made. The weighting yields a final value range based on the most reliable factors in the analysis.

Steps in the Sales Comparison Approach

1. Identify comparable sales.
2. Compare comparables to the subject and make adjustments to comparables.
3. Weight values indicated by adjusted comparables for the final value estimate of the subject.

Identifying comparables

To qualify as a comparable, a property must:

> - resemble the subject in size, shape, design, utility and location
> - have sold recently, generally within six months of the appraisal
> - have sold in an arm's-length transaction

An appraiser considers three to six comparables, and usually includes at least three in the appraisal report.

Appraisers have specific guidelines within the foregoing criteria for selecting comparables, many of which are set by secondary market organizations such as FNMA. For example, to qualify as a comparable for a mortgage loan appraisal, a property might have to be located within one mile of the subject. Or perhaps the size of the comparable must be within a certain percentage of improved area in relation to the subject.

The time-of-sale criterion is important because transactions that occurred too far in the past will not reflect appreciation or recent changes in market conditions.

An arm's length sale involves objective, disinterested parties who are presumed to have negotiated a market price for the property. If the sale of a house occurred between a father and a daughter, for example, one might assume that the transaction did not reflect market value.

Principal sources of data for generating the sales comparison are tax records, title records, and the local multiple listing service.

Adjusting comparables

The appraiser adjusts the sale prices of the comparables to account for competitive differences with the subject property. Note that the sale prices of the comparables are known, while the value and price of the subject are not. Therefore, adjustments can be made *only to the comparables' prices, not to the subject's*. Adjustments are made to the comparables in the form of a value deduction or a value addition.

Adding or deducting value. If the comparable is *better* than the subject in some characteristic, an amount is *deducted* from the sale price of the comparable. This neutralizes the comparable's competitive advantage in an adjustment category.

For example, a comparable has a swimming pool and the subject does not. To equalize the difference, the appraiser deducts an amount, say $6,000, from the sale price of the comparable. Note that the adjustment reflects the contribution of the swimming pool to market value. The adjustment amount is not the cost of the pool or its depreciated value.

If the comparable is *inferior* to the subject in some characteristic, an amount is *added* to the price of the comparable. This adjustment equalizes the subject's competitive advantage in this area.

Adjustment criteria. The principal factors for comparison and adjustment are *time of sale, location, physical characteristics, and transaction characteristics.*

> ▶ **time of sale**
>
> An adjustment may be made if market conditions, market prices, or financing availability have changed significantly since the date of the comparable's sale. Most often, this adjustment is to account for appreciation.

> ▶ **location**
>
> An adjustment may be made if there are differences between the comparable's location and the subject's, including neighborhood desirability and appearance, zoning restrictions, and general price levels.

▸ **physical characteristics**

Adjustments may be made for marketable differences between the comparable's and subject's lot size, square feet of livable area (or other appropriate measure for the property type), number of rooms, layout, age, condition, construction type and quality, landscaping, and special amenities.

▸ **transaction characteristics**

An adjustment may be made for such differences as mortgage loan terms, mortgage assumability, and owner financing.

Weighting comparables

Adding and subtracting the appropriate adjustments to the sale price of each comparable results in an adjusted price for the comparables that indicates the value of the subject. The last step in the approach is to perform a weighted analysis of the indicated values of each comparable. The appraiser, in other words, must identify which comparable values are more indicative of the subject and which are less indicative.

An appraiser primarily relies on experience and judgment to weight comparables. There is no formula for selecting a value from within the range of all comparables analyzed. However, there are three quantitative guidelines: the total number of adjustments; the amount of a single adjustment; and the net value change of all adjustments.

As a rule, *the fewer the total number of adjustments, the smaller the adjustment amounts, and the less the total adjustment amount, the more reliable the comparable.*

Number of adjustments. In terms of total adjustments, the comparable with the fewest adjustments tends to be most similar to the subject, hence the best indicator of value. If a comparable requires excessive adjustments, it is increasingly less reliable as an indicator of value. The underlying rationale is that there is a margin of error involved in making any adjustment. Whenever a number of adjustments must be made, the margin of error compounds. By the time six or seven adjustments are made, the margin becomes significant, and the reliability of the final value estimate is greatly reduced.

Single adjustment amounts. The dollar amount of an adjustment represents the variance between the subject and the comparable for a given item. If a large adjustment is called for, the comparable becomes less of an indicator of value. The smaller the adjustment, the better the comparable is as an indicator of value. If an appraisal is performed for mortgage qualification, the appraiser may be restricted from making adjustments in excess of a certain amount, for example, anything in excess of 10-15% of the sale price of the comparable. If such an adjustment would be necessary, the property is no longer considered comparable.

Total net adjustment amount. The third reliability factor in weighting comparables is the total net value change of all adjustments added together. If a comparable's total adjustments alter the indicated value only slightly, the comparable is a good indicator of value. If total adjustments create a large dollar amount between the sale price and the adjusted value, the comparable is a poorer indicator of value. Fannie Mae, for instance, will not accept the use of a comparable where total net adjustments are in excess of 15% of the sale price.

For example, an appraiser is considering a property that sold for $1,000,000 as a comparable. After all adjustments are made, the indicated value of the comparable is $1,210,000, a 21% difference in the comparable's sale price. This property, if allowed at all, would be a weak indicator of value.

Broker's comparative market analysis

A broker or associate who is attempting to establish a listing price or range of prices for a property uses a scaled-down version of the appraiser's sales comparison approach called a comparative market analysis, or CMA (also called a competitive market analysis). While the CMA serves a useful purpose in setting general price ranges, brokers and agents need to exercise caution in presenting a CMA as an appraisal, which it is not. Two important distinctions between the two are objectivity and comprehensiveness.

First, the broker is not unbiased: he or she is motivated by the desire to obtain a listing, which can lead one to distort the estimated price. Secondly, the broker's CMA is not comprehensive: the broker does not usually consider the full range of data about market conditions and comparable sales that the appraiser must consider and document. Therefore, the broker's opinion will be less reliable than the appraiser's.

The following exhibit illustrates the sales comparison approach. An appraiser is estimating market value for a certain house. Four comparables are adjusted to find an indicated value for the subject. The grid which follows the property and market data shows the appraiser's adjustments for the differences between the four comparables and the subject.

Sales Comparison Approach Illustration

Data

Subject property: 8 rooms-- 3 bedrooms, two baths, kitchen, living room, family room; 2,000 square feet of gross living area; 2-car attached garage; landscaping is good. Construction is frame with aluminum siding.

Comparable A: Sold for 1,000,000 within previous month; conventional financing at current rates; located in subject's neighborhood with similar locational advantages; house approximately same age as subject; lot size smaller than subject; view similar to subject; design less appealing than subject's; construction similar to subject; condition similar to subject; 7 rooms-- two bedrooms, one bath; 1,900 square feet of gross living area; 2-car attached garage; landscaping similar to subject.

Comparable B: Sold for 1,200,000 within previous month; conventional financing at current rates; located in subject's neighborhood with similar locational advantages; house six years newer than subject; lot size smaller than subject; view is better than the subject's; design is more appealing than subject's; construction (brick and frame) better than subject's; better condition than subject; 10 rooms-four bedrooms, three baths; 2,300 square feet of gross living area; 2-car attached garage; landscaping similar to subject.

Comparable C: Sold for 1,150,000 within previous month; conventional financing at current rates; located in subject's neighborhood with similar locational advantages; house five years older than subject; lot size larger than subject; view similar to subject; design and appeal similar to subject's; construction similar to subject; condition similar to subject; 8 rooms-- three bedrooms, two baths; 2,000 square feet of gross living area; 2-car attached garage; landscaping similar to subject.

Comparable D: Sold for 1,090,000 within previous month; conventional financing at current rates; located in a neighborhood close to subject's, but more desirable than subject's; house approximately same age as subject; lot size same as subject; view similar to subject; design less appealing than subject's; construction (frame) poorer than subject's; poorer condition than subject; 7 rooms-- two bedrooms, one and one half baths; 1,900 square feet of gross living area; 2-car attached garage; landscaping similar to subject.

Sales Comparison Approach Illustration, cont.

Adjustments

	Subject	A	B	C	D
Sale price		1,000,000	1,200,000	1,150,000	1,090,000
Financing terms		standard	standard	standard	standard
Sale date	NOW	equal	equal	equal	equal
Location		equal	equal	equal	-20,000
Age		equal	-12,000	+10,000	equal
Lot size		+10,000	+10,000	-10,000	equal
Site/view		equal	-10,000	equal	equal
Design/appeal		+10,000	-12,000	equal	+5,000
Construction quality	good	equal	-30,000	equal	+10,000
Condition	good	equal	-50,000	equal	+20,000
No. of rooms	8				
No. of bedrooms	3	+5,000	-5,000	equal	+5,000
No. of baths	2	+10,000	-15,000	equal	+5,000
Gross living area	2,000	+10,000	-20,000	equal	+10,000
Other space					
Garage	2 car/attd.	equal	equal	equal	equal
Other improvements					
Landscaping	good	equal	equal	equal	equal
Net adjustments		+45,000	-144,000	0	+35,000
Indicated value	1,120,000	1,045,000	1,056,000	1,150,000	1,125,000

For comparable A, the appraiser has made additions to the lot value, design, number of bedrooms and baths, and for gross living area. This accounts for the comparable's *deficiencies* in these areas relative to the subject. A total of five adjustments amount to $45,000, or 4.5% of the purchase price.

For comparable B, the appraiser has deducted values for age, site, design, construction quality, condition, bedrooms, baths, and living area. This accounts for the comparable's superior qualities relative to the subject. The only addition is the lot size, since the subject's is larger. A total of nine adjustments amount to $144,000, or 12% of the sale price.

For comparable C, the appraiser has added value for the age and deducted value for the lot size. The two adjustments offset one another for a net adjustment of zero.

For comparable D, one deduction has been made for the comparable's superior location. This is offset by six additions reflecting the various areas where the comparable is inferior to the subject. A total of seven adjustments amount to $35,000, or 3.2% of the sale price.

In view of all adjusted comparables, the appraiser developed a final indication of value of $1,120,000 for the subject. Underlying this conclusion is the fact that Comparable C, since it only has two minor adjustments which offset each other, it is by far the best indicator of value. Comparable D might be the second best indicator, since the net adjustments are very close to the sale price. Comparable A might be the third best indicator, since it has the second fewest number of total adjustments. Comparable B is the least reliable indicator, since there are numerous adjustments, three of which are of a significant amount. In addition, Comparable B is questionable altogether as a comparable, since total adjustments alter the sale price by 12%.

ESTIMATING INCOME PROPERTY VALUE

Steps in the income approach

The income capitalization approach, or income approach, is used for income properties and sometimes for other properties in a rental market where the appraiser can find rental data. The approach is based on the principle of anticipation: the expected future income stream of a property underlies what an investor will pay for the property. It is also based on the principle of substitution: that an investor will pay no more for a subject property with a certain income stream than the investor would have to pay for another property with a similar income stream.

The strength of the income approach is that it is used by investors themselves to determine how much they should pay for a property. Thus, in the right circumstances, it provides a good basis for estimating market value.

Steps in the income approach

The income capitalization method consists of estimating annual net operating income from the subject property, then applying a capitalization rate to the income. This produces a principal amount that the investor would pay for the property.

Steps in the Income Approach

1. Estimate potential gross income.
2. Estimate effective gross income.
3. Estimate net operating income.
4. Select a capitalization rate.
5. Apply the capitalization rate.

- - - - - - - - - - - - - - - -

Estimate potential gross income. Potential gross income is the scheduled rent of the subject plus income from miscellaneous sources such as vending machines and telephones. Scheduled rent is the total rent a property will produce if fully leased at the established rental rates.

Scheduled rent
+ Other income

Potential gross income

Market rent is determined by market studies in a process similar to the sales comparison method. Contract rent is used primarily if the existing leases are not due to expire in the short term and the tenants are unlikely to fail or leave the lease.

Estimate effective gross income. Effective gross income is potential gross income minus an allowance for vacancy and credit losses.

Potential gross income
- Vacancy & credit losses

Effective gross income

The allowance for vacancy and credit loss is usually estimated as a percentage of potential gross income.

Estimate net operating income. Net operating income is effective gross income minus total operating expenses.

Effective gross income
- Total operating expenses

Net operating income

Operating expenses include fixed expenses and variable expenses. Fixed expenses are those that are incurred whether the property is occupied or vacant, for example, real estate taxes and hazard insurance. Variable expenses are those that relate to actual operation of the building, for example, utilities, janitorial service, management, and repairs.

Operating expenses do not include debt service, expenditures for capital improvements, or expenses not related to operation of the property.

Select a capitalization rate. The capitalization rate is an estimate of the *rate of return* an investor will demand on the investment of capital in a property such as the subject.

Apply the capitalization rate. An appraiser now obtains an indication of value from the income capitalization method by dividing the estimated net operating income for the subject by the selected capitalization rate

$$\frac{NOI}{capitalization\ rate} = value$$

Using traditional symbols for income (I), rate (R) and value (V), the formula for value is

$$\frac{I}{R} = V$$

Income Capitalization Method Illustration

I. ESTIMATE POTENTIAL GROSS INCOME

Potential gross rental income	192,000
Plus: other income	2,000
Potential gross income	194,000

II. ESTIMATE EFFECTIVE GROSS INCOME

Less: vacancy and collection losses	9,600
Effective gross income	184,400

III. ESTIMATE NET OPERATING INCOME

Operating expenses	
Real estate taxes	32,000
Insurance	4,400
Utilities	12,000
Repairs	4,000
Maintenance	16,000
Management	12,000
Reserves	1,600
Legal and accounting	2,000
Total expenses	84,000
Effective gross income	184,400
Less: total expenses	84,000
Net operating income	100,400

IV. SELECT CAPITALIZATION RATE

$$\frac{NOI}{capitalization \quad rate} = value$$

Capitalization rate: 7%

V. APPLY CAPITALIZATION RATE

$$\frac{I}{R} = V = \frac{100,400}{.07} = 1,434,300 \text{ (rounded)}$$

Indicated value by income approach: 1,434,300

10 Estimating Property Value
Snapshot Review

CONCEPTS OF VALUE

Basic value determinants
- supply: goods or services available for sale, lease, or trade
- demand: goods or services desired for purchase, lease, or trade
- price mechanism: quantified value of an exchange
- value components: desire; utility; scarcity; purchasing power

Valuation principles
- anticipation, substitution, contribution, change, highest and best use, conformity, supply, demand, progression, regression, assemblage, subdivision, utility, transferability

DEFINING MARKET VALUE

opinion of the price that a willing seller and willing buyer would probably agree on for a property at a given time
conditions for market value: must be cash equivalent; sufficiently exposed to market; knowledgeable principals; no duress; arm's length conditions

ESTIMATING RESIDENTIAL PROPERTY VALUE
- most commonly used; relies on principles of substitution and contribution

Steps in the approach
- compare sale prices, adjust comparables to account for differences with subject

Identifying comparables
- must be physically similar, in subject's vicinity, recently sold in arm's length sale

Adjusting comparables
- deduct from comp if better than subject; add to comp if worse than subject

Weighting comparables
- best indicator has fewest and smallest adjustments, least net adjustment from the sale price

Broker's comparative market analysis
- abridged sales comparison approach by brokers and agents to find a price range

ESTIMATING INCOME PROPERTY 'VALUE
- used for income properties and in a rental market with available rental data

Steps in the approach
- value = NOI divided by the capitalization rate

SECTION TEN QUIZ: Estimating Property Value

1. As a component of real estate value, the principle of substitution suggests that

   a. if two similar properties are for sale, a buyer will purchase the cheaper of the two.
   b. if one of two adjacent homes is more valuable, the price of the other home will tend to rise.
   c. if too many properties are built in a market, the prices will tend to go down.
   d. people will readily move to another home if it is of equal value.

2. Highest and best use of a property is that use which

   a. is physically and financially feasible, legal, and the most productive.
   b. is legal, feasible, and deemed the most appropriate by zoning authorities.
   c. entails the largest building that zoning ordinances will allow developers to erect.
   d. conforms to other properties in the area.

3. The concept of market value is best described as

   a. the price a buyer will pay for a property, assuming other similar properties are within the same price range.
   b. the price an informed, unhurried seller will charge for a property assuming a reasonable period of exposure with other competing properties.
   c. the price a buyer and seller agree upon for a property assuming stable interest rates, appreciation rates, and prices of other similar properties.
   d. the price that a willing, informed, and unpressured seller and buyer agree upon for a property assuming a cash price and the property's reasonable exposure to the market.

4. A significant difference between an appraisal and a broker's opinion of value is

   a. the appraiser tends to use only one or two of the approaches to value.
   b. the broker may not be a disinterested party.
   c. the broker is subject to government regulation in generating the opinion.
   d. the appraiser uses less current market data.

5. A notable weakness of the sales comparison approach to value is that

   a. there may be no recent sale price data in the market.
   b. the approach is not based on the principle of substitution.
   c. the approach is only accurate with unique, special purpose properties.
   d. sale prices cannot be compared, since all real estate is different.

6. The steps in the market data approach are

   a. choose nearby comparables, adjust the subject for differences, estimate the value.
   b. gather relevant price data, apply the data to the subject, estimate the value.
   c. select comparable properties, adjust the comparables, estimate the value.
   d. identify previous price paid, apply an appreciation rate, estimate the value.

7. In the sales comparison approach, an adjustment is warranted if

   a. the buyer obtains conventional financing for the property.
   b. the seller offers below-market seller financing.
   c. a comparable is located in another, albeit similar neighborhood
   d. one property has a hip roof and the other has a gabled roof.

8. To complete the sales comparison approach, the appraiser

    a. averages the adjustments.
    b. weights the comparables.
    c. discards all comparables having a lower value.
    d. identifies the subject's value as that of the nearest comparable.

9. One weakness of the cost approach for appraising market value is that

    a. builders may not pay market value for materials or labor.
    b. market value is not always the same as what the property cost.
    c. comparables used may not have similar quality of construction.
    d. new properties have inestimable costs and rates of depreciation.

10. The cost of constructing a functional equivalent of a subject property is known as

    a. reproduction cost.
    b. replacement cost.
    c. restitution cost.
    d. reconstruction cost.

11. An office building lacks sufficient cooling capability to accommodate modern computer equipment. This is an example of

    a. physical deterioration.
    b. economic obsolescence.
    c. incurable depreciation.
    d. functional obsolescence.

12. A home is located in a neighborhood where homeowners on the block have failed to maintain their properties. This is an example of

    a. curable external obsolescence.
    b. incurable economic obsolescence.
    c. functional obsolescence.
    d. physical deterioration.

13. In appraisal, loss of value in a property from any cause is referred to as

    a. deterioration.
    b. obsolescence.
    c. depreciation.
    d. deflation.

14. The first two steps in the cost approach are to estimate the value of the land and the cost of the improvements. The remaining steps are

    a. estimate depreciation, subtract depreciation from cost, and add back the land value.
    b. subtract deterioration from cost, estimate land depreciation, and total the two values.
    c. estimate depreciation of land and improvements, subtract from original cost.
    d. estimate obsolescence, subtract from the cost of land and improvements.

15. The roof of a property cost $10,000. The economic life of the roof is 20 years. Assuming the straight-line method of depreciation, what is the depreciated value of the roof after 3 years?

    a. $10,000
    b. $8,500
    c. $7,000
    d. $1,500

16. The income capitalization approach to appraising value is most applicable for which of the following property types?

    a. Single family homes
    b. Apartment buildings
    c. Undeveloped land
    d. Churches

17. The steps in the income capitalization approach are:

    a. estimate gross income, multiply times the gross income multiplier.
    b. estimate effective income, subtract tax, apply a capitalization rate.
    c. estimate net income, and apply a capitalization rate to it.
    d. estimate potential income, apply a capitalization rate to it.

18. Net operating income is equal to

    a. gross income minus potential income minus expenses.
    b. effective gross income minus debt service.
    c. potential gross income minus vacancy and credit loss minus expenses.
    d. effective gross income minus vacancy and credit loss.

19. If net income on a property is $20,000 and the cap rate is 5%, the value of the property using the income capitalization method is

    a. $100,000.
    b. $400,000.
    c. $1,000,000.
    d. $4,000,000.

20. The principal shortcoming of the gross rent multiplier approach to estimating value is that

    a. numerous expenses are not taken into account.
    b. the multiplier does not relate to the market.
    c. the method is too complex and cumbersome.
    d. the method only applies to residential properties.

21. If the monthly rent of a property is $3,000, and the gross rent multiplier (GRM) is 80. The formula for value using the GRM is (gross rent x multiplier = value) Therefore , what is the value of the property?

    a. $45,000
    b. $240,000
    c. $267,000
    d. $288,000

22. If total adjustments create a large dollar amount between the sale price and the adjusted value, the comparable is _____ indicator of value.

    a. a better
    b. a perfect
    c. a poorer
    d. not an

23. The principle of _____ focuses on the degree to which a particular improvement affects market value of the overall property.

    a. highest and best
    b. contribution
    c. change
    d. conformity

24. What supply-demand conditions indicate a scarcity in available properties?

    a. When supply exceeds demand
    b. When real estate values drop
    c. When demand and supply are equivalent
    d. When demand exceeds supply

25. Which value principle states that there is a use for a property that produces the greatest income and return?

    a. Anticipation principle
    b. Progression principle
    c. Highest and best use principle
    d. Income principle

11 Real Property Investment Analysis

Real Estate as an Investment
Taxation of Real Estate Investments
Investment Analysis of a Residence
Investment Analysis of an Income Property

REAL ESTATE AS AN INVESTMENT

Risk and reward
Illiquidity
Management requirements

Real estate investments participate in the general risks and rewards of all investments. However, real estate investments are often complex. They are also distinguished by their lack of liquidity and by the amount of management they require. In addition, each investor has specific aims and circumstances that affect the viability of any particular real estate investment for that individual. Licensees who lack expertise in the area of real estate investment analysis should refer potential investors to a competent advisor. Nevertheless, a licensee should be familiar with the basics of real estate as an investment.

Risk and reward
Capital put into real estate is always subject to the full range of risk factors: market changes, income shortfalls, negative leverage, tax law changes, and poor overall return.

Market demand for a specific type of property can decline. For example, a business district's retailers may vacate stores in an area in order to obtain better space in a new shopping center. Market downturns leave the income property investor with an unmarketable property or one which can only be re-leased at a loss of some portion of the original investment. Thus the expected reward from income or appreciation may never be obtained.

Another risk of the investment property is the cost of development or operation. If start-up costs or ongoing operating costs exceed rental income, the owner must dip into additional capital resources to maintain the investment until its income increases. If income does not rise, or if costs do not decline, the investor can simply run out of money.

Leverage is a constant risk in real estate investment. If the property fails to generate sufficient revenue, the costs of borrowed money can bankrupt the owner, just as development and operating costs can. Investors often overlook the fact that leverage only works when the yield on the investment exceeds the costs of borrowed funds.

Tax law is an ongoing risk in long-term real estate investment. If the investor's tax circumstances change, or if the tax laws do, the investor may end up paying more capital gains and income taxes than planned, undermining the return on the investment. An investor needs to consider carefully the value of such potential tax benefits as deductions for mortgage interest, tax losses, deferred gains, exemptions, and tax credits for certain types of real estate investment.

Illiquidity

Compared with other classes of investment, real estate is relatively illiquid. Even in the case of liquidating a single-family residence, one can expect a marketing period of at least several months in most markets. In addition, it takes time for the buyer to obtain financing and to complete all the other phases of closing the transaction. Commercial and investment properties can take much longer, depending on market conditions, leases, construction, permitting, and a host of other factors. The investor who is in a hurry to dispose of such an investment can expect to receive a lower sales price than may be ideal. Compare this with the ease of drawing money out of a bank account or selling a stock.

Management requirements

Real estate tends to require a high degree of investor involvement in management of the investment. Even raw land requires some degree of maintenance to preserve its value: drainage, fencing, payment of taxes, and periodic inspection, to name a few tasks. Improved properties often require extensive management, including repairs, maintenance, onsite leasing, tenant relations, security, and fiscal management.

TAXATION OF REAL ESTATE INVESTMENTS

Taxable income
Cost recovery
Gain on sale
Interest

Real estate investments are taxed on the income they produce and on the increase in value, or gain, when the investment is sold. These forms of taxation are distinct from the ad valorem taxation of real estate.

Taxable Income

Taxable income from investment real estate is *the gross income received minus any expenses, deductions or exclusions that current tax law allows*. Taxable income from real estate is added to the investor's other income and taxed at the investor's marginal tax rate. The "Investment Analysis of an Income Property" section below gives details.

Cost recovery

Cost recovery, or **depreciation**, allows the owner of income property to deduct a portion of the property's value from gross income each year over the life of the asset. The "life of the asset" and the deductible portion are defined by law. In theory, the owner recovers the full cost of the investment if it is held to the end of the asset's economic life as defined by the Internal Revenue Service. At the time of selling the asset, the accumulated cost recovery is subtracted from the investment's original value as part of determining the taxable capital gain.

Cost recovery is allowed only for income properties and that portion of a non-income property which is used to produce income. It applies only to improvements. Land cannot be depreciated. The part of a property which can be depreciated is called the **depreciable basis**.

Depreciation schedules. Residential rental properties are depreciated over a period of 27.5 years. The basic annual deduction for such property is 3.636%, with adjustments for the month of the taxable year in which the property was placed in service. Non-residential income properties placed in service after 1994 are depreciated over a period of 39 years (basic annual percentage is 2.564%). The proper method of depreciation should be determined in consultation with a qualified tax advisor.

Gain on sale

When real estate, whether non-income or income, is sold, a *taxable event* occurs. If the sale proceeds *exceed* the original cost of the investment, subject to some adjustments, there is a **capital gain** that is subject to tax. If the sales proceeds are less than the original cost with adjustments, there is a **capital loss**.

An investor can sometimes defer the reporting of gain or loss, and, hence, taxation of gain, by participating in an exchange of like-kind assets. The legislation that deals with like-kind exchanges is contained in Section 1031 of the IRS code. These tax-deferred exchanges are sometimes called **Section 1031 exchanges** and **Starker exchanges**, named for an investor who won a case against the IRS.

To qualify under Section 1031, there must have been a legitimate exchange of the assets involved. The property being transferred must have been held for productive use in a trade or business or held as an investment and must be exchanged for property that will also be used in a trade or business or be held as an investment. Tax on gain is deferred until the investment or business property is sold and not exchanged.

Interest

Mortgage interest incurred by loans to buy, build, or materially improve a primary or secondary residence is deductible from gross income. The interest on a home equity loan may be deducted only if the loan is used to "buy, build or substantially improve" the home that secures the loan. Principal payments on a loan are *not* deductible.

For income properties that are held as investments, interest on debts incurred to finance the investment is deductible as **investment interest** up to the amount of net income received from the property.

INVESTMENT ANALYSIS OF A RESIDENCE

Appreciation
Deductibles
Tax liability
Gains tax exclusion

Investment analysis examines the economic performance of an investment. The analysis includes costs, income, taxation, appreciation, and return.

A property acquired and used as a primary residence is an example of a non-income property. If a portion of a residence is used for business (i.e., a home office), this portion only may be treated as an income property for tax purposes. Since, by definition, a non-income property does not generate income, its value as an investment must come from one or more of the other sources: appreciation, leverage, or tax benefits.

Appreciation

Appreciation is the increase in value of an asset over time. A simple way to estimate appreciation on a primary residence is to subtract the price originally paid from the estimated current market value:

$$Current\ value - original\ price = total\ appreciation$$

For example, if a house was bought for $300,000 and its estimated market value now is $400,000, it has appreciated by $100,000.

Original price:	$300,000
Current market value:	$400,000
Total appreciation:	$100,000

Total appreciation can be stated as a percentage increase over the original price by dividing the estimated total appreciation by the original price.

The house in the last example has appreciated by 33%:

$$\frac{(Total\ appreciation)}{Original\ price} = \%\ appreciated$$

$$\frac{100,000}{300,000} = 33\%$$

To estimate the percentage of *annual appreciation*, divide the percent appreciated by the number of years the house has been owned:

$$\frac{\%\ total\ appreciation}{years\ owned} = \%\ appreciation\ per\ year$$

If the house in the previous example has been owned for three years, the annual appreciation has been 11%.

$$\frac{33\%}{3 \ years} = 11\% \ appreciation \ per \ year$$

Deductibles

The primary tax benefit available to the owner of a non-income property is the *annual deduction for mortgage interest*. The portion of annual mortgage payments that goes to repay principal must be subtracted to determine the amount paid for interest. Principal repayment is not deductible. Furthermore, depreciation is not allowed for non-income properties.

Tax liability

The seller of a principal residence may owe tax on capital gain that results from the sale. The IRS defines gain on the sale of a home as **amount realized** from the sale minus the **adjusted basis** of the home sold.

Amount realized. The amount realized, also known as **net proceeds from sale**, is expressed by the formula:

sale price

\-   <u>costs of sale</u>

amount realized

The sale price is the total amount the seller receives for the home. This includes money, notes, mortgages or other debts the buyer assumes as part of the sale.

Costs of sale include brokerage commissions, relevant advertising, legal fees, seller-paid points and other closing costs. Certain *fixing-up expenses*, as discussed further below, can be deducted from the amount realized to derive an **adjusted sale price** for the purpose of postponing taxation on gain.

For example, Larry and Mary sold their home for $350,000. Their selling costs, including the commission they paid Broker Betty and amounts paid to inspectors, a surveyor, and the title company, amounted to ten percent of the selling price, or $35,000. The amount they realized from the sale was therefore $315,000.

Adjusted basis. Basis is a measurement of how much is invested in the property for tax purposes. Assuming that the property was acquired through purchase, the **beginning basis** is the cost of acquiring the property. Cost includes cash and debt obligations, and such other settlement costs as legal and recording fees, abstract fees, surveys, charges for installing utilities, transfer taxes, title insurance, and any other amounts the buyer pays for the seller.

The beginning basis is increased or decreased by certain types of expenditures made while the property is owned. Basis is increased by the cost of **capital improvements** made to the property. Assessments for local improvements such as roads and sidewalks also increase the basis. Examples of capital improvements are: putting on an addition, paving a driveway, replacing a roof, adding central air conditioning, and rewiring the home.

Basis is decreased by any amounts the owner received for such things as easements.

The basic formula for **adjusted basis** is:

> Beginning basis
> \+   capital improvements
> \-   <u>exclusions, credits or other amounts received</u>
>   adjusted basis

For example, Mary and Larry originally paid $200,000 for their home. They spent an additional $10,000 on a new central heating and cooling unit. Their adjusted basis at the time of selling it is therefore $210,000.

Gain on sale. The gain on sale of a primary residence is represented by the basic formula:

> amount realized (net sales proceeds)
> \-   <u>adjusted basis</u>
>   gain on sale

Gain on sale, if it does not qualify for an exclusion under current tax law, is taxable.

Gain on Sale

	Selling price of old home	$350,000
-	Selling costs	35,000
=	Amount realized	315,000
	Beginning basis of old home	200,000
+	Capital improvements	10,000
=	Adjusted basis of old home	210,000
	Amount realized	315,000
-	Adjusted basis	210,000
=	Gain on sale	105,000

In the case of Mary and Larry, their capital gain was $315,000 - $210,000, or $105,000. They will owe tax on this amount in the year of the sale unless they qualify for the exclusion described below.

Gains tax exclusion   Tax law provides an exclusion of $250,000 for an individual taxpayer and $500,000 for married taxpayers filing jointly. The exclusion of gain from sale of a residence can be claimed *every two years*, provided the taxpayer

1. <u>owned</u> the property for at least two years during the five years preceding the date of sale;

2. <u>used</u> the property as principal residence for a total of two years during that five-year period;

3. has waited two years since the last use of the exclusion for any sale.

Losses are not deductible, and there is no carry-over of any unused portion of the exclusion. Postponed gains from a previous home sale under the earlier rollover rules reduce the basis of the current home if that home was a qualifying replacement home under the old rule.

INVESTMENT ANALYSIS OF AN INCOME PROPERTY

Pre-tax cash flow
Tax liability
After-tax cash flow
Investment performance

Income properties are those which are held primarily for the generation of income. In addition to commercial and investment properties such as office buildings, this category includes residential rental properties. An important difference between income and non-income properties is that deductions for depreciation are allowed on income properties. Income properties, like non-income properties, generate a gain (or loss) on sale, and they also create an annual income stream. The annual income streams are determined on both a pre-tax and after-tax basis in order to determine the productivity of the investment.

Pre-tax cash flow

Cash flow is the difference between the amount of actual cash flowing into the investment as revenue and out of the investment for expenses, debt service, and all other items. Cash flow concerns cash items only, and therefore excludes depreciation, which is not a cash expense **Pre-tax cash flow**, or cash flow before taxation, is calculated as follows:

	potential rental income
-	vacancy and collection loss
=	effective rental income
+	other income
=	gross operating income (GOI)
-	operating expenses
-	reserves
=	net operating income (NOI)
-	debt service
=	pre-tax cash flow

Potential rental income is the annual amount that would be realized if the property is fully leased or rented at the scheduled rate. **Vacancy and collection loss** is rental income lost because of vacancies or tenants' failure to pay rent. **Effective rental income** is the potential income adjusted for these losses. To that is added any **other income** the property generates, such as from laundry or parking charges, to obtain **gross operating income**. **Operating expenses** paid by the landlord include such items as utilities and maintenance. These are deducted from gross operating income. Some owners also set aside a cash **reserve** each year to build up a fund for capital replacements in the future, for example, to replace a roof or a furnace. Cash reserves are <u>not</u> deductible for tax purposes until spent as deductible repairs or maintenance. The remainder is **net operating income (NOI)**. When the annual amount paid for **debt service**, including principal and interest, is subtracted, the remainder is the **pre-tax cash flow**.

For instance, a small office building of 3,500 square feet rents at $20 per square foot. If fully rented, the annual rental income would be $70,000. Historically, the property averages $4,200 in vacancy and collection losses. Equipment rental will provide an additional $2,000 per year in income. The owner will have to pay operating expenses amounting to ten dollars per square foot, or $35,000 per year. The owner sets aside one dollar per square foot, or $3,500 per year, for reserves. The owner financed the purchase of the building with a loan that requires annual debt service in the amount of $20,000. The pre-tax cash flow for the building is illustrated in the following exhibit.

Pre-tax Cash Flow

	potential rental income	$70,000
-	vacancy and collection loss	4,200
=	effective rental income	65,800
+	other income	2,000
=	gross operating income (GOI)	67,800
-	operating expenses	35,000
-	reserves	3,500
=	net operating income (NOI)	29,300
-	debt service	20,000
=	pre-tax cash flow	9,300

Tax liability

The owner's tax liability on taxable income from the property is based on *taxable income* rather than cash flow. Taxable income and tax liability are calculated as follows:

	net operating income (NOI)
+	reserves
-	interest expense
-	cost recovery expense
=	taxable income
x	tax rate
=	tax liability

Taxable income is net operating income minus all allowable deductions. Cost recovery expense is allowed as a deduction, while allowances for reserves and payments on loan principal payback are not allowed. Thus, since reserves were deducted from gross operating income to determine NOI, this amount must be added back in. As only the interest portion of debt service is deductible, the principal amount must be removed from the debt service payments and the *interest expense* deducted from NOI. Taxable income, multiplied by the owner's marginal tax bracket, gives the **tax liability**.

Note on tax rate: when a rental property is owned as an individual or by way of a pass-through entity (partnership, LLC treated as a partnership for tax purposes, or S corporation), its net income is taxed at the individual's personal marginal income tax rate. The next exhibit shows the tax liability for the previous example using an individual rate of 24%.

Tax Liability

	net operating income (NOI)	29,300
+	reserves	3,500
-	interest expense	10,000
-	cost recovery expense	22,000
=	taxable income	800
x	tax rate (24%)	
=	tax liability	192

After-tax cash flow

After-tax cash flow is the amount of income from the property that actually goes into the owner's pocket *after income tax is paid*. It is figured as:

	pre-tax cash flow
-	tax liability
=	after-tax cash flow

The after-tax cash flow for the sample property is illustrated in the following exhibit.

After-tax Cash Flow

	pre-tax cash flow	9,300
-	tax liability	192
=	after-tax cash flow	9,108

Investment performance

Investors measure the investment performance of an income property in many different ways, depending on their needs. A few of the common measures are:

$$\frac{Net\ operating\ income}{price} = return\ on\ investment\ (ROI)$$

$$\frac{cash\ flow}{cash\ invested} = cash\text{-}on\text{-}cash\ return\ (C\ on\ C)$$

$$\frac{cash\ flow}{equity} = return\ on\ equity\ (ROE)$$

11 Real Property Investment Analysis Snapshot Review

REAL ESTATE AS AN INVESTMENT

Risk and reward
- the real estate investor must weigh the potential risks and returns inherent in market variability, expected vs. real income, use of borrowing leverage, changes in tax treatment of capital gains and income, and the cost of capital

Illiquidity
- real estate is generally less liquid than other investment types: it takes time to market a property

Management requirements
- real estate tends to require more investor involvement than other investments do: maintenance, management, operation

TAXATION OF REAL ESTATE INVESTMENTS

Taxable income
- gross income received minus allowable expenses, deductions and exclusions

Cost recovery
- deduction of a portion of a property's value from gross income each year over the

Gain on sale
- an excess of proceeds from sale of a property over the original cost of the property, subject to adjustments

Interest
- mortgage interest is deductible from annual gross income from a property, subject to limitations

Passive activities
- business activities in which the taxpayer does not materially participate, including interests in limited partnerships and rental activities; losses from such activities can be used to offset income from other passive activities

INVESTMENT ANALYSIS OF A RESIDENTIAL PROPERTY

Appreciation
- increase in the value of an asset over time; may be stated as a difference between the original price and current market value, or as a percentage increase over the original price; not a true measure of investment return

Deductibles
- for non-income properties, primary tax benefit is annual deduction for mortgage

Tax liability
- the seller of a principle residence owes tax on any capital gain that results from the sale unless excluded; capital gain is defined as the amount realized minus the adjusted basis

Gains tax exclusion
- up to $250,000 for a single seller and $500,000 for a married couple can be excluded from gains tax every two years

INVESTMENT ANALYSIS OF AN INCOME PROPERTY

Pre-tax cash flow
- annual pre-tax cash flow is net operating income minus debt service

Tax liability
- tax liability on income from a property is based on taxable income: net operating income minus interest expense and cost recovery

After-tax cash flow
- annual after-tax cash flow is pre-tax cash flow minus tax liability

Investment performance
- a few common measures of investment performance are:
  - return on investment (net operating income divided by price)
  - cash-on-cash return (cash flow divided by cash invested)
  - return on equity (cash flow divided by equity)

SECTION ELEVEN QUIZ: Real Property Investment Analysis

1. All investors desire their investments to increase in value. However,

    a. the degree of return is inversely related to the degree of risk.
    b. the more the investor stands to gain, the greater the risk that the investor may lose.
    c. investments requiring intense management have lesser returns.
    d. the more liquid an investment is, the greater the chances are that the investment will not appreciate.

2. Two of the rewards that investments offer are

    a. income and tax benefits.
    b. negative leverage and appreciation.
    c. appreciation and taxation.
    d. positive leverage and prestige.

3. An investor invests in fifteen diversified bond funds. This is an example of an investment in

    a. money.
    b. equity.
    c. debt.
    d. real estate.

4. A real estate investment can take a long period of time to sell. For the investor, this means that real estate is

    a. management intensive.
    b. insensitive to marketing.
    c. vulnerable to seller's markets.
    d. relatively illiquid.

5. Compared to a stock portfolio, a real estate investment would be considered

    a. a riskier investment.
    b. a more management-intensive investment.
    c. a shorter-term investment.
    d. a more leveraged investment.

6. Six investors purchase a shopping center. One investor manages the tenants and another handles the marketing and leasing. Two investors manage accounting and finance, and the remaining two run the management office. This is a possible example of

    a. a general partnership.
    b. a limited partnership.
    c. a real estate investment trust.
    d. an investment conduit.

7. Taxable income produced by an income property is

    a. gross income minus expenses plus land and building depreciation.
    b. gross income minus expenses minus land and building depreciation.
    c. gross income minus building depreciation plus land depreciation.
    d. gross income minus expenses minus building depreciation.

8. As a general rule, in deriving taxable income on an investment property, it is legal to

   a. deduct principal and interest payments from income.
   b. deduct principal payments from income.
   c. deduct interest payments from income.
   d. deduct principal and interest payments from income and capital gain.

9. Which of the following is true of the tax treatment of a principal residence?

   a. The owner may deduct the property's interest and principal from ordinary income.
   b. The owner may depreciate the property and deduct depreciation expenses.
   c. The owner can deduct any capital gain when the property is sold.
   d. The owner may be able to exclude capital gain from taxable income when the property is sold.

10. An investment property seller pays $14,000 in closing costs. These costs

   a. may be deducted from personal income.
   b. may be deducted from the property's income.
   c. may be deducted from the sale price for gains tax purposes.
   d. may be deducted from the adjusted basis for gains tax purposes.

11. Capital gain tax is figured by multiplying one's tax bracket times

   a. the sum of the beginning basis plus gain.
   b. the difference between net sale proceeds and adjusted basis.
   c. the sum of net sale proceeds and capital gain.
   d. the difference between net sale proceeds and capital gain.

12. Cash flow is a measure of how much pre-tax or after-tax cash an investment property generates. To derive cash flow it is therefore necessary to exclude

   a. cost recovery expense.
   b. interest expense.
   c. loan principal payments.
   d. net operating income.

13. One way investors measure the yield of an investment is by

   a. dividing net operating income by cash flow.
   b. multiplying the investor's required yield times after-tax cash flow.
   c. dividing cash flow by the investor's equity.
   d. multiplying cash flow times the price paid for the property.

14. What is synonymous with depreciation?

   a. Obsolescence
   b. Capital gain
   c. Gain on sale
   d. Cost recovery

15. The basic formula for adjusted basis is:

Beginning basis + capital improvements -_____

    a. Depreciation
    b. Cash and debt obligations
    c. Legal and recording fees
    d. Appreciation

16. Tax law provides an exclusion of _____ for an individual taxpayer and _____ for married taxpayers filing jointly.

    a. $100,000; $500,000
    b. $250,000; $500,000
    c. $150,000; $600,000
    d. $300,000; $600,000

17. What is total appreciation?

    a. It is an increase over the current price found by dividing the estimated total appreciation by the original price.
    b. It is a percentage increase over the original price found by dividing the estimated total appreciation by the current price.
    c. It is a percentage increase over the original price found by dividing the estimated total appreciation by the original price.
    d. It is an increase over the original price found by dividing the estimated total appreciation by the current price.

18. What is another name for a tax-deferred exchange?

    a. Starker 1031 exchange
    b. Section 1060 exchange
    c. Capital gains exchange
    d. Gain on sale exchange

12 Property Insurance

Basic Insurance Concepts
Standard Policy Features
Flood Insurance
Insurance Issues

BASIC INSURANCE CONCEPTS

Purpose
Homeowners' insurance
Agents
Insurance companies
Insurance brokers

Purpose

The purpose of insurance is to protect an asset against possible loss, whether that loss be related to property, flood, auto, health, business, life or pets. Some types of insurance are required because of where one lives and what one owns. For example, most mortgage lenders require homeowner's insurance to protect a property that is collateral for the lender's loan. A lender may require flood insurance on a property located in a flood zone.

In the world of real estate, the types of insurance of most common concern are homeowners' insurance and flood insurance.

Homeowners' insurance

Homeowners' insurance covers the home itself, personal property or contents of the home, and liability for injury others may suffer on the insured property.

Lender-placed insurance. Most lenders will place homeowner's insurance on a home if the owner has let the insurance lapse. Premiums for lender-placed, or forced-place, insurance are considerably higher than those for insurance an owner would buy. The coverage is also typically much less and limited to the structure itself. The lender will usually add the amount of the premium payment to the mortgage payments and require the homeowner to pay the higher amount. The lender will do this until the homeowner obtains a policy on his or her own.

Owner-placed insurance. A property owner should consider the following when seeking homeowner's insurance coverage:

> ▸ the size and value of the property
> ▸ the potential for an increase or decrease in the property's value
> ▸ the value of the items contained in the home
> ▸ the age of the items in the home and how much depreciation will impact their coverage if they need replacing

- ▸ the area where the property is located and what weather conditions may threaten the home
- ▸ what type of structure is being insured
- ▸ whether the property is rented or owner occupied
- ▸ the lender's coverage requirements
- ▸ the cost and terms of the policy

Another factor to consider is where the insurance will be purchased. Insurance can be purchased from an agent, an insurance company, or a broker.

Agents

Agents can be independent and sell insurance for several different companies, or they can be employed by only one company and sell insurance for that company alone. Independent agents can offer a larger selection of price and terms and reduce or eliminate the need shop around for the best policy. On the other hand, some companies sell their policies only through their own agents. Consequently, a homeowner who prefers one company over others will have to go directly to an agent who works for that company. Either kind of agent can provide coverage and loss prevention advice and help with losses and claims.

Insurance companies

Insurance companies sell insurance through agents, sales representatives, and the Internet. Agents and sales representatives provide advice, while the Internet facilitates comparing similar coverage from different companies and often allows purchase of a policy online. Most major companies also have local offices that provide walk-in assistance.

Insurance brokers

Insurance brokers work for the client and not an insurance company. They perform the search for the best policy and terms for the client. They negotiate terms and prices, assist with claims, and provide risk management advice. Brokers may be authorized to issue a policy or to bind an insurance company to issue a policy. The client pays the broker, who then pays the company.

STANDARD POLICY FEATURES

Content
Policy types
Coverage
Deductibles
Homeowners' policies

Content

The content of a policy explains in detail what is covered and to what extent. If the policy does not include a specific peril or threat, then a loss caused by that peril will not be covered. For example, if the property is located in Florida, where hurricanes are prevalent, but a policy does not include coverage for hurricanes, then the homeowner will be responsible for repairing damage to the home caused by a hurricane. The same is true for mold. Many homeowner's policies specifically exclude coverage for mold. Therefore, if mold is discovered in the home, the insurance policy will not cover the cost of remediating the mold or for the loss of the use of the home while the mold is being remediated.

Declarations. The declarations page includes the basic details of the policy, effective dates, deductibles, endorsements, and the name of any mortgagee. It also states the insurance rating of the property as determined by the property description.

Policy types

Insurance policies can be either monoline or package policies.

Monoline policy. These policies include only one kind of coverage. Examples include liability policies and homeowners' policies.

Package policy. These policies include more than one kind of coverage, such as homeowner's insurance and liability insurance in the same policy . Package policies typically cost less than separate policies for similar coverages.

Coverage

Each policy contains certain types of coverage. The coverages can be basic or comprehensive, providing more extensive coverage. The main types of coverage and those most commonly included in homeowners' policies are as follows.

Dwelling coverage. This pays for damage to the home itself and any structures or fixtures attached to the home. Coverage would include attached garages, plumbing, electrical systems, HVAC systems, and so forth. This is the most basic and common coverage and typically includes fire, windstorm, hail, tornadoes, vandalism, smoke, etc. It may not cover hurricanes, earthquakes, or mold unless specifically added.

Other structures coverage. This pays for damage to structures not attached to the home. These include unattached garages, fences, sheds, pool houses, or any other structure located on the property but not attached to the home.

Personal property coverage. This pays for the loss of personal belongings that are not considered to be the home itself. Examples include furniture, appliances, clothing, computers, televisions, home décor, books, and so forth. This coverage typically includes damage, loss, and theft of the personal property, whether or not it is actually on the property. For example, if the homeowner is traveling and loses a laptop computer during the trip, the personal property coverage on the owner's policy would pay for the laptop.

Loss of use coverage. This pays some expenses to live elsewhere after the home has been damaged or destroyed by a covered peril. Again, if the peril is not covered, the policy will not pay for loss of use. If there is no earthquake coverage under the policy and a home in California is damaged by an earthquake, the policy holder will not receive loss of use payment while the home is being repaired.

Liability coverage. This pays if the homeowner is sued and found to be responsible for someone being injured on the owner's property. If the stairs leading up to a home are covered with ice and the homeowner has not cleared the stairs, the owner might be held responsible for a visitor's injuries from a fall on the stairs. Liability insurance would cover the financial penalty imposed by the injured visitor's lawsuit. Liability also covers damage to someone else's property caused by the policyholder's negligence.

Medical payment coverage. This pays the medical bills if someone is hurt on the homeowner's property. When that same visitor slips on the icy stairs and is injured, the medical payment coverage would pay for the visitor's hospital and medical bills related to the fall. Also, if the homeowner owns a dog that injures someone, the medical payments coverage would pay for the resulting medical bills. However, some insurance companies exclude dogs altogether or exclude certain breeds of dogs that they deem to be dangerous breeds. In this case, if the policy excluded pit bulls and it was the homeowner's pit bull which bit someone, the policy would not pay for those medical bills.

Exclusions. It is worth mentioning again that numerous perils are typically excluded. These include hurricanes, earthquakes, and mold. However, for an increased premium, these perils can be added to the policy. Some types of coverage are always excluded from homeowners' policies, for example, flood. Separate flood policies are purchased through federal insurance programs.

Endorsements. An endorsement (or rider) provides coverage for property or perils not covered in the original policy. An example of an endorsement would be coverage for expensive jewelry.

Conditions. A condition is a specific requirement for coverage in a policy. For example, a car may be covered only when it is parked in the garage.

The 80% rule. Homeowner policies should insure the home for at least 80% of the home's replacement cost. With this coverage, the insurance company will pay losses in full up to the face amount of the policy, minus the deductible. For example, if the total coverage amount is $300,000 and the deductible is $500, a total loss of the home would pay $299,500.

However, if the home is not insured for 80% of the replacement cost, the loss would be paid based on the actual cash value of the property. This coverage amount would be based on depreciation and the home's age. For example, the recovery from a total loss of the same $300,000 home may be considerably less than the cost to replace the home if the home is 10 years old. A 10-year depreciation amount would be figured into the loss, and the company would pay the loss based on that factor.

Deductibles

Most policies include a deductible, which is a stated amount of money the policy holder must pay before the insurance benefits commence. The deductible amount will be determined by the premium amount – the lower the deductible, the higher the premium. The typical deductible on a homeowner's policy is $500 to $1,000.

Individuals renting or leasing an apartment or a house may carry a renters' insurance policy. This policy will pay for damage or loss of the renter's personal property by any peril covered in the policy. Renters' insurance is similar to homeowners' insurance except it does not cover the actual dwelling. The landlord still needs to carry homeowners' insurance to cover the dwelling itself.

Homeowners' policies

Homeowners' insurance policies are based on the Homeowners 2000 Program which made revisions to forms and endorsements in 2010. Under HO 2000, there are six major policies that cover homeowners, renters, and condominium or cooperative owners. Mobile homes or house trailers can only be covered by other insurance policies.

HO-1 is the basis for most homeowners' policies. It provides coverage for losses from the following perils:

- theft
- lightning, wind, and hail
- fire and smoke
- theft and vandalism
- explosion
- civil damage and riots
- war and terrorism
- damage from vehicles and aircraft
- glass breakage
- damage to property being removed in an emergency situation such as fire

In addition, the **HO-1** policy includes liability coverage for

- personal injury – resulting from negligence on the part of the insured
- medical payments – for injuries occurring to guests or resident employees of the insured
- physical damage – caused by the insured to the property of others

HO-2, also known as a peril policy, covers items in addition to those included in the HO-1 policy. These items include electric current, accidental discharge of water, weight of ice and snow, falling objects and building collapse. In a peril policy, if the item is not listed, it is not covered.

HO-3 is a more comprehensive all-risk policy that differs from the HO-2 in that it covers all perils unless they are listed in the policy.

HO-4 is a policy is for renters. This policy covers personal property and liability for damage to the property or injuries to other people in the rented unit.

HO-5 policies have the most comprehensive coverage of all the homeowners' policies. It includes coverage for structures, personal property and loss of use.

HO-6 policies are specific to condominiums and cooperatives. This policy type does not cover the structure itself but does cover semi-permanent structures such as cabinets, carpeting, wallpaper, etc. It also covers personal property. The condominium association or cooperative would carry coverage for the actual structure.

HO-7 policies provide an extended form of real and personal property coverage designed specifically for very expensive houses.

HO-8 policies are for older homes with replacement costs higher than the home's market value. This policy type pays to repair or replace damaged property with cheaper common construction materials and methods, referred to as functional replacement.

FLOOD INSURANCE

FEMA and the NFIP
Flood zones
Insurance requirement
Disclosure
Cost of insurance

FEMA and the NFIP   The Federal Emergency Management Agency (FEMA) administers the National Flood Insurance Program (NFIP). The purpose of the NFIP is to reduce the financial impact of flooding on both private and public structures. In addition to providing affordable flood insurance, it also encourages the development of floodplain management regulations as well as their enforcement.

Flood zones   **Flood hazard.** Flood zones as designated by FEMA are areas that border rivers and streams where flooding is a concern. Designated flood hazard zones are subject to restrictions on the location, type, and elevation of all improvements to the land (residential, agricultural, commercial, and industrial). Flood maps generally show a community's flood zones, floodplain boundaries, and Base Flood Elevation. This information, when examined together, determines the risk of flooding.

Flood hazards will change over time. The flow of water and how it drains can change due to natural or manmade causes. New land use and community development, natural forces such as climate change, terrain changes, and wildfires all can impact the risk of flooding.

To better reflect the current flood risk conditions, FEMA uses the latest technology to update and issue new flood maps nationwide to aid communities, property owners, businesses, and other stakeholders in taking steps to address flood risks. For informative videos and more information including flood maps, visit www.fema.gov and www.floodsmart.gov.

Insurance requirement   If a property is in a FEMA-designated flood hazard area, and financing is being obtained through a federally regulated mortgage loan, flood insurance is required. Flood insurance, which is a separate policy, cannot be purchased directly from the NFIP but must be purchased through the same companies that provide regular homeowners' insurance.

If an entire structure is above the 100-year flood plain, it has a 1% annual chance of flooding, and the requirement for flood insurance may be waived. The zone it is located in is called the Special Flood Hazard Area (SFHA), also known as the **1% annual chance flood** zone. Properties located in low- to moderate-risk flood hazard areas such as the SFHA are not federally mandated to be covered by flood insurance; however, a lender may still require it. As flood hazard area maps are revised and properties move from low- to high-risk areas, flood insurance becomes a requirement.

Residents in a high-risk flood zone who have received federal disaster assistance in the form of grants from FEMA or low-interest disaster loans from the U.S.

Small Business Administration (SBA) following a Presidential Disaster Declaration must maintain flood insurance in order to be considered for any future federal disaster aid.

Disclosure   Brokers have the responsibility to disclose if any portion of a property is located in a flood hazard area, as this is a material fact. Buyers should be advised to consult FEMA flood maps and/or check with the local planning office to determine the precise location of any flood zones and restrictions.

Cost of insurance   Charges for flood insurance are based on the following:

> ‣ flood zone classification (this determines the risk of flooding)
> ‣ age of the building and number of floors
> ‣ occupancy as well as contents and their location
> ‣ location of the lowest floor of the building in relation to the base flood elevation
> ‣ amount of coverage
> ‣ deductibles

INSURANCE ISSUES

Insurability
CLUE report
Residential sales contract concerns

Insurability   Determining the insurability of a property should always be part of a purchaser's due diligence process, and brokers should advise their clients accordingly.

If a purchaser has a large claims history, obtaining insurance may be difficult, or premiums may be very expensive, as companies try to mitigate their risk. Claims that attract particular attention include slips and falls, water damage, and dog bites. Companies commonly keep a list of the dogs most likely to bite as determined by the Centers for Disease Control and Prevention. Owning a dog on the CDC's list can make it difficult to obtain coverage. Higher premiums can also be expected in high-risk areas such as those prone to hurricanes or fire.

CLUE report   Insurance companies are required to report all claims for which they set up a file for a possible claim, deny a claim, or pay out money for a claim. The consumer reporting agency **LexisNexis** compiles claim report files and generates Comprehensive Loss Underwriting Exchange (**CLUE**) reports.

A CLUE report goes back for up to seven years, listing both personal property and personal auto claims, and includes the following information:

> ‣ name
> ‣ date of birth
> ‣ policy number
> ‣ date of loss
> ‣ type of loss

- description of covered property
- amount paid out by the insurance company
- property address (for property claims) or vehicle information (for auto claims)

Residential sales contract concerns

Brokers may encounter transactions where a property is or has been vacant for a period of time, a buyer wants to take possession before closing, or a seller wants to continue possession for a time after closing. All of these situations carry specific insurance concerns. Brokers should advise sellers to maintain coverage until after closing as the Risk of Loss remains the responsibility of the seller.

Vacant property. Vacant property is not inhabited and does not contain the personal property needed to support occupancy. Vacant properties carry a higher risk for vandalism and damage that goes undiscovered for an extended period of time. Homeowners' policies typically contain vacancy exclusions that include water damage, theft, vandalism, and glass breakage if the property has been vacant and the damage occurs within 30-60 days of becoming vacant (the exact terms depend on state law and the type of policy).

A vacant home is more difficult and expensive to insure; however, no property should ever go without coverage, so owners are advised to discuss obtaining a vacancy policy with their insurance provider. When available, vacant home coverage can be three times more expensive than the coverage for an occupied home.

Unoccupied property. Unoccupied property is different from vacant property. An unoccupied property is one that still contains all the furnishings needed so the owner could return at any time. Unoccupied properties are often vacation homes where the owner spends significant time away from the property. In this situation, the home may still be covered under the normal homeowners' policy. Owners should consult with their insurance provider to determine whether their policy excludes unoccupied building coverage and prevents the recovery of damages if the property is vacant for more than 60 consecutive days.

Commercial property. A commercial property must have at least 31% of its total square footage occupied to avoid being considered vacant. Like homeowners' policies, commercial policies exclude coverage for water damage, theft, and vandalism when a property has been vacant for 60 days. In addition, commercial policies typically reduce coverage for perils by 15% when the property is vacant.

Early or late possession. For many reasons, early or late possession are tricky situations for all buyers, sellers, and brokers. Brokers are reminded to use the appropriate addenda for these situations and to advise their clients to confirm coverage for their particular situation with their insurance provider ahead of time.

For early possession by the buyer, the seller will most likely need to obtain a landlord's policy, as homeowners' policies typically do not cover the home if it is not owner occupied. Buyers assuming possession early are advised to purchase renters' insurance to cover their personal property and to obtain regular homeowners' coverage beginning on the day of closing.

On the other side, sellers who maintain possession after closing will need to purchase renters' insurance and the new owner (buyer) will need to obtain a landlords' policy.

12 Property Insurance
Snapshot Review

BASIC INSURANCE CONCEPTS

Purpose
- insurance is to protect against losses related to property, flood, auto, health, business, life, pets
- requirements based on location, type of asset

Homeowner's insurance
- protects assets and complies with lender requirements; lender-placed more expensive than owner-placed
- homeowner should consider size, age, location, type, and value of property and contents and terms of policy

Agents, companies, brokers
- agents, insurance companies, and insurance brokers all sell insurance policies

STANDARD POLICY FEATURES

Content
- explains what is covered, and to what extent; exclusions; basic details in declarations page

Policy types
- monoline includes one type of insurance; package includes multiple types in one policy

Coverage
- dwelling coverage protects home and attached structures or fixtures
- other structures coverage protects unattached structures such as fences and sheds
- personal property coverage protects personal belongings and contents of home even when not located on the property
- loss of use coverage pays some expenses to live away from the home during repairs from covered perils
- liability coverage protects homeowner when sued for injuries to others
- medical payment coverage pays medical bills for someone injured on homeowners property
- exclusions of some perils such as earthquakes are typical; must be added at increased premium; flood is always excluded and requires separate policy

Deductibles
- when purchasing insurance, must consider deductible amount, replacement cost, or actual cash value, all of which impact premium amount

Homeowners' policies
- HO-1 is basic policy; HO-2, HO-3, and HO-5 are most common for modern homes; HO-2 has least coverage; HO-5 has most comprehensive coverage; all include structure and personal property
- HO-6 for condominiums and cooperatives; covers semi-permanent structures such as cabinets and personal property
- HO-8 for older or unique homes with replacement costs higher than property market value
- HO-4 for renters covers personal property and liability; HO-7 for extended coverage of expensive homes

FLOOD INSURANCE

FEMA and NFIP
- NFIP Administered by FEMA

Flood zones
- FEMA-designated flood hazard areas abutting rivers, streams
- Zones are subject to usage and improvement restrictions; affect insurance requirements
- Depicted on flood maps and subject to change over time

Insurance requirement
- required for homes in high risk areas
- may be required by lenders for homes in a Special Flood Hazard Area (SFHA)
- required if the homeowners have received federal disaster grants or loans and want to be considered for federal disaster aid in the future

Disclosure
- location of a property in a flood zone is a material fact to be disclosed

Cost of insurance
- based on: flood zone, age and height, occupancy, contents, location, amount, deductibles

INSURANCE ISSUES
- claims history affects insurability; due diligence requires investigation
- Comprehensive Loss Underwriting Exchange (CLUE) report tracks history for up to seven years

Residential sales contract concerns
- homeowners policies typically contain vacancy exclusions
- unoccupied property is different from vacant property in that the homeowner may return at any time
- if a buyer takes possessions early, he/she should purchase renters' insurance and the homeowner should purchase a landlord's policy
- if a seller maintains possession for a time after closing, he/she should purchase renters insurance and the new owner should purchase a landlords' policy

SECTION TWELVE QUIZ: PROPERTY INSURANCE

1. What will likely happen if a homeowner lets his or her homeowners' insurance coverage lapse?

   a. The mortgage lender will place coverage on the home.
   b. The mortgage lender will foreclose on the home.
   c. The home will not be protected if there is a flood.
   d. The homeowner will not be allowed to purchase a new policy.

2. Depending on a home's location, a mortgage lender may require the borrower to carry

   a. liability insurance.
   b. health insurance.
   c. personal property insurance.
   d. flood insurance.

3. Which of the following would NOT be handled by an independent insurance agent?

   a. Comparison shopping for policy terms and prices
   b. Providing loss prevention advice
   c. Helping with a loss or claim
   d. Offering coverage from a company who only employs its own agents

4. If a homeowner wanted coverage for his home and all structures on the property as well as coverage in case a visitor is injured on his property, what type of policy should he buy?

   a. Dwelling
   b. Monoline
   c. Package
   d. Liability

5. Which homeowners' policy covers condominiums?

   a. HO-3
   b. HO-4
   c. HO-5
   d. HO-6

6. Which homeowners' policy covers older homes with replacement costs higher than the home's market value?

   a. HO-4
   b. HO-5
   c. HO-8
   d. HO-6

7. Which homeowners' policy is also known as renters' insurance?

   a. HO-1
   b. HO-3
   c. HO-4
   d. HO-5

8. Which of the following is a true statement about the "80% rule" for homeowner's policies?

   a. 80% of replacement value is the maximum an insurance company will pay.
   b. If insured for less than 80% of replacement cost, a home's coverage will include a deduction for depreciation.
   c. If insured for 80% of replacement cost, a home is covered for the full cost of replacement.
   d. Insurance companies will not insure residences for less than 80% of their replacement cost.

9. A limitation of coverage on an insurance policy is called a(n)

   a. deductible.
   b. condition.
   c. exclusion.
   d. package.

10. Which of the following is not covered in the standard HO-1 policy?

   a. Damage caused by terrorism
   b. Damage caused by aircraft
   c. Damage caused by cars
   d. Damage caused by earthquakes

11. Flood insurance

   a. is a regular part of all homeowners' policies.
   b. can only be purchased from FEMA.
   c. is paid by the state for property in a flood zone.
   d. is required in high-risk flood hazard areas for properties finances by federally backed mortgage loans.

12. Which of the following is NOT true regarding flood insurance

   a. Flood insurance is purchased from the same providers as homeowners' insurance.
   b. Flood insurance is sold by the NFIP.
   c. Flood insurance may be required by mortgage lenders for properties in the SFHA.
   d. Flood insurance is designed to reduce the impact of flooding on public and private buildings.

13. Brokers should do all of the following EXCEPT

   a. assist clients with determining if a property is located in a flood zone.
   b. omit information indicating a property is in a flood zone because it is the buyer's responsibility to discover during the DDP.
   c. ask a seller client if the client's property is covered by flood insurance.
   d. check flood maps and be familiar with the flood zones in their market area.

14. Insurance companies may remove coverage for certain perils when a commercial property has been vacant for

   a. one year.
   b. 120 days.
   c. 90 days.
   d. 60 days.

15. All of the following can impact the insurability of a property EXCEPT

    a.   certain dog breeds.
    b.   presence of a metal roof.
    c.   claims filed by the owner.
    d.   claims filed on the property.

16 An unoccupied property is different from a vacant property in that

    a.   the water is still turned on.
    b.   the property is rented for at least a year.
    c.   the property is furnished so the owners could return at any time.
    d.   the property has been condemned by the city.

17. The CLUE report

    a.   is required to be purchased along with homeowners' insurance.
    b.   goes back for up to seven years, listing both personal property and personal auto claims.
    c.   is short for the comprehensive loss underwriting event report.
    d.   is available for free from the FEMA website.

18. A homeowner who allows the buyer to move in early (early possession) should

    a.   purchase a renter's policy.
    b.   add an exclusion to the homeowner's HO-3 policy.
    c.   cancel the homeowner's insurance three days after the buyer takes early possession.
    d.   purchase a landlord's policy.

19. Insurance policies can either be package or _____ policies

    a.   personal property
    b.   monoline
    c.   all coverage
    d.   dwelling

20. The Special Flood Hazard Area (SFHA) has a _____ annual chance of flooding.

    a.   1%
    b.   5%
    c.   90%
    d.   99%

13 Risk Management

Risk Management Strategies
Risk Management Procedures
Primary Areas of Risk

Risk is the chance of losing something. Its two dimensions are the probability of occurrence and the extent of exposure to monetary or non-monetary consequences. Since most risks are related to judgments and decisions, the real estate licensee, who makes numerous complex decisions every day, faces a high degree of *risk potential*.

Risk management is a structured approach to dealing with the uncertainties and consequences of risk. In real estate practice, the aim is to reduce risk to an acceptable level through anticipation and planning.

RISK MANAGEMENT STRATEGIES

Avoidance
Reduction
Transference
Retention

Four well-established strategies for managing risk are:

▶ Avoidance (elimination)
▶ Reduction (mitigation, sharing)
▶ Transference (outsourcing, insuring)
▶ Retention (acceptance and budgeting)

Not all of these strategies are always possible or available, but a real estate firm or licensee who fails to make a conscious effort to employ one or more of them increases the likelihood of loss from the many potential risks that are always present in the real estate business.

Avoidance   Avoidance includes refraining from an activity that carries risk. One can avoid the risks of being in an automobile accident by not riding in automobiles. Avoiding risks also means missing the opportunity to benefit from the avoided activity. By avoiding automobile travel, one is confined to modes of transportation, such as buses and walking, that do not offer the same high degree of personal freedom and efficiency. Complete avoidance of risk in real estate practice is almost impossible. A broker, for instance, may believe that hiring only experienced affiliates eliminates the risk that affiliates will commit license law violations. However, even experienced practitioners may not know the law, and, sometimes, people break the law deliberately. The risk may be reduced, but it remains.

Reduction

Reduction involves taking steps to reduce the probability or the severity of a potential loss. However, this strategy may result in reducing risk in one area only to increase it in another. A familiar example is a sprinkler system that dispenses water to reduce the risk of fire but at the same time increases the risk of water damage.

In real estate practice, one risk reduction tactic is to share responsibility for making a decision. The agent provides the consumer with expertise, and perhaps some advice, but lets the consumer decide how much to offer. In this way, the agent gets some relief from the risks inherent in the buyer's decision to purchase.

Transference

Transference means passing the risk to another party, by contract or other means. An insurance policy is the common example, but sometimes the wording of a sales or personal services contract can transfer risk without resorting to insurance.

In the real estate business, transference is typically and most successfully accomplished by means of an errors and omissions (E&O) insurance policy, either on the individuals in a firm or on the firm itself. State law may require such insurance.

Retention

Retention of risk means entering into an activity in spite of known risks and taking full responsibility for the consequences. This is, in effect, self-insurance, the only strategy left when risk cannot be reduced or transferred and one has decided not to avoid it because of the desirability of the potential benefits.

RISK MANAGEMENT PROCEDURES

Education
Disclosure
Documentation and record keeping
Insurance

Experience shows that the most practical strategies for risk management in real estate practice are reduction and transference, with procedures focusing on:

- ▶ Education
- ▶ Disclosure
- ▶ Documentation
- ▶ Insurance

Education

Education is the first line of defense against risk. When agents are familiar with the forms provided by the office, how and when to complete them and where to send them, the likelihood of errors is reduced. Likewise, agents need to be able to identify and understand common contract elements, complete contract forms developed by attorneys, and evaluate offers received from co-op agents on their listings without committing a license violation or breach of law.

In most states, brokers have a legal obligation to provide training to affiliated licensees. Licensees also have the obligation to seek out appropriate education and training outside the brokerage to ensure that they know how to comply with the law. In addition, licensees must satisfy legal requirements for continuing education, while those who care about personal excellence will seek further education and training to enhance their professional skills.

Disclosure

By ensuring that all parties have the information they are entitled to, proper disclosure reduces the risk that clients and customers will accuse a licensee of misleading or inducing them to make a decision with incomplete information. Further, laws in every state require disclosures of one kind or another.

Disclosure may be made in writing or verbally and may or may not require written acknowledgment from the receiving party.

Required disclosures usually include:

- agency relationships
- property condition
- duties and obligations
- personal interest in the transaction
- personal interest in referrals

Documentation and Record keeping

Documentation provides evidence of compliance with laws and regulations. It proves what clients and customers and licensees said and did in a transaction. Some documentation is required by law.

The components of a thoroughly documented paper trail include:

- Policy and procedure manuals
- Standard forms
- Communication records
- Transaction records
- Contracts
- Accounting
- Other important documents

Policy manual. A written and uniformly enforced company policy lets everyone in the firm know what to expect before problems arise. The policy manual should cover the company's rules in such areas as floor duty privileges, assignment of relocation properties to agents, referrals between agents within the company, and requirements for continuing education, sales meeting participation, and property tours.

Procedures manual. A company procedures manual should spell out how to handle every aspect of the company's business that agents and brokers need to know—from handling consumers' funds and documents, conducting consumer transactions, dealing with MLS-related matters, and placing signage, to all procedures prescribed by state or federal law, especially license, banking and fair housing laws. Adherence to a procedures manual reduces the risk that an individual will inadvertently commit an unlawful act. Whenever changes are made to the policy or procedures manual, each agent should sign the revised manual as evidence that the agent has examined it.

Standard forms. Standard forms save time and protect against the unauthorized practice of law. Since they are most often prepared by lawyers familiar with the market area, they can address contingencies that are common in the area in a manner that reflects the real estate laws of the state. On the other hand, a licensee often needs to adapt a standardized form for a client by assisting with filling in blanks, modifying terms, and attaching addenda. The licensee must always remain aware of the limitations the state has placed on such activities.

Here are a few of the standard forms a brokerage should provide for its agents and affiliates:

- buyer and seller representation agreements, exclusive and non-exclusive
- agreement to show property
- purchase and sale agreement
- agency disclosure form
- property condition disclosure, disclaimer, and exemption form
- lease agreement
- personal interest disclosure form
- referral for service disclosure form
- lead-based paint disclosure form
- special disclosure forms (mold, radon, subsurface sewage system, impact fees/adequate facilities taxes, etc.)
- referral agreement
- independent contractor agreement
- closing checklist

Communication records. Some communications with transaction parties are good and necessary for business. Others are required by law, such as certain disclosures. A transaction checklist is a good tool for managing risk associated with the failure to make required communications to all principals and for keeping track of required communications from co-op agents.

Retaining evidence that information has been communicated is a necessary procedure. Electronic communications should be archived on suitable electronic media. Copies of mailed or faxed communications should be maintained in the transaction folder.

It is always difficult to document telephone or face-to-face conversations, especially with the constant use of cell phones from a variety of locations. It is a good practice to make brief notes at the time and then write them up later for mailing or faxing to the other party. Be sure, however, that you can produce these notes on demand, lest you be accused later of withholding documentation that has been promised.

Maintaining a good record of communications is useful for resolving disagreements where parties dispute what has been said because it allows the agent to produce a dated document that resolves the issue definitively.

Transaction records. State laws require licensees to document transactions. Firms are required to keep written records of all real estate transactions for a number of years (usually three to five) after closing or termination. Required records typically include:

- listing agreements
- offers
- contracts
- closing statements
- agency agreements
- disclosure documents
- correspondence and other communication records
- notes and any other relevant information

Accounting. In addition to other accounting records, there is the requirement to maintain written accounting of escrow funds. For each transaction, property, and principal, escrow records will include:

- depositor
- date of deposit
- date of withdrawal
- payee
- other information deemed pertinent by the real estate commission

Other documents. Additional documents may be required by law or regulation, or should be kept simply as protection in case of disputes and lawsuits. These would include copies of advertising materials, materials used in training agents, records of compliance with continuing education requirements, safety manuals, and anything else that shows how the firm conducts its business and safeguards its staff as well as the rights of consumers.

Insurance

Many forms of insurance are available for property owners and managers. Some of these types are also used to manage certain risks of brokers and licensees.

General Liability. General liability insurance provides coverage for risks incurred by a property owner when the public or a licensee enters the owned property (**public liability**). The insurer pays the covered claim and legal fees, costs, and expenses, including medical expenses, resulting from owner negligence or other causes. This type of insurance does not cover **professional liability,** for which an Errors & Omissions policy is necessary.

Errors and Omissions. Professional liability is of two general types:

1. Unprofessional conduct – a claim that one has failed to carry out fiduciary duties and provide an acceptable standard of care

2. Breach of contract – a claim that one has failed to perform services under the terms of a contract in a timely manner

The primary method for transferring the professional liability risks of brokers, managers, and licensees is Errors & Omissions (E&O) insurance. A standard E&O policy provides coverage for "damages resulting from any negligent act, error or omission arising out of Professional Services." A standard policy does NOT cover:

- violations of law
- fraudulent, dishonest, criminal or malicious acts
- mishandling of escrow moneys, earnest money deposits, or security deposits
- antitrust violations
- sexual harassment
- Fair Housing violations
- agent-owned properties
- environmental violations
- failure to detect or disclose environmental conditions, including mold
- acts committed prior to licensure or after termination of active status
- activities as an appraiser if licensing other than a real estate license is required

E&O insurance, in short, covers "mistakes" but not crimes.

Fire and hazard. The risks of property damage caused by fire, wind, hail, smoke, civil disturbance, and other such causes are covered by fire and hazard insurance.

Flood. The risks of property damage caused by floods, heavy rains, snow, drainage failures, and failed public infrastructures such as dams and levies are covered by a specialized flood policy. Regular hazard policies do not include flood coverage.

Other insurance. Other common types of insurance coverage for income and commercial properties include:

- **casualty**—coverage for specific risks, such as theft, vandalism, burglary, illness and accident, machinery damage

- **workers' compensation**—hospital and medical coverage for employees injured in the course of employment, mandated by state laws

- **contents and personal property**—coverage for building contents and personal property when they are not actually on the building premises

- **consequential loss, use, and occupancy**—coverage for the business losses resulting from a disaster, such as loss of rent and other revenue, when the property cannot be used for business

- **surety bond**—coverage against losses resulting from criminal or negligent acts of an employee

PRIMARY AREAS OF RISK

Agency
Property disclosures
Listing and selling process
Contracting process
Fair Housing
Antitrust
Rules and regulations
Misrepresentation
Recommending providers
Financing and closing
Trust fund handling

Risks for licensees are present every day in business transactions. Many of these risks carry legal implications as well as possible financial and professional consequences.

Agency

The risks of agency will occur in one of two areas:

▶ the requirement to inform and disclose
▶ the requirement to carry out an agency duty.

Most states require agency relationships to be in writing and to be disclosed to all parties to a transaction. State law may spell out agency duties, or the duties may be a part of general agency law. In states that do not use agency, there is still the obligation to explain and disclose the nature of the relationship.

Disclosure requirements. A licensee may be acting in a transaction as facilitator, agent, subagent, designated agent, single agent, dual agent, non-agent or in some capacity. Regardless of status, the licensee must follow state disclosure requirements. These are, typically, to:

▶ disclose status *verbally* to other licensees on initial contact
▶ disclose status *verbally* to buyer and seller before providing real estate services
▶ confirm the disclosure *in writing* before signing a listing agreement or presenting a purchase offer (to an unrepresented seller) or before preparing a purchase offer (to an unrepresented buyer)
▶ get a *signed receipt* indicating the written disclosure has been made

Carrying out the duties of agency also require disclosures of :

▶ personal interest the agent has in a transaction (such as owner or buyer)
▶ personal benefit the agent will derive from a service referral
▶ required property and market information
▶ information about customers a client is entitled to have

Duties. A licensee who acts for a principal in a real estate transaction is required by law to assume certain responsibilities toward the parties to the transaction. Whether a state applies the fiduciary duties of agency law or specifies its own duties toward clients and consumers, the basic duties remain:

To all parties

- ▶ honesty
- ▶ fairness
- ▶ reasonable care and skill
- ▶ disclosures

To clients

- ▶ skill
- ▶ care
- ▶ diligence
- ▶ loyalty
- ▶ obedience
- ▶ confidentiality
- ▶ accounting
- ▶ full disclosure

The duty to exercise **skill, care and diligence** means that licensees may not be casual or negligent in their actions. Licensee negligence is actionable when principals are harmed by the licensee's failure.

The duty of **loyalty** requires the agent to *put the client's interests above those of everyone else*, including his or her own.

The duty of **obedience** requires the agent to act on the principal's wishes regarding the transaction as long as they do not result in any illegal action. The duty of obedience never overrides the legal obligation of agents to deal fairly and honestly with all parties.

The duty of **confidentiality** requires the agent to hold in confidence any information that would harm the client's interests or bargaining position or anything else the client wishes to keep secret, unless the law requires disclosure. The duty of confidentiality survives the termination of the listing contract.

The duty of **accounting** applies to all funds involved in a real estate transaction. Accounts must be maintained as required by law, and escrow funds are to be handled strictly in accordance with the law.

The duty of **disclosure** applies to both parties to a transaction, although usually with some differences. Proper disclosure to customers primarily concerns agency, property condition, and environmental hazards. To the client, it generally concerns all known facts regarding the property and the transaction, including information about the other transaction party. State laws prescribe what may, must, and must not be disclosed. Licensees must be vigilant to avoid oversights and conflicts of interest that can lead to a disclosure to the wrong party or disclosure of information that is confidential.

Conflicts of interest. Conflicts of interest arise when an agent forgets to put the best interests of a client ahead of those of everyone else. This can happen in situations involving undisclosed dual agencies, broker-owned listings, licensees buying for their own account, vendor referrals, and property management subcontracting of services, among many others. Even ordinary, everyday transactions carry a built-in risk of conflict of interest. Consider the fact that a licensee usually receives no compensation for a failed transaction. Therefore, it is in the licensee's interest to see the transaction completed, even if it may not be in the client's best interest. A negative result from a home inspection or other test has the potential to cause a buyer to back out of a contract. A licensee who has forgotten whose best interest should be primary might be tempted to recommend inspectors who will overlook problems in exchange for receiving referrals. Licensees must always disclose any self-interest they have in a transaction, and always remember their duties to clients and consumers.

Confidentiality. Licensees have a responsibility to maintain the confidentiality of certain kinds of information they obtain concerning clients and customers. The duty to maintain confidentiality generally survives the termination of a listing agreement into perpetuity. If it seems that revealing confidential information might benefit the client, the licensee should obtain the client's written permission to proceed.

Confidential information generally includes information about a client's motivations in a transaction, financial and personal details, and information specifically designated as confidential by the client. Public information, such as that contained in public records, information that becomes known without the licensee's participation, or that the client reveals to another, is not considered confidential.

State laws often require businesses to provide security for the personal information they obtain about consumers. Security procedures should protect personal information from unauthorized access, destruction, use, modification, or disclosure. Confidential information, when it is not to be retained, must be disposed of in a secure manner.

Penalties. Possible penalties for breach of agency relationships include:

- rescission of transaction
- loss of compensation
- fees and costs
- punitive damages
- ethics discipline
- license discipline

Property disclosures

Property condition. Most states require the seller of a residential property to deliver to the buyer a written disclosure or disclaimer about the property's condition, including any material defects the owner knows about. The disclosure is usually required before any purchase contract is accepted.. A second disclosure may be required at closing. The licensee should always obtain the parties' signatures acknowledging receipt of these disclosures.

Depending on the state, the licensee may have no further duty to disclose property condition after properly informing parties of their rights and obligations. However, the licensee may still be subject to legal action for

▶ deliberately distorting the facts (intentional misrepresentation)
▶ cheating any party (fraud)
▶ concealing or failing to disclose adverse facts which the licensee knew about or should have known about (intentional or unintentional misrepresentation)

Lead-based paint and other disclosures. Federal law requires sellers of houses built before 1978 to make a lead-based paint disclosure before accepting an offer to purchase. The licensee must tell the seller about this requirement, give the seller the proper disclosure form, and make sure that the buyer receives it.

The licensee must also make sure the seller discloses any other circumstances the situation and the law require, which may include:

▶ wood infestation inspection report
▶ soil test report
▶ subsurface sewage disposal system permit disclosure
▶ impact fees or adequate facilities taxes disclosure
▶ mold and radon reports or treatments

Listing and selling process

Nature and accuracy of the listing agreement. In most states, a listing agreement is enforceable only if it is in writing. Most states forbid net listings, because they violate the requirement that a valid listing agreement must specify a selling price and the agent's compensation. The licensee, in accordance with the duty of due diligence, must verify the accuracy of the statements in the listing regarding the property, the owner, and the owner's representations. Especially important facts for a broker or agent to verify are:

▶ the property condition
▶ ownership status
▶ the client's authority to act

An agent who does not to act with a reasonable degree of due diligence in these matters may be exposed to liability if it turns out that the property is not as represented or the client cannot perform the contract as promised.

Comparative Market Analysis (CMA). In preparing a Comparative Market Analysis, licensees should guard against using the terms "appraisal" and "value," which are reserved for the use of certified appraisers. Misuse of these terms could lead to a charge of misrepresenting oneself as an appraiser. In discussing listed properties with clients or customers, real estate licensees should be careful to use guarded terms such as "recommended listing price," "recommended purchase price,' and "recommended listing price range."

Agents should make every effort to help the sellers find a reasonable listing price based on the current market. If the CMA leads the seller to list at a price that is too high, the seller may blame the agent when the transaction fails because of an appraisal that comes in below the selling price. To minimize this risk, it is best to be conservative in the CMA and retain documentation that the seller went above the recommended price in spite of the agent's advice.

Estimate of Closing Costs. In preparing an estimate of closing costs for a seller or buyer, there is the risk of forgetting something, leading to an unpleasant surprise when the consumer suddenly faces unexpected costs or conditions. Licensees should use their broker's form, if there is one, and make it clear to the consumer that it is only an estimate of likely costs, not a statement of actual costs. In some states, brokers and agents do not prepare closing cost estimates, leaving that task to the lender.

Advertising. State and federal laws regulate advertising, including the federal Fair Housing laws as they pertain to discriminatory advertising and providing of services. Advertising includes electronic communication, social media/networking, and internet marketing. Usage must be consistent with company image and legal requirements. The license laws of most states list illegal advertising actions subject to discipline such as:

> ▸ making any substantial and intentional misrepresentation
>
> ▸ making any promise that might cause a person to enter into a contract or agreement when the promise is one the licensee cannot or will not abide by
>
> ▸ making continued and blatant misrepresentations or false promises through affiliate brokers, other persons, or any advertising medium
>
> ▸ making misleading or untruthful statements in any advertising, including using the term "Realtor" when not authorized to do so and using any other trade name, insignia or membership in a real estate organization when the licensee is not a member.

Committing such acts may result in license suspension or revocation.

Authorizations and Permissions. Licensees should stay within the bounds of the authority granted by the agency agreement or must not do anything requiring permission without first getting that permission in writing. For instance, permission should be obtained before doing any of the following unless the listing agreement specifically grants the authority:

> ▸ post a sign on the property
> ▸ remove other signs
> ▸ show the property
> ▸ hand out the property condition disclosure
> ▸ distribute marketing materials
> ▸ advertise in various media
> ▸ use a multiple listing service
> ▸ cooperate with other licensees
> ▸ divide the commission or negotiate a commission split
> ▸ share final sales data with the MLS
> ▸ place a lock box on the property

- appoint subagents
- appoint a designated agent
- change agency status

Scope of expertise. Real estate licensees are not, by nature, financial consultants, accountants, appraisers, soil scientists, well diggers, lawyers, decorators, contractors, builders, plumbers, carpenters, inspectors, prognosticators, and a number of other kinds of expert. However, in today's competitive environment, consumers often demand much more from a licensee than the traditional basic services. An agent who fails to live up to prevailing standards may be held liable for negligence, fraud, or violation of state real estate license laws and regulations. At the same time, agents must be particularly careful about the temptation to misrepresent themselves as experts and offer inappropriate expert advice. Disclaimer and referral are always the best risk control procedures to forestall an accusation of misrepresentation from a consumer who claims to have been harmed by reliance on the licensee's non-existent expertise. The exact nature of the services to be provided should be stated as clearly as possible in the listing agreement.

Contracting process According to the Statute of Frauds, all contacts for real estate must be in writing to be enforceable. Contracts that contain incorrect information or are inadequately prepared can pose a serious liability for a licensee. To avoid such a situation, it is imperative for the contract to reflect the terms that the parties have agreed upon in the most accurate and honest manner. The agent must also be careful to comply with the letter of the real estate law. Violations can jeopardize the enforceability of a listing or sales contract, in addition to resulting in criminal prosecution.

Common risks and errors in the contracting process include:

- using an illegal form

  A licensee may be punished for using any real estate listing agreement form, sales contract form, or offer to purchase form that lacks a *definite termination date*.

- failing to state inclusions and exclusions

  The parties should identify as included in or excluded from the transfer any ambiguous items. Unwritten agreements between the parties are a source of later dispute and trouble.

- failing to track the progress of contingency satisfaction

  The time period for completing contingencies such as inspections is specific and limited. Failure to meet or waive a condition may terminate the contract. A "time is of the essence" clause in the standard agreement makes the time period for contingencies critical.

- mistakes in entering data in a form

  All data should be checked and verified: dates, times, amounts, warranties, descriptions, names, representations, promises, procedures, authority, etc. One way to reduce risk in the contracting process is to use a checklist that covers all the contract items.

Unauthorized practice of law. The unintentional practice of law without a license is a great risk in the contracting process, as well as in the representation process. It is illegal for real estate professionals who are not attorneys to draw up contracts for transactions they are not involved in or to charge a separate fee for preparing a contract.

Such licensees may fill in blanks or make deletions on a preprinted contract form prepared by a lawyer. While a licensee may make deletions, additions to a form should be drafted by an attorney. The principals themselves can make changes as long as each change is signed or initialed by all signers. Preprinted riders can often be attached as addenda to a contract without an attorney.

It is also illegal for real estate licensees who are not lawyers to give legal advice or interpret contract language. Licensees, however, may express opinions. For instance, if a licensee believes that a party has grasped the meaning of a contract, it is permissible to say something like, "Though I am not an attorney, in my opinion your understanding of this contract is correct." It would be questionable to make a definitive statement like, "That's correct."

Fair Housing

The risk of violating fair housing laws can be minimized through ongoing education that addresses both the content and the intent of the laws. It is especially necessary for paperwork and documentation to be accurate and concise in a situation where a fair housing issue could arise.

Advertising. The Fair Housing Act forbids real estate advertising that mentions race, color, religion, national origin, sex, handicap, or familial status in any way that suggests preference or discrimination. State laws may add other protected categories, such as creed and age.

Risk can be reduced by the use of street names or other non-biased geographical references when stating where the property is located, and by describing the property rather than the type of persons who might live in or around it. Even if a home appears "ideal for a young family," it is best not to advertise it as such. Such advertising would exclude other groups such as singles, the elderly, and older families.

In advertising the sale or rental of housing covered by the Fair Housing Act, HUD recommends using the Fair Housing Logo or phrase "Equal Housing Opportunity."

Answering questions. When faced with questions that might lead to a *steering* charge or other violation of fair housing laws, it is best for the licensee to limit the response to features of the home and to the process of selling, buying, and listing properties, and refer the questioner to someone else to answer questions about such matters as the demographic make-up of the neighborhood. It is illegal for the licensee to voice an opinion based on race, religion, color, creed, national origin, sex, handicap, elderliness, or familial status. The agent should explain this fact to the buyer and be wary of any situation where the agent's behavior might be construed as discriminatory.

Listing agreements. Before entering into a listing agreement, a licensee should explain that it is necessary to comply with fair housing laws and obtain the potential client's acknowledgment and agreement. The agent should make it clear that the agent will

> ▸ reject the use of terms indicating race, religion, creed, color, national origin, sex, handicap, age or familial status to describe prospective buyers.

> ▸ terminate the listing if the seller uses race, religion, creed, color, national origin, sex, handicap, age, or familial status in the consideration of an offer.

> ▸ inform the broker if the seller makes any attempt to discriminate illegally.

Offers. A seller cannot refuse to sell a property to an individual based on the individual's belonging to a protected class, and if this is attempted, the real estate professional must not be involved. If the seller asks about the color, religion, creed, national origin, ethnicity, age, or familial status of a buyer, the agent must explain that it is illegal to give out such information. The best risk reduction procedure is to treat all buyers and sellers equally, showing no preference for one over another.

Antitrust

Antitrust laws forbid brokers to band together to set a price on their services in listing and selling property. Even being overheard discussing commission rates or being present at such a conversation can lead to charges of *price fixing*.

The law recognizes that some cooperative arrangements between firms – such as joint development projects – may help consumers by allowing these firms to compete more effectively against each other. Even so the government does not prosecute all agreements between companies, but only those that will raise prices for the public or deny the public new and better products.

Sherman Antitrust Act. The *Sherman Antitrust Act* makes illegal all contracts, agreements, and conspiracies among competitors that would unfairly restrict interstate trade by fixing prices, rigging bids, or other means. An unlawful monopoly is created when one company becomes the only supplier of a product or service by getting rid of competition via secret agreements with other companies.

Clayton Act. The *Clayton Act* prohibits mergers or acquisitions that are likely to lessen competition and increase prices to consumers. The Act also prohibits certain other business practices that under certain circumstances may harm competition. Private parties injured by an antitrust violation may sue in federal court for three times their actual damages, plus court costs and attorneys' fees.

Federal Trade Commission Act. The *Federal Trade Commission Act* forbids unfair competition in interstate commerce but establishes no criminal penalties.

Enforcement. Federal antitrust laws are enforced in three main ways:

> ▸ the Antitrust Division of the Department of Justice (DOJ) brings criminal and civil enforcement actions

> ▸ the FTC brings civil enforcement actions

> ▸ private parties bring lawsuits claiming damages

To collect evidence, Department of Justice lawyers often work with the Federal Bureau of Investigation (FBI) on court-authorized searches of a business, monitoring phone calls and employing informants equipped with secret listening devices.

State attorneys general may sue under the Clayton Act on behalf of injured consumers in their states, and groups of consumers often bring lawsuits on their own.

Anyone associated with an organization found guilty of an antitrust violation and determined to have had knowledge of that violation may also suffer legal consequences.

Penalties. Penalties for Violation of Antitrust Laws include:

> ▸ fines for individuals and corporations, as well as possible imprisonment.

> ▸ Under the Clayton Antitrust Act, parties can sue antitrust violators and recover three times the damages they incurred plus court costs and attorneys' fees.

Rules and regulations

State real estate laws and commissioners' rules and regulations attempt to cover every possible risky situation. Non-compliance poses a direct threat to the legal and financial status of licensee and license in the following general ways:

> ▸ license expiration
> ▸ license revocation or suspension
> ▸ licensee discipline
> ▸ suit for damages

License expiration. Licenses expire because licensees neglect to:

> ▸ maintain E & O insurance when required
> ▸ meet education requirements
> ▸ observe correct renewal procedures

License revocation or suspension. Licenses are typically revoked or suspended when a licensee is found guilty of:

- obtaining a license under false pretenses
- committing a "prohibited act"
- neglecting to present every written offer as required
- neglecting to deliver signed copies of accepted offers to transaction parties as required
- failing to make sure that all required terms and conditions are present in a contract to purchase
- handling earnest money and other escrow funds improperly

Licensee discipline. A state real estate commission may assess a civil penalty for violations of a statute, rule, or order. Licensees are disciplined for:

- acting without a license when a license is required
- demanding a referral fee without reasonable cause
- entering into a net listing
- trying to induce another licensee's client to end or change an existing agency contract
- paying a commission to an unlicensed individual or company
- receiving an illegal referral fee, rebate or kickback
- practicing with an expired license

Citations. Citations are issued for specific violations that are determined to not pose a substantial threat to public health, safety, and welfare. The maximum citation that may be issued by DBPR investigators of FREC is $500. Citations must be paid or disputed within 30 days. Licensees may be issued a citation for:

- licensure issues
- renewal violations
- advertising violations

Licensee lawsuits. A licensee may be sued by the Department of Justice, Federal Trade Commission, a state real estate commission, a human rights commission, another licensee or firm, or an individual consumer. Licensees are mainly sued for:

- fair housing violations
- antitrust violations
- license law and other state law violations
- breach of contract
- agency duty violations
- illegal practice of law
- failures to disclose
- customer or client dissatisfaction
- fraud
- theft

Misrepresentation　　Misrepresentation may be unintentional or intentional.

Unintentional misrepresentation. This type of misrepresentation occurs when a licensee _unknowingly_ conveys inaccurate information to a consumer concerning a property, financing or agency service. False or inaccurate information that the licensee, as a professional, should have known to be false or inaccurate may be included in the definition. Those found guilty generally have to pay fines and may be disciplined by state real estate regulators and professional organizations.

Risky areas for unintentional misrepresentation include:

- making and reporting measurements
- describing property
- offering opinions about future growth and development of a neighborhood or neighboring property
- making declarative statements about the presence or absence of hazardous materials

The risks of unintentional misrepresentation are reduced if an agent

- learns to measure and calculate areas accurately
- relies on measurements reported by others only with extreme caution and specific disclaimers
- refrains from exaggeration
- avoids stating opinions a consumer might take for expertise

Intentional misrepresentation. Also known as fraud, this kind of misrepresentation occurs when a licensee _knowingly_ conveys false information about a property, financing or service. Fraud is a criminal act that may result in fines and incarceration, in addition to discipline from state regulators and professional organizations.

Recommending providers

There are several risks attending the recommendation of vendors and service providers to a consumer. First, the consumer may not be satisfied with the performance of the recommended party and blame the licensee. Second, in cases where a recommended provider performs illegal acts, there may be legal consequences for the licensee. Third, if a licensee has a business relationship with a recommended vendor or provider and neglects to disclose the fact, there are license violation consequences.

The major risk management technique is to shift the responsibility for choosing a vendor to the consumer. This can be done by refusing to recommend vendors at all; by presenting a broad range of choices and allowing the consumer to select; or by presenting a short list of thoroughly vetted vendors and allowing the consumer to make the decision, always with the disclaimer that *to the best of the licensee's knowledge*, the vendors on the list are competent and honest, but that the consumer is responsible for investigating and making his or her own judgment before hiring or buying.

Financing and closing

In the financing and closing phases of a transaction, a consumer may feel that a licensee has been incompetent or misleading. Licensees have an obligation to inform and educate their clients throughout the transaction process. Surprises and accusations of incompetence or misrepresentation are among possible results of failing to keep the party informed.

Discrimination. Of course, it is important to comply with relevant laws. Licensees must be mindful of the requirements of ECOA and refrain from participating in any manner of discriminatory lending. It is illegal to:

> ▶ threaten, coerce, intimidate or interfere with a person who is exercising a fair housing right or assisting another other to exercise that right.

> ▶ indicate a limitation or preference based on race, color, national origin, religion, sex, familial status, or handicap in any advertisement or communication. Single-family and owner-occupied housing that is otherwise exempt from the Fair Housing Act is subject to this prohibition against discriminatory advertising.

Progress reporting. All inspections and tests must comply with local and state laws and with the purchase contract. Progress reports should be accurate, timely, in writing, and free of speculation. If a consumer has a question about the meaning of something in an inspection report, the licensee should refer the consumer to the person who wrote the report rather than trying to explain it. This method transfers some of the risk inherent in interpreting the report.

Qualifying buyers. Many transactions fail because a buyer has been improperly qualified before the offer is presented. Using a lender to qualify the buyer saves time and protects the agent against leading a seller to believe a purchaser is fully qualified when this may not be the case. Also, lenders and loan agents are better able to look into the buyer's qualifications than a real estate licensee is. If it becomes necessary to show a property to a potential buyer who has not been qualified by a lender, the licensee can gain some protection by performing an informal qualification and documenting the fact that it was based on the information provided by the buyer. The buyer's signature on this documentation indicates the buyer's acceptance of at least partial responsibility for the qualification.

Lending fees disclosure. The licensee should explain loan fees, charges,

amounts, timing, and responsibilities. Agents can assist in the loan decision by explaining how to compare loans with differing charges and interest rates. The fact that a high origination fee and points may make a loan with a low interest rate unattractive to a borrower is important information for the agent to provide, and providing it may protect the agent against a later complaint that the buyer suffered a loss because of the agent's failure to inform.

Appraisal problems. Delays and appraised value are the typical problem areas. Failure to inform parties about delays can compromise the transaction. An under-appraisal will require the buyer to make a larger down payment or the seller to lower the price. If the property appraises for more than the purchase price, the seller may blame the agent for suggesting the lower price. In such a case, the seller's agent's defense is that the seller agreed to the listing price and that the price was a factor in attracting the buyer to the property.

RESPA Violations. The **Real Estate Settlement Procedures Act (RESPA)** stipulates that the parties to certain purchase transactions must be given accurate information reflecting their closing costs. It also prohibits certain business practices that are not considered to be in the consumer's best interest.

The licensee's risks regarding RESPA primarily relate to

> ▶ failing to ensure that the consumer is informed about his or her rights under the law

> ▶ giving or receiving an illegal kickback.

RESPA currently requires lenders to:

> ▶ give a copy of a Consumer Financial Protection Bureau loan information booklet to the applicant. The booklet explains RESPA provisions, general settlement costs, and the required **Closing Disclosure** form. The lender must provide the estimate of closing costs within three business days following the borrower's application.

> ▶ give the applicant a Loan Estimate (Form H-24) of expected closing costs within three business days of receiving the application. Actual closing costs may not vary from the estimate beyond certain limits.

> ▶ give the buyer the Closing Disclosure (Form H-25) specifying costs to be paid by buyer and seller at closing three business days before consummation.

> ▶ give the *buyer* the opportunity to review the final settlement statement *one business day prior to closing*.

RESPA specifically *prohibits* any fee or kickback paid to a party for a service when the party has not actually rendered the service. For example, it is prohibited for an insurance company to pay a real estate agent or a lender for referring a client.

Fees for referring clients to the following services are strictly forbidden:

> ▶ title services (search, insurance)
> ▶ appraisals
> ▶ inspections
> ▶ surveys
> ▶ loan issue
> ▶ credit report
> ▶ attorney services

The sharing of commissions and the payment of referral fees among cooperating brokers and multiple-listing services are not RESPA violations.

Trust fund handling   State laws prescribe how licensees must handle any escrow or earnest money deposits they receive. Those laws usually state that a broker must hold money received in connection with the purchase or lease of real property in a trust fund account. The type of account and financial depository are specified. The broker must record receipt of the money and place that money in the trust account within a specified time period. Usually, the law allows the broker to hold an earnest money check uncashed until the offer is accepted, provided the buyer gives written permission and the seller is informed.

Typical trust fund handling requirements include:

- the broker named as trustee of the account
- a federally-insured bank or recognized depository located in the state
- an account that is not interest-bearing if the financial institution ever requires prior written notice for withdrawals
- maintenance of records in a particular accounting format
- separate records kept for each beneficiary, property, or transaction
- records of funds received and paid out regularly reconciled with bank statements
- withdrawals only by the broker-trustee or other specifically authorized person

Commingling and conversion. Mixing of personal or company funds with client funds is grounds for the revocation or suspension of a real estate license. Depositing client funds in a personal or business account, or using them for any purpose other than the client's business, is also grounds for suspension or revocation of a license. It is important for the broker to remove commissions, fees or other income earned by the broker from a trust account within the period specified by law to avoid committing an act of commingling.

13 Risk Management
Snapshot Review

RISK MANAGEMENT STRATEGIES
- two dimensions of risk: size, probability; risk management: structured approach to uncertainty

Avoidance
- refrain from risky activity

Reduction
- reduce probability; share responsibility

Transference
- pass risk by contract; insurance

Retention
- accept risk; self-insurance

RISK MANAGEMENT PROCEDURES

Education
- train in laws, forms and procedures, job performance

Disclosure
- provide information to reduce misunderstanding & lawsuits; agency, property condition, duties, personal interest

Documentation and record keeping
- maintain evidence of compliance; manuals, forms, records, contracts, accounting, other documents

Insurance
- general liability, E & O, fire and hazard, flood, casualty, workers, personal property, consequential loss, surety bond

PRIMARY AREAS OF RISK

Agency
- main failures: to inform and disclose, to fulfill duties
- disclosures: verbal, written, signed receipt; agency relationship and duties; personal interest in transaction; required information
- duties: to all– honesty, fairness, care, skill, required disclosures; additional to clients– diligence, loyalty, obedience, confidentiality, accounting, full disclosure
- conflicts of interest arise from failing to put client's interest first
- confidentiality duty lasts forever; laws define what is confidential, how to treat and dispose of information
- penalties include loss of transaction, compensation, fees and costs, damages, license

Property disclosures
- property condition, lead-based paint, other conditions; disclosure may discharge liability; failure to disclose may be construed as misrepresentation

Listing and selling process
- areas of risk include listing agreement accuracy, Comparative Market Analysis results, closing cost estimates, advertising, authorizations and permissions, exceeding expertise

Contracting process
- contracts for real estate must be in writing; inaccuracy endangers contract; other risks: illegal form, omitted elements, lapsed contingencies, wrong data
- unauthorized practice of law: non-lawyers may fill in blanks and delete words on standard contract forms; no legal advice to public allowed

Fair Housing	• advertising may not state preference, limitation or discrimination based on race, color, religion, national origin, sex, handicap, familial status
	• agent must not be involved with discriminatory actions of a client or customer
Antitrust	• government prosecutes cooperative arrangements that raise prices or reduce consumer choices: Sherman Antitrust Act outlaws restraint of trade; Clayton Act outlaws practices that harm competition; Federal Trade Commission Act outlaws unfair methods of competition
	• violations punishable by government criminal and civil actions as well as by private lawsuits; fines, damages, and imprisonment possible
Rules and regulations	• violators of state rules and regulations risk license expiration, revocation, suspension, and other discipline
	• prime causes of discipline include commission of prohibited acts, practicing with an expired license, disclosure failures, earnest money mishandling
Misrepresentation	• unintentional: inaccurate information conveyed unknowingly; subject to fines and license discipline; occurs most often in measurements, property descriptions
	• intentional: fraud, knowingly conveying false information; criminal act subject to fines, license discipline, and incarceration
Recommending providers	• risks include consumer dissatisfaction, possible vicarious liability for illegal acts committed by a recommended provider, undisclosed business relationship (RESPA violation as well as license violation)
	• best practice: do not recommend any vendors, or provide a list of trusted vendors with no recommendation and a disclaimer
Financing and closing	• risk areas include fair housing and ECOA violations; failed transactions because of agent failure to monitor contingency period; failure to ensure proper disclosure of closing costs; RESPA violations
Trust fund handling	• risk areas include mishandling of earnest money deposits; commingling and conversion of trust funds; errors in use of trust

SECTION THIRTEEN QUIZ: Risk Management

1. Of the following risk management strategies, the one that aims at minimizing both the severity and the likelihood of loss is

   a. avoidance.
   b. reduction.
   c. transference.
   d. retention.

2. Insurance is a method of

   a. risk elimination.
   b. risk mitigation.
   c. risk outsourcing.
   d. risk acceptance.

3. How does disclosure manage risk?

   a. It deflects and reduces risk by preventing others from claiming they were misled.
   b. It eliminates the risk of committing an error.
   c. It accepts the risk of revealing confidential information.
   d. It transfers the risk of a code violation to the client.

4. Which of the following statements about a company procedures manual as a risk management device is true?

   a. It places all the responsibility for compliance on the broker.
   b. It relieves the licensee of responsibility for knowing and obeying the law.
   c. It can be a guide to compliance with the law.
   d. It adds to the risk of misleading the public.

5. In what sense is the use of standardized forms a risk management procedure?

   a. It eliminates the risk of being unable to draft a contract correctly.
   b. It reduces the risk of losing a client by having to make a referral to an attorney.
   c. It reduces the risk of committing an unauthorized practice of law.
   d. It eliminates the risk of wasting valuable time in creating custom forms.

6. Keeping thorough records of every transaction is not only a risk management technique, it is

   a. good for company morale.
   b. necessary for obtaining market share.
   c. a technique for discovering market trends.
   d. a legal requirement.

7. Which of the following communication records must (as opposed to should) be kept?

   a. Notes on every conversation.
   b. Copies of required communications to principals.
   c. Notes from company training sessions.
   d. Business cards of licensees one meets at open houses.

8. The standard E & O policy covers damages resulting from

    a. failure to disclose an environmental condition.
    b. antitrust violations.
    c. mishandling of earnest money deposits.
    d. negligence, error or omission in carrying out professional services.

9. Which of the following is a common risk relating to the agency relationship?

    a. Failing to inform and disclose properly.
    b. Failing to take a personal interest in a transaction.
    c. Acting as an exclusive agent without an oral agency agreement.
    d. Forgetting to record the listing agreement.

10. Even after giving buyer and seller the required information about property condition disclosures, the licensee may still be subject to legal action for

    a. failing to detect customer misrepresentations.
    b. failing to disclose known adverse facts.
    c. relying on publicly available market information.
    d. advising the purchaser to exercise due diligence.

11. In performing a comparative market analysis, a licensee must be careful to

    a. use the term "market value" whenever possible in the report.
    b. show a low suggested selling price to avoid a complaint of misrepresenting the value.
    c. include the results of a certified appraisal in the analysis.
    d. avoid creating a false impression that the licensee is a certified appraiser.

12. In fulfilling a listing agreement, one of the major risk areas is

    a. finding a buyer who turns out to be unqualified.
    b. exceeding the authority of the agreement.
    c. showing the property without the presence of the owner.
    d. cooperating with other licensees.

13. A simple way of reducing the risk of committing an error or omission in the contracting process is

    a. use a checklist of all items, contingencies, dates and responsibilities that must be met.
    b. delegate some of your responsibilities to the licensee who represents the other party in the contract.
    c. call the buyer and seller daily to check on progress.
    d. cut the list of necessary tasks down to a few essentials and concentrate on tracking those.

14. Regarding contracts and forms,

    a. once written and signed they cannot be changed except by a lawyer.
    b. real estate licensees may alter forms but not contracts.
    c. whoever originates them can make changes without the risk of unauthorized practice of law.
    d. the principals may make changes as long as they sign or initial each change.

15. The best way to minimize the risk of violating fair housing laws is to

    a. deal only with consumers who do not belong to a protected class.
    b. obtain education in the content and intent of the laws.
    c. make sure there is always a witness present at all meetings with consumers.
    d. stay away from transactions involving public housing.

16. A licensee risks violating antitrust law by

    a. being present at a conversation where the setting of commission rates is discussed.
    b. being present at a discussion of antitrust laws.
    c. charging a commission rate that happens to be the same as that charged by another firm.
    d. cooperating with another firm to do market research.

17. How is an intentional misrepresentation penalized?

    a. License discipline, fines, and possible incarceration.
    b. License discipline and fines, but no incarceration.
    c. License discipline only.
    d. Fines only.

18. All of the following are areas of risk for unintentional misrepresentation EXCEPT

    a. measuring and reporting property dimensions.
    b. describing properties and amenities.
    c. stating that a client should seek legal counsel.
    d. making statements about the presence or absence of hazardous substances.

19. To reduce risks inherent in reporting transaction progress to a client, the licensee should

    a. make reports orally only, never in writing.
    b. leave progress reporting to the inspectors and other experts.
    c. advise the client that it is company policy to make no progress reports until the contingency period is over.
    d. avoid statements of opinion and speculation in all reports.

20. How does sharing the qualifying function with a lender protect a licensee?

    a. It guarantees that a buyer will have a loan.
    b. It reduces the chance of presenting an offer from an unqualified buyer.
    c. It relieves the licensee of his or her due diligence responsibilities.
    d. It allows the licensee to avoid asking embarrassing questions.

21. General liability insurance coverage does not cover _____.

    a. professional liability.
    b. risks incurred by property owner when public enters his or her property.
    c. public liability.
    d. medical expenses resulting from owner negligence.

22. The insurance coverage needed if an employee is injured at work is called _____

   a. casualty insurance.
   b. consequential loss.
   c. workers' compensation.
   d. injury insurance.

23. A surety bond provides coverage against losses resulting from negligent or _____ acts of an employee.

   a. dangerous
   b. harmful
   c. medical
   d. criminal

24. How long should a licensee maintain client confidentiality regarding their listing agreement?

   a. Up until the listing agreement is terminated
   b. Forever
   c. 180 days after a listing agreement is ended
   d. 90 days after the listing agreement ends

25. Why is the time period of contingencies critical?

   a. Because of the "time is of the essence" clause
   b. Because there are deadlines
   c. It does not matter
   d. Because transactions have to close quickly

14 Property Management

Management Functions
The Management Agreement
Leasing Considerations
The Management Business

MANAGEMENT FUNCTIONS

Reporting
Budgeting
Renting
Property maintenance
Construction
Risk management

Property management is a specialty within the real estate profession. Many states require persons who manage real estate on behalf of other persons or entities to be licensed as real estate brokers. Other states license such persons specifically as property managers. Real estate firms that handle the sale of commercial and investment properties are in a natural position to manage those properties for their owners. Some property managers work for firms that manage multiple properties under blanket management contracts. Others are independent agents. Some are employees of the owner. They generally fall into one of the following categories:

▶ **individual property manager**-- usually a real estate broker who manages properties for one for one or more owners; may belong to a small property management firm devoted to full-time property management, be self-employed, or be one of several managers in a large real estate firm.

▶ **individual building manager**-- usually manages a single large property; may be employed by a property manager or directly by an owner; may or may not have a real estate license.

▶ **resident manager** (residential properties only)-- lives on the property and may be employed by a real estate broker, a managing agent or an owner to manage a property on a part-time or full-time basis; may be required by state law for properties of certain types and sizes.

A manager has a fiduciary relationship with the principal and, in general, is charged with producing the greatest possible net return on the owner's investment while safeguarding the value of the investment for the owner/investor. At the same time, the manager has some responsibilities to tenants, who want the best value and the best space for their money. Professional managers are therefore much more than rent collectors. They need technical expertise in marketing, accounting, finance, and construction. Property managers often specialize in one type of property - apartment, office, retail, industrial, farm, single-family-and acquire specialized knowledge of that property type. Whatever the property type and management arrangement, the manager's work involves leasing, managing, marketing, and maintaining the property. The services a manager provides thus can be seen to fall into three areas: financial, physical, and administrative. Specific functions, duties, and responsibilities are determined by the management agreement, although most agreements will include at least the following functions.

Reporting

Financial reporting to the principal is a fundamental responsibility of the property manager. Reports may be required monthly, quarterly, and annually. Required reports typically include an annual operating budget (see below); monthly cash flow reports indicating income, expenses, net operating income, and net cash flow; profit and loss statements based on the cash flow reports and showing net profit; and budget comparison statements showing how actual results match the original budget.

Budgeting

An operating budget based on expected expenses and revenues is a necessity for management. The budget will determine rental rates, amounts available for capital expenditures, required reserve funds, salaries and wages of employees, amounts to be paid for property taxes and insurance premiums and mortgage or debt service. It will indicate the expected return, based on the previous year's performance. A typical budget will contain a projection, also based on past performance and on current market information, of income from all sources, such as rents and other services, and of expenses for all purposes, such as operating expenses, maintenance services, utilities, taxes, and capital expenditures. Operating statements itemizing income and expenses are then presented to the owner on a regular basis so that the owner can evaluate the manager's performance against the budget.

Income. The total of scheduled rents plus revenues from such sources as vending services, storage charges, late fees, utilities, and contracts is the *potential gross income*. Subtracting losses caused by uncollected rents, vacancies and evictions gives *effective gross income*. Operating expenses are subtracted from this total to show *net operating income*. When debt service and reserves (which are not counted as operating expenses) are subtracted, the result is *cash flow*.

Expenses. Expenses may be fixed or variable. Fixed expenses are those that remain constant and may include operating expenses, regular maintenance costs, and administration. Variable expenses are those that may change from month to month or occur sporadically, such as specific repairs or capital expenditures.

Capital expenditures. Expected expenditures for major items such as renovation or expansion should be included as a budgeting item. Large-scale projects are typically budgeted over a period of years.

Cash reserve. A cash reserve is a fund set aside from operating revenues for variable expenses, such as supplies, redecorating, and repairs. The amount of the reserve is based on experience with variable expenses in previous years.

Renting

The property manager, whose full responsibilities include maintaining and managing the property in accordance with the owner's financial goals, include seeing that the property is properly rented and tenanted. The manager may use the services of a leasing agent, whose concern is solely to rent the space. In such a situation, some of the manager's tasks may be performed by the leasing agent. Renting the property includes the following tasks, regardless of which party is actually performing them.

Controlling vacancies. There are many possible reasons for vacancies in a building:

- rent too high or too low
- ineffective marketing
- management quality
- poor tenant-retention program
- image and appearance problems
- high market vacancy rate

Successful managers look for these factors and take steps to limit or counteract their effects.

Marketing. Finding and attracting the right kind of tenants for a property is the aim of a marketing program. A marketing plan based on the property's features and the relationship between supply and demand in the market area, and consonant with the money available, will determine the best mix of advertising and promotional activities. Marketing methods include:

- billboard advertising
- brochures and fliers
- meetings and presentations
- networking
- newspaper ads
- radio and television advertising
- signs
- tenant referrals
- websites and online services

The efficiency of marketing activities can be judged in terms of how many prospects per completed lease they generate. The lower the cost per prospect per lease, the more effective and efficient the program.

Setting rents. Rental income must be sufficient to cover fixed expenses, operating expenses, and desired return on investment. But rental rates must also be realistic, taking into account what is happening in the market. The manager must consider prevailing rents in comparable properties as well as vacancy rates in the market and in the property. The manager makes a detailed survey of competitive space and makes adjustments for differences between the subject property and competing properties before setting the rental rates for the property. Residential apartment rates are stated in monthly amounts per unit, while commercial rates are usually stated as an annual or monthly amount per square foot. If vacancy rates in the managed property are too high, the manager may have to lower rates or identify problems in the property or its management that are contributing to vacancy level. On the other hand, if the property's vacancy rate is significantly lower than market rates, the manager may conclude that higher rental rates are called for.

Selecting tenants. To ensure that the property produces the desired level of income from rent, it is essential to find the most suitable tenants. For commercial space, the manager must determine that:

> ▶ the space meets the tenant's needs for size, configuration, location, and quality.
> ▶ the tenant will be able to pay for the space.
> ▶ the tenant's business is compatible with that of other tenants.
> ▶ there is room for expansion if the tenant's need for space is likely to grow.

For residential space, in addition to ascertaining the tenant's creditworthiness, the manager must be careful to comply with all federal and local fair housing laws. A manager should collect the same type of information on all prospective tenants. However, even though the law prohibits discrimination on the basis of race, sex, age and other protected classes, a manager may discriminate in certain other ways. For example, a manager has the right to refuse to rent to a person who has a history paying rent late, damaging property, fighting with other tenants, or spotty employment.

Collecting rents. The lease agreement should clearly specify the terms of rental payment. The manager must establish a system of notices and records as well as a method of collecting rents on schedule. Compliance with all state laws and regulations concerning collecting and accounting for rents is a necessity to avoid unwanted legal complications. As for monies received, the manager must follow trust fund handling procedures established by law and laid out in the rental and management agreements. If authorized by the management agreement, the manager may also collect security deposits and handle them as required by law.

Maintaining tenant relations. Happy tenants remain in a rented space longer than unhappy tenants. High tenant turnover adds to increased advertising and redecorating expenses. For these reasons, it is incumbent on the manager to

> ▶ communicate regularly with tenants

- respond promptly and satisfactorily to maintenance and service requests
- enforce rules and lease terms consistently and fairly
- comply with all relevant laws, such as fair housing and ADA (Americans with Disabilities Act) regulations

Legal issues (Fair Housing, ADA, and ECOA). Fair housing laws govern landlords and tenants just as they do sellers and buyers. They ensure that persons receive fair treatment regardless of race, color, religion, national origin, sex, handicap, or familial status. Families with children must receive equal treatment with those who do not have children. Landlords cannot charge higher rents or security deposits because of the presence of children. Managers must make sure that their marketing and leasing practices are in accordance with fair housing laws.

The Americans with Disabilities Act similarly requires landlords in certain circumstances to make housing and facilities available to disabled persons without hindrance. Familiarity with this law and with the latest state, federal, and local fair housing laws is essential.

The Equal Credit Opportunity Act, which prohibits discrimination in lending, applies to how property managers evaluate potential tenants. The manager must be consistent in evaluating the creditworthiness of applicants. The same application forms and the same credit requirements should be used with all applicants.

Property maintenance

Physical maintenance of the property is one of the property manager's primary functions. The costs of services provided must always be balanced with financial objectives and the need to satisfy tenant needs. The manager will also be concerned with staffing and scheduling requirements, in accordance with maintenance objectives.

Maintenance objectives. The foremost maintenance objective is generally to preserve the value of the physical asset for the owner over the long term. Although not every property is best served by vast expenditures on top-level maintenance, it is almost always important to maintain the viability of the property as a rental. Three general types of maintenance are required to keep a property in serviceable condition: routine, preventive, and corrective.

Routine maintenance. Routine maintenance activities are those necessary for the day-to-day functioning of the property. Regular performance of these activities helps to keep tenants satisfied as well as forestall serious problems requiring repair or correction. Routine activities are such things as:

- regular inspections
- scheduled upkeep of mechanical systems-heating, air-conditioning, rest rooms, lighting, landscaping
- regular cleaning of common areas
- minor repairs
- supervision of purchasing

Preventive maintenance. Preventive maintenance goes beyond the routine in attempting to deal with situations that can become serious problems if ignored. Seasonal or scheduled replacement of appliances and equipment, regular painting of exterior and interior areas, and planned replacement of a roof are a few examples.

Corrective maintenance. When routine and preventive maintenance fail, repairs and replacements become mandatory to keep the property operational. A boiler may develop a leak, an air-conditioning unit may break down, an elevator may cease to function properly.

Maintenance contracting. Depending on building type and size, tenant needs, and budgetary constraints, a manager may decide to hire an outside firm to handle maintenance services rather than hiring on-site employees. Efficiency, competence, responsiveness, and effective cost will be major deciding factors.

Construction

Commercial and industrial property managers are regularly called upon to make alterations to existing space to accommodate a tenant's needs. They may also have to undertake or oversee construction that alters or expands common areas or the entire building itself. Again, such work may be contracted out or done by in-house employees.

Tenant improvements. Alterations made specifically for certain tenants are called build-outs or tenant improvements. The work may involve merely painting and re-carpeting a rental space, or erecting new walls and installing special electrical or other systems. In new buildings, spaces are often left incomplete so that they can be finished to an individual tenant's specifications. In such cases, it is important to clarify which improvements will be considered tenant property (trade fixtures) and which will belong to the building.

Renovations. When buildings lose functionality (become functionally obsolescent), they generally also lose tenants, drop in class, and suffer declining rental rates. Maintenance becomes more expensive because of the difficulties of servicing out-of-date building components. Renovation may solve some of these problems, but the manager will have to help the owner determine whether the costs of renovation can be recovered by increased revenues resulting from the renovation.

Environmental concerns. A variety of environmental concerns confronts a property manager, ranging from air quality to waste disposal, tenant concerns, and federal, state and local environmental regulations. The managed property may contain asbestos, radon, mold, lead, and other problematic substances. Tenants may produce hazardous waste. The manager must be aware of the issues and see that proper procedures are in place to deal with them, including providing means for proper disposal of hazardous materials, arranging for environmental audits and undertaking possible remediation. For instance, an audit may show that a building is causing tenants to become sick because of off-gassing from construction materials combined with a lack of ventilation. Remediation may consist of nothing more than replacing carpets and improving ventilation, and the manager, if empowered to do so, should take the necessary steps.

Legal concerns (ADA). The Americans with Disabilities Act requires managers to ensure that disabled employees and members of the public have the same level of access to facilities as is provided for those who are not disabled. Employers with at least fifteen employees must follow nondiscriminatory employment and hiring practices. Reasonable accommodations must be made to enable disabled employees to perform essential functions of their jobs. Modifications to the physical components of the building may be necessary to provide the required access to tenants and their customers, such as widening doorways, changing door hardware, changing how doors open, installing ramps, lowering wall-mounted telephones and keypads, supplying Braille signage, and providing auditory signals. Existing barriers must be removed when the removal is "readily achievable," that is, when cost is not prohibitive. New construction and remodeling must meet a higher standard, Managers must be aware of the laws and determine whether their buildings meet requirements. If not, the manager must determine whether restructuring or retrofitting or some other kind of accommodation is most practical.

Risk management

Many things can go wrong in a rented property, from natural disaster to personal injury to terrorism to malfeasance by employees. Huge monetary losses for the owner, in the form of civil and criminal penalties, legal costs, fines, damages, and costs of remediation can be the result. A manager must consider the possibility of such events and have a plan for dealing with them.

Risk management strategies. Depending on the nature of the risk, the size of the potential losses, the likelihood of its happening, and the costs of doing something about it, a manager and owner will generally choose one or more of the following risk management strategies:

> ▸ avoidance-removing the source of the risk, such as by closing off a dangerous area of the building

> ▸ reduction-taking action to forestall the event before it happens, such as by installing fire alarms, sprinklers, and security systems

> ▸ transference-shifting the risk to someone else by buying an insurance policy

> ▸ retention-taking the chance that the event is not likely enough to occur to justify the expense of one of the other strategies; self-insurance

Security and safety. A court may hold a manager and owner responsible for the physical safety of employees, tenants, and customers in leased premises. In addition to standard life safety and security systems such as sprinklers, fire doors, smoke alarms, fire escapes, and door locks, a manager may have to provide electronic and human monitoring systems (security cameras, security guards) and be prepared to take action against tenants who allow, conduct or contribute to dangerous criminal activities such as assault and drug use.

Insurance. Many types of insurance are available to allow for the shifting of liability away from the owner. An insurance audit by a competent insurance agent will indicate what kind of and how much coverage is advisable. Common types of insurance coverage for income and commercial properties include:

- ▶ casualty-coverage for specific risks, such as theft, vandalism, burglary, illness and accident, machinery damage

- ▶ liability-coverage for risks incurred by the owner when the public enters the building; medical expenses resulting from owner negligence or other causes

- ▶ workers' compensation-hospital and medical coverage for employees injured in the course of employment, mandated by state laws

- ▶ fire and hazard-coverage for damage to the property by fire, wind, hail, smoke, civil disturbance, and other causes

- ▶ flood-coverage for damages caused by heavy rains, snow, drainage failures, and failed public infrastructures such as dams and levies; flood insurance is not included in regular hazard policies

- ▶ contents and personal property-coverage for building contents and personal property when they are not actually on the building premises

- ▶ consequential loss, use, and occupancy-coverage for the business losses resulting from a disaster, such as loss of rent and other revenue, when the property cannot be used for business

- ▶ surety bond-coverage against losses resulting from criminal or negligent acts of an employee

The owner may opt for a multi-peril policy which combines standard types of commercial policies and may allow special coverage for floods, earthquakes, and terrorism.

The amount of coverage provided by certain types of policies may be based on whether the property is insured at depreciated value or current replacement value. Depreciated value is its original value minus the loss in value over time. Current replacement value, which is more expensive, is the amount it would cost to rebuild or replace the property at current rates.

Commercial policies include coinsurance clauses requiring the insured to bear a portion of the loss. Fire and hazard policies usually require the coverage to be in an amount equal to at least 80 percent of the replacement value.

Owner's policies do not cover what is owned by the tenant. Tenants should obtain their own renter's or tenant's insurance to cover personal belongings. Residential and commercial or business variants are available. The question of who owns tenant improvements is not only important when it is time for the tenant to leave the premises. It is also likely to determine whether the tenant's or the landlord's insurance company will be paying if the improvements are damaged or destroyed.

Handling of trust funds. Managers are responsible for proper handling of monies belonging to other parties that come into the manager's hands in the *course of doing business. For property managers, such funds include rents collected from tenants, security deposits, and capital contributions from the property owner. State laws, usually incorporated into real estate commission rules* and the state's real estate law, specify how a property manager is to manage trust funds. In general, the agent is to maintain a separate bank account for these funds, with special accounting, in a qualified depository institution. The rules for how long an agent may hold trust funds before depositing them, and how the funds are to be disbursed, are spelled out. The fundamental requirements are that the owners of all funds must be identified, and there must be no commingling or conversion of client funds and agent funds. Mishandling carries heavy penalties.

THE MANAGEMENT AGREEMENT

Components
Rights, Duties, and Liabilities

Components

The management agreement establishes an agency agreement between manager and owner as well as specifying such essentials as the manager's scope of authority, responsibilities, objectives, compensation, and the term of the agreement. Property managers are usually considered to be general agents empowered to perform some or all of the ongoing tasks and duties of operating the property, including the authority to enter into contracts. The agency relationship creates the fiduciary duties of obedience, care, loyalty, accounting, and disclosure. The contractual relationship ensures that the manager will strive to realize the highest return for the owner consistent with the owner's objectives and instructions. The agreement should be in writing and include at least the basics of any real estate contract, as follows.

> ▸ **Names of the parties**--owner, landlord, manager, tenant or other party to be bound by the contract

> ▸ **Property description**--street address, unit number and location, square footage, and other information that specifies the leased premises

> ▸ **Term**--time period (**months**, years) covered by the contract; termination conditions and provisions

- ▶ **Owner's purpose--maximize** net income, maximize asset value, maximize return, minimize expenditure, maintain property quality, etc.; long-term goals for the property

- ▶ **Owner's responsibilities--management** fees, plus any management expenses such as payroll, advertising and insurance that the manager will not be expected to pay

- ▶ **Manager's authority--**the **scope** of powers being conveyed to the manager: hiring and staffing, setting rents, contracting with vendors, ordering repairs, limits on expenditures without seeking owner permission

- ▶ **Manager's responsibilities--specification** of duties, such as marketing, leasing, maintenance, budgeting, reporting, collecting and handling rents; the manager should be included as an additional insured on the liability policy for the property

- ▶ **Budget--**amounts, or percentages of revenues, allotted for operations, taxes, insurance, capital expenditures, etc.

- ▶ **Allocation of costs--**who is to pay certain expenses, that is, which will be treated as expenses of the manager vs. which will be paid directly by the owner

- ▶ **Reporting--**how often and what kind of reports are to be made

- ▶ **Compensation--**the management fee or other means of compensation to the manager; there may be a flat fee based on square footage, a rental commission based on a percentage of annual rent, a combination of these, or some other arrangement; in compliance with anti-trust laws, management fees are not standardized but must be negotiated by agent and principal

- ▶ **Equal opportunity statement--**the HUD statement or equivalent concerning availability to all persons and classes protected by law, incorporated into the agreement in the case of a residential property

Rights, duties, liabilities

Both the manager and the landlord have rights, duties and liabilities under the terms of the management contract. How these are apportioned should be clearly stated in the agreement.

Landlord. The landlord has the right to receive rent according to the agreement, and to receive the premises in the specified condition at the end of the agreement term. The landlord and his or her agents may have the right to enter and inspect the premises, examine the books, hire and fire staff, and choose vendors. The landlord may retain or grant the power to enter into contracts, to set rents, and to select tenants. The landlord will have the right to terminate the management contract according to the terms of the contract. The landlord will have the duty to pay the agreed management fee, and to make other such payments as detailed in the agreement. State law will determine to what extent a principal is liable for the acts of the manager and the manager's employees. As owner, the landlord is liable for failures to comply with certain local, state, and federal laws, particularly the Environmental Protection Act and fair housing laws.

Manager. Depending on the degree of authority granted by the agreement, the manager may have the right to hire and fire, enter into contracts, and perform routine management tasks without interference from the owner. The manager has the duties described earlier: to maintain financial records and make reports; to budget; to find, retain, and collect from tenants; to maintain and secure the property; to meet the owner's objectives. The manager's liabilities include the consequences of mishandling trust funds, violating fiduciary responsibilities, and violating fair housing laws, credit laws, and employment laws.

Exhibit Abbreviated Sample Management Agreement

MANAGEMENT AGREEMENT

Agreement made_____[date], between_____, a corporation organized under the laws of the State of _____, having its principal office at_____[address],_____[city],_____[state], here referred to as owner, and_____, a corporation organized under the laws of the State of_____, having its principal office at a*ddress],*_____[city],_____[state], here referred to as agent.

RECITALS

1. Owner holds title to the following-described real property:_____[insert legal or other appropriate description], here referred to as the property.
2. Agent is experienced in the business of operating and managing real estate similar to the above-described property.
3. Owner desires to engage the services of agent to manage and operate the property, and agent desires to provide such services on the following terms and conditions.

In consideration of the mutual covenants contained herein, the parties agree:

EMPLOYMENT OF AGENT. Agent shall act as the exclusive agent of owner to manage, operate, and maintain the property.

BEST EFFORTS OF AGENT. On assuming the management and operation of the property, agent shall thoroughly inspect the property and submit a written report to owner concerning the present efficiency under which the property is being managed and operated, and recommended changes, if necessary.

LEASING OF PROPERTY. Agent shall make reasonable efforts to lease available space of the property, and shall be responsible for all negotiations with prospective tenants. Agent shall also have the right to execute and enter into, on behalf of owner, month-to-month tenancies of units of the property.

ADVERTISING AND PROMOTION. Agent shall advertise vacancies by all reasonable and proper means; provided, agent shall not incur expenses for advertising in excess of____Dollars ($_____) during any calendar quarter without the prior written consent of owner.

MAINTENANCE, REPAIRS, AND OPERATIONS. Agent shall use its best efforts to insure that the property is maintained in an attractive condition and in a good state of repair. Expenditures for repairs, alterations, decorations or furnishings in excess of_____Dollars ($____) shall not be made without prior written consent of owner.

EMPLOYEES. Agent shall employ, discharge, and supervise all on-site employees or contractors required for the efficient operation and maintenance of the property. All on-site personnel, except independent contractors and employees of independent contractors, shall be the employees of agent.

INSURANCE. Agent shall obtain the following insurance at the expense of owner, and such insurance shall be maintained in force during the full term of this agreement:

1. Comprehensive public liability property insurance of _____Dollars ($___) single limit for bodily injury, death, and property damage;

2. Comprehensive automobile insurance of _____ Dollars ($_____) single limit for bodily injury, death, and property damage;

3. Fire and extended coverage hazard insurance in an amount equal to the full replacement cost of the structure and other improvements situated on the property; and

4. A fidelity bond in the amount of_____ Dollars ($_____) on each employee who handles cash, and workers' compensation and employer liability insurance to cover the agents and employees of both employer and agent.

COLLECTION OF INCOME. Agent shall use its best efforts to collect promptly all rents and other income issuing from the property when such amounts become due. It is understood that agent does not guarantee the collection of rents.

BANK ACCOUNTS. Agent shall deposit (either directly or in a depositary bank for transmittal) all revenues from the property into the general property management trust fund of agent, here referred to as the trust account. From the revenues deposited in the trust account, agent shall pay all items with respect to the property for which payment is provided in this agreement, including the compensation of agent and deposits to the reserve accounts as provided for. Agent shall remit any balance of monthly revenues to owner concurrently with the delivery of the monthly report.

RESERVE ACCOUNT. Agent shall establish a reserve account for the following items: taxes, assessments, debt service, insurance premiums, repairs (other than normal maintenance), replacement of personal property, and refundable deposits.

RECORDS AND REPORTS. Agent shall furnish owner, no later than the end of the next succeeding month, a detailed statement of all revenues and expenditures for each preceding month. Within   days after the end of each calendar year, agent shall prepare and deliver to owner a detailed statement of revenues received and expenditures incurred and paid during the calendar year that result from operations of the property.

COMPENSATION OF AGENT. Agent shall receive a management fee equal to___percent (__ %) of the gross receipts collected from the operation of the property. Any management fee due agent hereunder shall be paid to agent within _____days after the end of each month.

TERMINATION AND RENEWAL. This agreement shall be for a term commencing on_____[date], and ending on _____[date].

MODIFICATION. This agreement may not be modified unless such modification is in writing and signed by both parties to this agreement.

IN WITNESS WHEREOF, the parties have executed this agreement at_[designate place of execution] the day and year first above written.

_____

_____

LEASING CONSIDERATIONS

Lease types
Owned and leased inclusions
Reversionary rights of owners
Landlord rights and responsibilities
Tenant rights and responsibilities
Evictions
Tenant improvements
Termination of a lease
Security deposit procedures
Universal Residential Landlord-Tenant Act

Lease types

A leasehold estate may grant tenancy for years, from period-to-period, at will, and at sufferance.

For years. An estate for years may be for any definite period—years, months, weeks, days. When the estate expires, the lessee must return the premises to the lessor and vacate the premises. Most commercial leases grant this type of estate.

Periodic. An estate from period-to-period does not have any definite period. Such an estate begins as a lease for a definite period but continues after the expiration of the lease, as long as the lessee continues to pay rent at the regular interval, the lessor accepts it, and no one gives notice to terminate the lease. This type of leasehold is common with residential properties.

At will. A tenancy at will is similar to the periodic tenancy, except that it does not begin with a definite period. It continues, with the consent of the lessor, as long as the tenant pays rent at regular intervals. It is terminated by the death of either party. The tenancy at will is rarely, if ever, used in a written lease.

At sufferance. A tenancy or estate at sufferance comes into existence when a tenant stays beyond the expiration of another type of lease without the lessor's permission. This type of tenancy is never intentionally used in a written lease.

Leases, depending on how rent is determined, are also defined as gross, net, percentage leases, and graduated leases.

Gross. In a gross lease, the tenant pays an established, fixed rent, and the landlord pays all property operating expenses, such as taxes, insurance, utilities, and other services. This is the arrangement commonly used in residential leases.

Net. Net leases have the tenant paying rent plus some or all of the operating expenses attributable to the rented space. This arrangement is commonly used in office and industrial leases.

Percentage. A percentage lease may be gross or net, but the rent is not fixed, but depends on the income generated by the tenant in the leased property. A common arrangement is to set a fixed base rent plus a percentage of the tenant's gross income or sales at the site. The percentage calculation may take effect only when the income reaches a certain level. This arrangement is commonly used in retail leases.

Graduated. Either a gross or a net lease may also be a graduated lease, in which the rental rate increases at specified times over the lease term.

Owned and leased inclusions

The lease should set forth items that are excluded or included in the leased property. For instance, a residential lease may include built-in appliances such as dishwashers but exclude freestanding ones, such as refrigerators. Furniture may be included or excluded. At issue for the landlord is the cost of maintenance. If a refrigerator is not included, it does not have to be maintained by the property manager.

Ownership also relates to insurance policies: one can only insure what one owns, so if a property item is destroyed by fire, the owner's policy will not provide any coverage for an item that is not included in the lease as belonging to the property. This may be of critical importance in a commercial lease where certain improvements might be owned by either the landlord or the tenant, according to the lease.

The lease should also have clear rules about making alterations. If the tenant is not satisfied with an item that is part of the property, the lease may provide for the tenant to make changes only with permission or with the obligation to return the premises to their original condition on termination, or that any alterations made to fixtures become the property of the landlord. Trade fixtures, by definition, belong to the tenant and can be removed when the tenant leaves.

Inclusions may also be of a financial nature-what is included in the rent. Principal and interest on a mortgage loan, homeowner's association dues, common area maintenance charges, liability and hazard insurance, and various operating expenses are items that might be included in the lease as the owner's or the tenant's responsibilities.

Reversionary rights of owners

Like the grantor of a life estate, the grantor of a leasehold estate retains a future interest in the estate. The lease grants a number of rights to the property, including, primarily, the rights to enter, possess, and use the property for the term of the lease. The lessee does not enjoy the full bundle of rights to the property. For instance, the lessee may not encumber or sell the property. When the lease expires (a condition subsequent), all rights revert to the original owner. A common example is the leasing of an apartment for a one-year period. When the lease expires, the lessee has no further rights in the property and full ownership reverts to the lessor. Another condition subsequent that may cause reversion of rights is tenant default.

Landlord rights and responsibilities

State law, often incorporating or modeling the Universal Residential Landlord Tenant Act (see below) prescribes rights and responsibilities for residential landlords and tenants.

Rights. Commonly, the landlord retains a right of entry into the premises in order to perform needed repairs and maintenance on a property. The lease and/or the law may specify that a landlord may enter the tenant's property only under one or more of the following conditions:

- ▸ An emergency requires the landlord to enter.
- ▸ The tenant gives consent to enter.
- ▸ The landlord enters during normal business hours and only after giving notice to either make repairs or to show the property to prospective tenants, purchasers or contractors.
- ▸ The tenant has abandoned or surrendered the property.
- ▸ The landlord has a court order allowing the entry.

Likewise, the landlord has the right to expect prompt payment of rent and adherence to building rules. At the end of the lease term, the landlord has the right to retake possession of the premises. In case of tenant breach or default, the landlord has the right to pursue the remedies provided by law, such as eviction, to take possession.

Responsibilities. The landlord (by way of the property manager), is expected to deliver a property that is habitable. This means that the landlord at the very least must:

- ▸ keep the heating, cooling, electrical, and plumbing systems in good working condition
- ▸ keep floors, stairways and railings safe and in good repair
- ▸ provide pest control as needed
- ▸ repair roof leaks and broken windows promptly.

Tenant rights and responsibilities

Rights. Beyond the right to quiet enjoyment (privacy) of a property received and maintained in a habitable condition, the tenant has other rights, depending on state law. For instance, a tenant may be able to take any of the following actions if a landlord fails to correct a problem that is the landlord's responsibility:

- ▸ move out without liability for back rent or the unexpired portion of the lease
- ▸ refer the problem to mediation, arbitration or small claims court
- ▸ after giving the owner written notification of an emergency situation, call a professional repair person and deduct the cost from the next month's rent.

Responsibilities. Depending on state law, a tenant generally must:

- ▸ Pay rent on time
- ▸ Follow the rules and regulations set out by the landlord
- ▸ Give a 30-day notice when terminating a month-to-month lease
- ▸ Return all door and mailbox keys when leaving the property
- ▸ Leave the unit in as clean a condition as it was at the start of the lease
- ▸ Keep the unit clean and sanitary
- ▸ Dispose of all rubbish, garbage and other waste in a sanitary manner

- ▸   Use and operate all electrical, gas and plumbing fixtures properly
- ▸   Refrain from destroying or damaging the property
- ▸   Prevent others from destroying or damaging the property
- ▸   Use the property and the rooms only for their intended purposes

Evictions

An *actual eviction* follows a procedure prescribed in state law and stated in the lease contract. The landlord must serve notice on the tenant a specified number of days before beginning the eviction suit. A court issues a judgment for possession, which requires the tenant to vacate. A court officer, such as a sheriff, may forcibly remove the tenant and possessions if the tenant refuses to vacate. The landlord can then enter and take possession.

A *constructive eviction* occurs when a tenant vacates the leased premises and declares the lease void, claiming that the landlord's actions have made the premises unfit for the purpose described in the lease. The tenant must prove that it was the landlord's actions that were responsible and may be able to recover damages.

Tenant improvements

As discussed earlier, leased spaces are often modified to a tenant's specifications. Such alternations may be made by the landlord on the tenant's behalf or by the tenant. Buildings usually have "standard" improvements, which any tenant improvements must equal or improve on. Many leases have a clause that requires the tenant to return the premises to the condition in which they were received at the end of the lease term. Who pays for improvements and who owns them are major matters for negotiation.

Termination of a lease

Like contracts in general, leases may terminate in a number of ways. Principal among these are the following.

Expiration. A lease with a term (estate for years) automatically expires at the end of the term.

Performance. Any contract terminates when all parties have performed their obligations.

Agreement. The parties may agree to terminate the lease before the end of the term.

Abandonment. The landlord may retake possession and pursue the tenant for default if the tenant abandons the premises and fails to fulfill lease obligations. The tenant's obligation to pay rent continues.

Default or Breach. A default occurs when either the tenant or landlord violates any of the terms or covenants of the lease. The damaged party may sue for damages, specific performance (of the breached obligation), or cancellation of the lease. When the default arises from the tenant's failure to pay rent or maintain the premises, the landlord may sue for possession and for eviction. Before filing suit, the landlord must give proper notice and allow the tenant to remedy the breach. The most common form of landlord default is failure to maintain the property and provide services. The tenant may vacate the premises and declare the lease cancelled if the landlord's default has made the premises unoccupiable. This action is called constructive eviction.

Notice. A periodic leasehold or tenancy at will may be terminated by proper notice given by either party.

Destruction. Property destruction is grounds for termination of the lease.

Condemnation. Eminent domain proceedings terminate leases.

Foreclosure. Foreclosure actions terminate lease obligations.

Death. A tenancy at will terminates on the death of either party. The landlord's death terminates any lease if the landlord held the leased property under a life estate, since the landlord cannot convey an interest that extends beyond the landlord's life.

Security deposit Procedures

As previously mentioned in the context of handling trust funds, state laws, real estate commission rules, and the state's real estate law, usually specify how a property manager is to manage security deposits. Such funds are normally held in a special trust account and may not be used for any purpose other than the intended one. Whether the deposit can earn interest, and to whom that interest belongs, are likewise prescribed by law. The law also prescribes when the deposit must be returned to the tenant, and under what circumstances any of it may be withheld. The contract language should clearly state the rules, among other things, governing what happens to the deposit when the lease terminates.

Uniform Residential Landlord-Tenant Act

The Uniform Residential Landlord-Tenant Act is model legislation that has been adopted to a greater or lessor extent in many states. In addition to addressing fair and equitable remedies for breaches by both landlord and tenant, the act aims to clarify imprecise language in residential leases that can lead to confusion or exploitation in such areas as:

- ▶ lease term
- ▶ rental amount
- ▶ security deposit
- ▶ landlord access
- ▶ procedures for default and eviction
- ▶ general obligations of landlord and tenant.

THE MANAGEMENT BUSINESS

Sources of business
Securing business
Professional development

Sources of business

Property management is increasingly a specialization within real estate. There is a growing need for skilled managers because of the increasing number and complexity of properties.

Specialist opportunities. Property managers with specialized training are in demand in a wide variety of property types, including shopping centers, commercial buildings, residential properties, and industrial parks. Within these property specialties are opportunities to specialize even further in such areas as:

▸ leasing
▸ asset management
▸ corporate property management
▸ resort management
▸ association management
▸ housing program management
▸ mobile home park management
▸ office building management

Owners and investors in these various property types are among the consumers of management services who represent potential clients for a professional property manager. Such owners and investors may be individuals, corporations, developers, landlords, banks, trusts, homeowners' associations, condominium associations, or investment syndicates.

Securing business

Reputation, demonstrated competence, professional training, and smart advertising are keys to finding management business. Before entering into a management agreement, the manager should make sure that the owner's management objectives are clear and that they are realistic.

Management plan. Developing a management plan is a necessary step in beginning a management project, and it may also be part of obtaining a management contract. The manager must consider the owner's objectives, including financial goals; the competitive market for the property, both local and regional, depending on the property type; and the features of the particular property. The plan will take into account market indicators such as vacancy rates, occupancy rates, absorption rates, and new supply coming onto the market. It will also include a budgetary component that considers sources of revenue and anticipated expenses. Finally, the plan will indicate what the manager intends to do with the property, given these considerations, to manage the property in a way that will meet the owner's objectives.

Professional development

A number of organizations provide valuable information and training in subjects related to property management. The certifications and designations provided by these organizations are often viewed as valuable signs of competence and can be a significant factor in getting hired as a manager. Important associations include:

- IREM-The Institute of Real Estate Management, offering the CPM (Certified Property Manager) designation

- BOMA and BOMI-The Building Owners and Managers Association International and the affiliated Building Managers and Owners Institute International, offering the RPA (Real Property Administrator), SMA (Systems Maintenance Administrator), and FMA (Facilities Management Administrator) designations

- NAA-The National Apartment Association, offering designations in apartment building management, maintenance, leasing, portfolio supervision and other related areas

- NARPM-The National Association of Residential Property Managers, offering the RPM (Residential Property Manager), MPM (Master Property Manager) and other related designations

- ICSC-The International Council of Shopping Centers, offering designations in retail property leadership, management, marketing, leasing, and development

- NACM-The National Association of Condominium Managers, offering the RCM (Registered Condominium Manager) designation

14 Property Management Snapshot Review

MANAGEMENT FUNCTIONS

- main manager types: individual broker or firm managing for multiple owners; building manager, employed by owner or other manager to manage a single property; resident manager, employed by owner, broker, or management firm to live and manage on site.

- manager is a fiduciary of the principal; duty to act in principle's best interests; may specialize in a property type

- needed skills: marketing, accounting, finance, construction; financial, physical, administrative services; specific functions determined by management agreement

Reporting

- monthly, quarterly, or annually; annual operating budget, cash flow reports, profit and loss statements, budget comparison statements

Budgeting

- operating budget based on expected expenses and revenues; determines rental rates, capital expenditures, reserves, salaries and wages; projects income based on past performance and current market

- potential gross income: total of scheduled rents plus revenues from other sources; effective gross income: total gross minus losses from vacancies, evictions, uncollected rents; net operating income: effective gross minus operating expenses; cash flow: net operating income minus debt service and reserves

- expenses are variable and fixed; capital expenditures are outlays for major renovations and construction; cash reserves set aside for variable expenses

Renting

- manager must keep property properly rented and tenanted; vacancies managed by rent setting, marketing, tenant relations, good service

- selecting compatible tenants and collecting scheduled rents are top priorities

- legal issues concern compliance with fair housing laws, Americans with Disabilities Act, and ECOA

Property maintenance

- main consideration: balance between costs of services, owner financial objectives, and tenant needs

- may be routine, preventive, or corrective; staffed in-house or contracted out

Construction

- tenant alterations, renovations, and expansion; also environmental remediation

- legal concerns: Americans with Disabilities Act; applies to employers with fifteen or more employees; manager to determine feasibility of restructuring, retrofitting, new construction, or other alternatives to comply

Risk management

- risk ranges from natural disaster to personal injury, terrorism, and employee malfeasance; handled by avoiding or removing the source, installing protective systems, buying insurance, self-insuring (risk retention)

- life safety systems include sprinklers, fire doors, smoke alarms, fire escapes, monitoring systems

- insurance includes casualty, liability, workers' comp, fire and hazard, flood, contents, consequential loss, surety bonds, multi-peril; tenants need their own insurance

- handling of trust funds is a major risk area; mishandling carries heavy penalties

MANAGEMENT AGREEMENT

Components
- names of parties; property description; lease term; owner's purpose; responsibilities; authority; budget; allocation of costs; reporting; compensation; Equal Opportunity statement

Rights, duties and liabilities
- landlord: receive rent; receive premises in specified condition; enter and inspect; examine books; enter into contracts, hire vendors, set rents; pay management; comply with laws
- manager: hire and fire; enter into contracts; perform management tasks; maintain records, make reports, budget, collect rent, find tenants, maintain the property, meet owner goals; handle trust funds; comply with laws

LEASING CONSIDERATIONS

Lease types
- for years, periodic, at will, at sufferance, gross, net, percentage, graduated

Owned and leased inclusions
- items included or excluded in the lease; owner's insurance covers only what is included; alterations to inclusions only with owner's permission
- "inclusion" also refers to financial items included as lessee's responsibility, such as operating expenses

Reversionary rights of owners
- all rights of ownership revert to owner at end of lease term

Landlord rights and responsibilities
- rights: enter premises, receive payment, retake on termination, pursue remedies; responsibilities: provide habitable conditions; maintain heating, cooling, electrical, plumbing; keep clean and in repair

Tenant rights and responsibilities
- rights: quiet enjoyment, habitable conditions, right to take action for default; responsibilities: pay rent, obey rules, give proper notice, return property in prescribed condition, use only for intended purpose

Evictions
- actual: prescribed legal procedure; notice, suit, judgment, taking of premises; constructive: tenant vacates for landlord failure to maintain premises

Tenant improvements
- ownership of and payment for improvements according to agreement

Termination of a lease
- causes: expiration, performance, agreement, abandonment, breach, notice, destruction of premises, condemnation, foreclosure, death of either party (tenancy at will), death of landlord (life estate)

Security deposit procedures
- determined by state law, commission rules, agreement

Universal Residential Landlord-Tenant Act
- model law regulating lease language and lease terms; adopted by many states

THE MANAGEMENT BUSINESS

Sources of business
- leasing, asset management, corporate properties, resorts, association management, housing programs, mobile home parks, office buildings; owners, investors, corporations, developers, landlords, condo and homeowners' associations, banks, trusts, syndicates

Securing business
- develop reputation and competence; obtain training; use effective advertising; make management plan in accordance with owner objectives

Professional development
- training, designations, certifications to increase and demonstrate competence

SECTION FOURTEEN QUIZ: Property Management

1. Property managers have a _____ relationship with the property owner.

    a. non-binding
    b. partnership
    c. fiduciary
    d. subagency

2. One of the property manager's fundamental responsibilities is

    a. obtaining construction loans for the principal.
    b. financial reporting to the principal.
    c. finding a buyer for the property.
    d. maintaining good standing in a managers' professional association.

3. Effective gross income is defined as

    a. the total of scheduled rents.
    b. the total of all rents and revenues generated by a property.
    c. potential gross income minus debt service and reserves.
    d. revenue from all sources minus losses from uncollected rents, vacancies, and evictions.

4. The efficiency of marketing activities can be measured in terms of

    a. cost per tenant prospect generated per lease.
    b. number of ads produced per marketing dollar.
    c. dollars expended per square foot of vacant space.
    d. percentage of reserves expended on marketing.

5. If a property's vacancy rate is significantly lower than market rates, it may be a sign that the manager needs to

    a. lower rental rates.
    b. raise rental rates.
    c. find better tenants.
    d. improve management quality.

6. Why does a manager need to keep tenants happy?

    a. Happy tenants make fewer demands for services.
    b. Managers are contractually required to please tenants.
    c. Unhappy tenants make the owner look bad.
    d. High tenant turnover increases expenses and reduces profits.

7. What are the three kinds of maintenance a manager has to carry out for a managed property?

    a. Constructive, deconstructive, and reconstructive
    b. Routine, preventive, and corrective
    c. Scheduled, planned, and improvised
    d. Emergency, elective, and optional

8. The Americans with Disabilities Act requires property managers to

   a. ensure that disabled employees have the same level of access to facilities that all employees have.
   b. hire the disabled whenever possible.
   c. remove all existing barriers to the free movement of disabled persons within the property, regardless of the cost.
   d. remodel the ground floor of the property in accordance with ADA standards if it was built before 1978.

9. Which of the following statements about the property manager's responsibility for security and safety is true?

   a. The manager has no responsibilities for building safety beyond ensuring that fire doors and sprinklers are working.
   b. The manager's security responsibilities are limited to the common areas.
   c. A court may hold the manager responsible for the physical safety of tenants, employees, and customers in leased premises.
   d. The manager's security responsibilities are limited to tenants and their employees in their leased premises.

10. Commercial fire and hazard insurance policies usually require coverage to equal at least 80 percent of the property's

    a. replacement value.
    b. reproduction value.
    c. original cost.
    d. depreciated basis.

11. Trust funds to be handled by a property manager are likely to include all of the following except

    a. rents collected from tenants.
    b. cash for the management firm's operating expenses.
    c. security deposits.
    d. capital contributions from the property owner.

12. What kind of agency is commonly created by a management agreement?

    a. Universal
    b. Specific
    c. General
    d. Vicarious

13. The rights, duties, and liabilities of the landlord and manager are

    a. apportioned under the terms of the management contract.
    b. dictated by common law.
    c. identical.
    d. regulated by the Universal Landlord Tenant Relations Act.

14. Which of the following describes a gross lease?

    a. The tenant pays a base rent plus some or all of the operating expenses.
    b. The tenant pays a fixed rent, and the landlord pays all operating expenses.
    c. The tenant pays a base rent plus an amount based on income generated in the leased space.
    d. The tenant pays a rent that increases at specified times over the lease term.

15. If an apartment contains a refrigerator that is not included in the lease,

    a. the lessee is required to buy it from the landlord.
    b. the landlord is required to remove it.
    c. the lease is invalidated because of an incomplete property description.
    d. the property manager does not have to maintain it.

16. A basic responsibility of a landlord is to

    a. provide leased space at market rental rates.
    b. deliver a habitable property.
    c. keep the rental space freshly painted.
    d. refrain from entering the leased space at any time during the lease term.

17. How does a constructive eviction occur?

    a. A landlord obtains a court order to force the tenant to vacate the leased premises.
    b. A court officer forcibly removes the tenant from the premises.
    c. A tenant declares a landlord in default and vacates the leased premises.
    d. A landlord declares a tenant in default and takes possession of the leased premises.

18. Among the essential elements of a management plan is consideration of

    a. the competitive market for the property.
    b. the property manager's career goals.
    c. the property owner's net worth.
    d. the management firm's income goals.

19. A _____ manages a property for one or more owners.

    a. building manager
    b. maintenance manager
    c. property manager
    d. rental agent

20. The Equal Credit Opportunity Act ensures that

    a. all property managers evaluate potential tenants fairly and equally.
    b. less-qualified tenants be given easier application guidelines.
    c. all real estate agents treat clients equally.
    d. applicants get different opportunities based on their credit score tiers.

21. If a landlord wants to evict a tenant, their first step is to _____.

    a. have a court issue a judgment for possession.
    b. serve notice on the tenant a specified number of days before beginning the eviction suit.
    c. require the tenant to vacate.
    d. have a sheriff forcibly remove a tenant.

22. A resident manager typically _____.

    a. lives on the property.
    b. manages a single large property.
    c. prepares retail leases for their tenants.
    d. manages commercial properties.

23. What happens to a lease if the landlord dies during the lease term?

    a. The lease will keep going no matter what.
    b. The lease will terminate 180 days after the death.
    c. The lease will be terminated if it was leased under a life estate.
    d. The lease will remain intact and the tenant will receive their security deposit back early.

24. Which of the following is a tenant's responsibility?

    a. Repair roof leaks
    b. Keep the electrical systems in working order
    c. Provide pest control
    d. Use the property and the rooms only for their intended purposes

25. A tenant must give a _____ notice when terminating a month-to-month lease.

    a. 60-day
    b. 30-day
    c. 90-day
    d. 14-day

15 Construction Terminology

HOUSE STYLES

bungalow - Originally a one-story house with prominent roof and large overhangs.

Cape Cod - A small one-story or one-and-a-half-story house with gable roof, clapboard or shingle siding, and no dormers (originally).

contemporary - A modern house that emphasizes materials and structure rather than any traditional or derivative style.

Dutch colonial revival - A house with a gambrel roof where the lower slope of the roof flares into the eave with a gentle curve.

Elizabethan - A house using or simulating half-timber construction; cross gables; steeply pitched roof; large chimney stacks.

English colonial - A saltbox, Cape Cod or other simple style with no ornamentations or classical details.

Federal - An adaptation of classical and Georgian styles, featuring tall windows, curved stairs, elliptical rooms, bowed projections and octagonal bays, virtually flat roof, balustrade along the eave line, fanlight transoms, decorated sidelights, porticoes and columns.

Georgian - A style characterized by symmetry, aligned windows, and conventional details; gambrel, gable or hip roof; windows capped with cornices or crown moldings; classical cornices on the eaves; pilasters often frame the doorway, but there is no covered porch at the front door; balustrade set high on the roof; building material varies regionally.

Gothic revival - A variety of irregular, picturesque, rambling designs; steeply-pitched gable and cross-gable roof, vertical siding in earthy colors; carved ornamentation; verandas and balconies.

Greek revival - A style based on the forms of the classical Greek temple; shallow-pitched gable roof, with gable end usually oriented toward the road; portico with columns; recessed front entrance with wide casings; white clapboard with dark green shutters.

mansard - A modern style featuring the mansard roof; often has arched dormer windows, double front doors, smooth stucco covering, and decorative corner features.

modern - A house built with up-to-date materials. May be contemporary in style, or a reproduction or derivative style.

neoclassical revival - A style featuring a two-story classical portico with columns, restrained decorative details, smooth exterior wall surfaces, often a hip roof.

prairie - Characterized by a low-pitched hip roof with wide overhangs; bands of casement windows; stucco covering; strong horizontal emphasis; low, heavy and solid appearance.

Queen Anne - A multi-story, wood-framed and (usually) clapboarded style featuring turrets, towers, verandahs, wrap-around porches, gazebos, scrollwork, varied shingle patterns.

ranch - Typically one-story; simple gable roof; built on a slab or shallow foundation; materials, coverings, ornamentation vary.

Romanesque - A style featuring masonry construction, massive walls, round arches, masonry mullions, steep multi-gabled roof, turrets.

saltbox - A two-story house with a gable roof, the back slope of which is elongated down to a one-story height; usually covered in clapboard siding.

Spanish mission - Characterized by red tile roof, wide eaves with exposed rafter ends, open porches with rectangular piers, a dominant curved parapet, and stucco.

split-level - A ranch-type house with a one-story section meeting a two-story section midway.

Tudor - A masonry or stucco building with parapeted gables, stone mullions, large leaded windows, and a Tudor arch.

Victorian - Not a single style; often used to refer to Queen Anne or Gothic revival styles.

Williamsburg colonial - A modern style featuring symmetrical facade, steeply-pitched gable roof with dormers; clapboard or brick covering.

DOOR TYPES AND PARTS

bifold - A two-paneled folding door mounted in a track, usually used with closets.

Dutch - A two-part door divided horizontally.

French - A two-part door divided vertically.

sidelight - Narrow window next to an entry door.

solid core - A door constructed of exterior surfaces with solid wood blocks filling the space between them.

steel - A door constructed of steel as a fire-proofing or security barrier.

threshold - The bottom part of a doorway.

ELECTRICAL SYSTEMS

240 volt service - The type of electrical supply required by such household appliances as air conditioners, washers and dryers. Usually separate from the normal household supply of 120 volts.

amperage - A measure of the overall capability of the household supply. 100 amp service is the modern minimum standard.

circuit breaker - A resettable device that interrupts a circuit when there is an overload or fault on the line.

conduit - Metal piping used to carry flexible wiring.

fuse - A device that interrupts a circuit when there is an overload or fault. The fuse must be replaced after it has performed the interruption.

ground fault circuit interrupter - A device that monitors the current entering and leaving a receptacle or circuit. When incoming and outgoing currents are unequal, the device instantly opens the circuit. Used particularly in bathroom, garage and outdoor receptacles.

junction box - A box that contains wire splices or cable connections, but devices.

outlet box - A box that protects wire connections and holds a device such as a switch or receptacle.

rheostat - A dimmer switch that allows gradient control of current.

EXTERIOR COVERINGS

beveled siding - Siding consisting of horizontally overlapped boards that are thinner on the upper edge than on the lower.

board and batten - Siding that is applied in vertical panels or boards with the vertical joints covered by narrow strips.

brick - Outside structural wall or veneer consisting of brick and mortar. In residences, generally regarded as low-maintenance, fireproof and decorative.

clapboard - A type of smooth beveled siding, generally narrow, that is common in older frame houses.

redwood siding - Siding, usually beveled, made of cedar or redwood. Noted for resistance to weather, it may be installed with rough or smooth side out, and may be stained, painted, or only sealed.

shingle - A type of thick, wooden shingle, also called a shake, which can be applied vertically as siding.

siding - Exterior finish or "skin" of a wall; typical types are vinyl, aluminum, beveled wood, shingle, and board and batten.

stucco - A cement-based material applied in semi-liquid form over metal lath. A kind of false stucco is sometimes applied to plywood panels.

tongue and groove - A type of wooden siding milled with a groove on one edge and a protruding "tongue" on the other so that the edge of one board fits into the edge of the next board.

FOUNDATION TYPES AND PARTS

brick - A foundation of brick laid on a concrete footing, found in some older houses.

cement block - A foundation of cast blocks laid on a concrete footing.

footing - The base on which the foundation walls sit. Usually poured concrete, twice the thickness of the walls.

poured concrete - A foundation in which the walls consist of concrete poured into forms.

slab - A horizontal concrete section used as a foundation.

stone - A foundation of field stone.

GENERAL STRUCTURE

balloon frame - A house framing method in which studs extend from foundation to roof. Floor joists are hung on the studs. Generally replaced by platform framing after 1945.

basement - An area below grade level, generally accessible from inside the house, with sufficient clearance that a person can stand up in it. A full basement covers the area of the entire first floor.

bay - A portion of a building that projects beyond the face of the building.

beam - A horizontal structural member. May be solid timber, laminated wood, or metal.

bearing wall - A wall that supports part of the load above it.

casing - Finish trim around a framed wall opening.

crawl space - The area between first floor joists and ground in a house without a basement. Often filled with gravel. Clearance is not sufficient to allow a person to stand up.

deck - A horizontal wooden surface attached to the exterior of a house.

dormer - A windowed structure with its own roof that projects from the main roof of a building.

downspout - An externally mounted vertical tube that carries rain water from gutter to ground or drain tile.

drain tile - An underground tube that carries water away from the foundation footing or from the top of the foundation wall at the downspout.

drywall - A type of smooth gypsum board used as an interior wall covering. Also called sheetrock and plasterboard.

eave - The part of a roof that hangs beyond the external supporting wall.

facade - The front face of a building.

fascia - A board that covers the ends of the roof rafters.

flashing - Metal sheets or strips installed as waterproofing at roof edges and around junctures of roof surfaces and other wall and roof locations where leakage must be prevented.

girder - A horizontal beam that supports other beams.

greenboard - A water-resistant type of gypsum board.

gutter - A trough at the roof eave or other low point that collects rain water from the roof and carries it to a downspout.

gypsum board - A wall paneling material composed of a core of gypsum between outer layers of heavy paper.

joist - One of the parallel, horizontal beams that supports a floor or ceiling.

masonry - Construction using brick, stone, or concrete block..

partition - A dividing wall, usually not a bearing wall.

post - A vertical structural member that supports a beam or girder.

rafter - One of the parallel supporting members that holds the roof decking. Usually 2 x 6 or 2 x 8 solid timber (2 x 4 in some older houses).

sheathing - The rough covering of the shell of a structure, fastened to studs, rafters or joists as a support for a finish covering; typically composition board, plywood, or solid lumber (in older houses).

sheetrock - Drywall.

sill - Bottom horizontal member of a door or window frame; horizontal framing member bolted to a slab or foundation wall.

soffit - The horizontal under-surface covering the area between the exterior wall and the end of rafters; the boxed-in area between the top of a row of cabinets and the ceiling

stud - One of the vertical, parallel structural elements of a framed wall. Metal or wood.

subfloor - Sheathing applied to floor joists as rough flooring.

suspended ceiling - A ceiling supported by hangers attached to joists rather than being attached directly to the joists.

termite shield - A metal or other barrier placed around foundation walls and wall penetrations to impede termites.

underlayment - Plywood or other type of panel applied to a subfloor as a support for finished flooring.

wallboard - Gypsum board or composition board used as an interior wall covering.

HEATING AND COOLING

central air - An air conditioning unit, mounted outside a house, that cools the entire house by way of ducting.

duct work - Sheet metal shafting and piping that carries hot and cold air in a house.

electric - Heating by electric resistance cable or panels in floors, walls, or ceilings, or some other electrically powered radiation system.

forced air - Heating by hot air blown by a furnace fan and carried in ducts.

gas - Heating by means of a furnace powered by natural gas. May be forced air or hot water.

heat pump - A device for recirculating heated air.

hot water - Heating by means of hot water carried through pipes to heating coils, floor radiators, or baseboard radiators.

oil - Heating by means of a furnace powered by fuel oil. May be forced air, hot water or steam.

register - A grating in wall or floor to permit heated or cooled air to enter a room.

return - A grating in wall or floor to remove cooled or warmed air from a room.

solar - Heating by means of collection of solar radiation.

steam - Heating by means of steam carried through pipes to radiators.

window unit - A self-contained air conditioning unit installed in a window.

INSULATION

asbestos - A fibrous mineral used for fireproofing, electrical insulation, around heating pipes and ducts, also applied as a spray covering on walls and ceilings; now regarded as a hazardous substance subject to environmental regulation.

batting - Fibrous material, usually fiberglass, wadded together, backed with foil or paper, and formed into a roll; designed to fit between studs of a standard stud wall.

blown - Loose insulating material blown into spaces between studs and wall surfaces.

fiberglass - A cotton-like material consisting of glass and resin.

firestop - A fire-resistant material used to impede the spread of flames.

foam - Polystyrene or other expanding foam sprayed into gaps.

foam board - Light-weight solid board composed of polystyrene foam and cut to fit between studs.

R-factor - A measure of the efficiency of insulation against heat transfer.

vapor barrier - A waterproof material that prevents warm, moisture-laden indoor air from meeting colder outdoor air and condensing.

PLUMBING

cleanout - A removable opening in a drain pipe that allows cleaning out of clogging material.

cast iron - Material traditionally used for soil stack and soil pipe, with joints poured of hot lead.

copper - Material traditionally preferred for piping hot and cold water supply within a house, with soldered joints.

lead - Material once commonly used to seal water supply pipes, now regarded as hazardous and subject to environmental regulation.

PVC - Polyvinyl chloride, a thermoplastic resin used for piping, with glued joints.

soil stack - Large-dimension vertical pipe that vents sewer gases through the roof

soil pipe - Drain pipe that carries waste to sewer or septic system.

sump pump - A pump installed in a basement to remove water from around and under the foundation and floor of the basement.

trap - A U-shaped section of drain pipe that holds water as a barrier against sewer gases and odors.

vent pipe - A pipe that allows sewer gases to vent above the roof line and prevents back pressure from building up; connects to a vent stack.

vent stack - A soil stack.

well and septic - A water supply and waste removal system that is self-contained on a parcel, usually in rural areas where city services are not available.

asphalt shingle - Heavy felt impregnated with asphalt and coated with mineral granules; come in a range of colors; life span of approximately 15 years.

built-up - A low-pitch or flat roof covered with layers of roofing felt laminated with tar, pitch or asphalt and topped with hot tar and gravel.

cross gable - A gable roof that intersects another gable roof at right angles.

decking - Boards or panels applied to the rafters as a support for the roof covering.

felt - Asphalt-impregnated paper installed over decking as an underlayment for the roof covering.

flat - A roof with little or no pitch; not suitable for shingles; requires a built-up or membrane type of covering.

gable - A triangular end wall defined by the two slopes of a roof and a line joining the eaves; a pitched roof that creates a triangular end wall.

gambrel - A roof that has two slopes on each side, the lower slopes being steeper than the upper slopes; typical of barns.

Gothic - A ridged roof with sides that curve, often ending in a flair.

hip - The outside corner formed by the perpendicular meeting of the outside edges of two roof slopes; a roof that ends in hips rather than gables or other end walls.

mansard - A roof that has two slopes on all four sides; the upper slope is close to horizontal and the lower slope is close to vertical.

membrane - A vulcanized sheet of rubber or other seamless material applied with adhesive directly to decking; used on flat and low-pitch roofs.

pitched - A roof that has a slope; pitch is usually stated as a ratio of rise (vertical distance) in inches per 12 inches of run (horizontal distance).

rafter - One of the parallel beams that supports the decking of a sloped roof.

rake - The slope of a gable.

ridge - The horizontal line formed by the juncture of two roof slopes; the board to which the upper ends of the rafters of two slopes are nailed.

roll roofing - Mineral-coated, asphalt-impregnated felt produced in long rolled-up sheets instead of as individual shingles; typically installed in overlapped pieces which are the length of the entire roof.

roofing paper - Felt.

shake - A wooden shingle, usually redwood or cedar, that can be installed as a roof covering or wall covering.

shed - A pitched roof with a single slope.

slate - A fine-grained rock that splits into thin, smooth layers that can be used as shingles; very heavy, but long-lasting.

tile - Curved ceramic or concrete elements that fit together in such a way as to form a waterproof roof covering.

truss - A framework of rafters and connecting beams installed as a unit to support part of a roof and tie together the opposite walls.

valley - The inside corner created where two roof slopes meet; the opposite of a hip.

WINDOW TYPES AND PARTS

awning - A window hinged along the top edge and designed to swing at the bottom.

bay - A window or group of windows in a structural bay.

SECTION FIFTEEN QUIZ: Construction Terminology

1. You pass by a house with a prominent roof and large overhangs- what architectural style is this?

   a. Cape cod
   b. Georgian
   c. Contemporary
   d. Bungalow

2. What type of roof is not suitable for shingles?

   a. Flat
   b. Gothic
   c. Felt
   d. Pitched

3. A _____ recirculates heated air.

   a. heat pump
   b. return
   c. steam pump
   d. hot water heater

4. Which plumbing material is now considered hazardous?

   a. PVC
   b. Lead
   c. Copper
   d. Cast iron

5. What is the front face of a building called?

   a. Fascia
   b. Drywall
   c. Facade
   d. Bearing wall

6. A horizontal timber component of a ceiling is also called a _____.

   a. dormer.
   b. beam.
   c. post.
   d. both b and c

7. Which door is typically used for a closet?

   a. Bifold door
   b. French door
   c. Dutch door
   d. None of the above

8. A _____ style home typically has a red tile roof.

    a. Queen Anne
    b. Spanish mission
    c. Mansard
    a. Prairie

9. What is a box that protects wire connections?

    a. Outlet box
    b. Fire box
    c. Vent stack box
    d. Power box

10. What is a tube that carries water away from the foundation footing called?

    a. Downspout
    b. Soil pipe
    c. Drain tile
    d. Vent pipe

11. An electrician is looking to insulate his electrical work, what should he use?

    a. Asbestos
    b. Vapor barrier
    c. Copper
    d. Plumber's tape

12. What is a U-shaped section of a drain pipe?

    a. Trap
    b. Soil pipe
    c. Sump pump
    d. Cleanout

13. What is a cement based material used as an non-load bearing exterior covering?

    a. Wainscoting
    b. Spanish tile
    c. Stucco
    d. Reinforced brick

14. A _____ is a framework of rafters and connecting beams installed as a unit to support part of a roof and tie together the opposite walls.

    a. truss
    b. membrane
    c. valley
    d. gambrel

15. What is a grating in a wall or floor used for airflow in heating or cooling of a home?

    a. Register
    b. An HVAC return
    c. Pump
    d. Vent-stack covering

16 Elements of the Listing Process

The Listing Agreement
Obtaining Listings
Marketing Listings
Pre-closing Activities
Communications and Technology

THE LISTING AGREEMENT

The most common way of creating an agency relationship is by listing agreement. The agreement sets forth the various authorizations and duties, as well as requirements for compensation. A listing agreement establishes an agency for a specified transaction and has a stated expiration.

A listing agreement, the document that puts an agent or broker in business, is a legally enforceable real estate agency agreement between a real estate broker and a client, authorizing the broker to perform a stated service for compensation. The unique characteristic of a listing agreement is that it is governed both by agency law and by contract law.

The cornerstones of agency law in the context of a listing agreement are:
- definition of the roles of parties involved
- fiduciary duties of the agent
- agent's scope of authority

Parties. The principal parties to the contract are the listing broker and the client. The client may be buyer, seller, landlord, or tenant in the proposed transaction. Legally, the broker is the client's agent. The principal party on the other side of the transaction is a customer or a potential customer, called a prospect. A broker who represents the party on the other side of the transaction is an agent of that party, and not an agent of the listing broker, unless a dual agency arrangement is specifically allowed.

Fiduciary duties. A listing agreement establishes an agency relationship between agent and client that commits the agent to the full complement of fiduciary duties to the client in fulfilling the agreement.

Scope of authority. Customarily, a listing is a special agency, or limited agency, agreement. Special agency limits the scope of the broker's authority to specific activities, generally those which generate customers and catalyze the transaction. A special agency agreement usually does not authorize a broker to obligate the client to a contract as a principal party, unless the agreement expressly grants such authorization, or the client has granted power of attorney to the broker. For example, a listing broker may not tell a buyer that the seller will accept an offer regardless of its terms. Telling the offeror that the offer is accepted would be an even more serious breach of the agreement.

Under agency law, a client is liable for actions the broker performs that are within the scope of authority granted by the listing agreement. A client is not liable for acts of the broker which go beyond the stated or implied scope of authority.

Thus, in the previous example, the seller would not be liable for the broker's statements that the offer would be accepted or was accepted, since the broker did not have the authority to make such statements. A broker who exceeds the scope of authority in the listing agreement risks forfeiting compensation and perhaps even greater liabilities.

A broker may represent any principal party of a transaction: seller, landlord, buyer, tenant. An owner listing authorizes a broker to represent an owner or landlord. There are three main types of owner listing agreement:
1.   exclusive right-to-sell (or lease)
2.   exclusive agency
3.   open listing.

Another type of listing, although legal yet frowned upon in Florida, is a net listing. The first three forms differ in their statement of conditions under which the broker will be paid. The net listing is a variation on how much the broker will be paid.

Exclusive right to sell. A buyer agency or tenant representation agreement authorizes a broker to represent a buyer or tenant. The most commonly used form is an exclusive right-to-represent agreement, the equivalent of an exclusive right-to-sell. However, exclusive agency and open types of agreement may be also used to secure a relationship on this side of a transaction.

Though not a distinct type of listing agreement, multiple listing is a significant feature of brokerage practice. Multiple listing is an authorization to enter a listing in a multiple listing service.

The exclusive right-to-sell, also called exclusive authorization-to-sell and, simply, the exclusive, is the most widely used owner agreement. Under the terms of this listing, a seller contracts exclusively with a single broker to procure a buyer or effect a sale transaction. If a buyer is procured during the listing period, the broker is entitled to a commission, regardless of who is procuring cause. Thus, if anyone--the owner, another broker-- sells the property, the owner must pay the listing broker the contracted commission.

The exclusive right-to-lease is a similar contract for a leasing transaction. Under the terms of this listing, the owner or landlord must pay the listing broker a commission if anyone procures a tenant for the named premises.

The exclusive listing gives the listing broker the greatest assurance of receiving compensation for marketing efforts.

Exclusive agency. An exclusive agency listing authorizes a single broker to sell the property and earn a commission, but leaves the owner the right to sell the property without the broker's assistance, in which case no commission is owed. Thus, if any party other than the owner is procuring cause in a completed sale of the property, including another broker, the contracted broker has earned the commission. This arrangement may also be used in a leasing transaction: if any party other than the owner procures the tenant, the owner must compensate the listing broker.

Open listing. An open listing, or, simply, open, is a non-exclusive authorization to sell or lease a property. The owner may offer such agreements to any number of brokers in the marketplace. With an open listing, the broker who is the first to perform under the terms of the listing is the sole party entitled to a commission. Performance usually consists of being the procuring cause in the finding of a ready, willing, and able customer. If the transaction occurs without a procuring broker, no commissions are payable.

Open listings are rare in residential brokerage. Brokers generally shy away from them because they offer no assurance of compensation for marketing efforts. In addition, open listings cause commission disputes. To avoid such disputes, a broker has to register prospects with the owner to provide evidence of procuring cause in case a transaction results. An open listing may be oral or written.

Net listing. A net listing is one in which an owner sets a minimum acceptable amount to be received from the transaction and allows the broker to have any amount received in excess as a commission, assuming the broker has earned a commission according to the other terms of the agreement. The owner's "net" may or may not account for closing costs. For example, a seller requires $750,000 for a property. A broker sells the property for $830,000 and receives the difference, $80,000, as commission.

Net listings are generally regarded as unprofessional today, and in many states they are illegal. They are legal in Florida, though seldom used. The argument against the net listing is that it creates a conflict of interest for the broker. It is in the broker's interest to encourage the owner to put the lowest possible acceptable price in the listing, regardless of market value. Thus the agent violates fiduciary duty by failing to place the client's interests above those of the agent.

Due diligence. Due diligence in the listing context refers to verifying the accuracy of the statements in the listing regarding the property, the owner, and the owner's representations. Especially important facts for a broker to verify are:
- the property condition
- ownership status
- the client's authority to act

Failure to perform a reasonable degree of due diligence may increase an agent's exposure to liability in the event that the property is not as represented or that the client cannot perform as promised.

OBTAINING LISTINGS

Listings are the traditional source of a broker's income. By obtaining a listing, a broker obtains a share of the commission generated whenever a cooperating broker finds a buyer. It is not so certain that working with a buyer will provide income. In the absence of an exclusive buyer representation agreement, a buyer may move from one agent to another without making any commitment. Agents can spend considerable time with a buyer and earn nothing. Hence the special value of a listing: it is likely to generate revenue.

Listing procedures. The marketing and self-promotional efforts of agents generate listings. New agents usually focus on becoming well known in a small geographical area and hope to encounter clients there who are willing to list with them. More experienced and better-known agents are able to rely to a greater extent on referrals in obtaining listings.

Prospecting. Prospecting is any activity designed to generate listing prospects: parties who intend to sell or lease property and who have not yet committed to a broker. Prospecting activities include mailing newsletters and flyers, selling directly and person-to-person, advertising, and selling indirectly via community involvement. The goal of prospecting is to reach a potential seller or landlord, make that person aware of the agent's and brokerage's services, and obtain permission to discuss the benefits of listing, often in the form of a formal selling presentation.

Listing presentation and negotiation of agreement. A listing presentation is an agent's opportunity to meet with a seller and present the merits of the agent's marketing plan, personal expertise, and company strengths. At the same time, an agent can explain the many phases and details of a real estate transaction and point out how the provisions of the listing agreement and the agent-principal relationship work to ensure a smooth transaction. Ultimately, the agent's aim in a presentation meeting is to have the principal execute a listing agreement. This result will set in motion the process of marketing the property. In practice, it may take an agent many meetings with a prospect before the prospect signs an agreement.

Pricing. It is almost always necessary for an agent seeking a listing to suggest a listing price or price range for the property. It is important to make a careful estimate, because underpricing a property is not in the best interests of the seller, and overpricing it often prevents a transaction altogether. In brief, an agent usually relies on an analysis of comparable properties which have recently sold in the same neighborhood. By making adjustments for the differences between the subject property and the comparables, the agent arrives at a general price range. Agents must be careful to caution sellers that they are not appraisers, and that the suggested price range is not an expert opinion of market value. If a more precise estimate of market value is desired, the seller should hire a licensed appraiser.

MARKETING LISTINGS

The process of marketing a listed property occurs in three broad steps, leading to the desired end of a completed sale contract. At each of these steps, there are critical skills an agent must master.

Marketing plan. After the broker formalizes the listing agreement, the agent initiates a marketing plan for the property. An ideal marketing plan is a cohesive combination of promotional and selling activities directed at potential customers. The best combination is one that aims to have maximum impact on the marketplace in relation to the time and money expended.

Selling the prospect. When marketing activities produce prospects, the agent's marketing role becomes more interpersonal. An agent must now:

- qualify prospects' plans, preferences, and financial capabilities
- show properties that meet the customer's needs
- elicit the buyer's reactions to properties
- report material results to the seller or listing agent

At the earliest appropriate time, an agent must make certain disclosures to a prospective customer. An agent is required to disclose the relevant agency relationship, the property's physical condition, and the possible presence of hazardous materials.

Obtaining offers. If a buyer is interested in purchasing a property, an agent obtains the buyer's offer of transaction terms, including price, down payment, desired closing date, and financing requirements. An agent must be extremely careful at this point to abide by fiduciary obligations to the client, whoever that party may be. Discussions of price are particularly delicate: whether the client is buyer or seller, the agent's duty is to uphold the client's best interests. Thus, it is not acceptable to suggest to a customer what price the client will or will not accept. With pricing and other issues, it is always a good practice to understand what role the client wants the agent to assume in the offering phase of the transaction; in other words, exactly how far the agent may go in developing terms on the client's behalf.

When a buyer or tenant makes an offer, the agent must present it to the seller or landlord at the earliest possible moment. If the terms of the offer are unacceptable, the agent may assist the seller in developing a counteroffer, which the agent would subsequently submit to the customer or customer's agent. The offering and counteroffering process continues until a meeting of the minds results in a sale contract.

PRE-CLOSING ACTIVITIES

Between the execution of the sale contract and the closing of the transaction, the property is "under contract" or "contract pending." During this period, buyer and seller have certain things to do to achieve a successful closing. The buyer often needs to arrange financing and dispose of other property; the seller may need to clear up title encumbrances and make certain property repairs. The sale contract should specify all such required tasks. The time period between contracting and closing is referred to as the contingency period, or pre-closing period.

Agent's responsibilities. As dictated by custom and the circumstances of a transaction, an agent has a range of duties and responsibilities during the pre-closing period. An agent's foremost duty following acceptance of an offer is to submit the contract and the earnest money to the sponsoring broker without delay.

Other possible responsibilities are:
- assisting the buyer in obtaining financing
- recommending inspectors, appraisers, attorneys, and title companies
- assisting in communications between principals
- assisting in the exchange of transaction documents

Broker's responsibilities. The listing broker has the primary responsibility for handling deposit monies and for overseeing the agent's pre-closing activities. State license laws require that earnest money deposits be placed in an account which is separate from the broker's operating accounts. They also require the broker to keep accurate records and follow accepted accounting procedures. These precautions protect the buyer and seller and safeguard the deposited funds. A broker must be careful to avoid two common violations of escrow regulations: commingling and conversion.

Commingling. Commingling is the act of mixing the broker's personal or business funds with escrow funds. A broader definition of commingling includes the failure to deposit earnest money into escrow in a timely manner. In most states, commingling funds constitutes grounds for license suspension or revocation.

Conversion. Conversion is the act of misappropriating escrow funds for the broker's business or personal use. More serious than mere commingling, conversion is effectively an act of theft: using monies which do not belong to the broker. Conversion carries serious consequences, including license revocation.

COMMUNICATIONS AND TECHNOLOGY

Multiple listing services and websites. The posting and sharing of property listings and data among broker websites, firm websites, and multiple listing services (MLS) is one of the most effective marketing tools available to today's licensees. Broker cooperation assures sellers of maximum exposure for their properties, just as it assures buyers of seeing the widest possible range of listed properties.

To ensure fair use of MLS facilities, the National Association of REALTORS® has developed an Internet Data Exchange (IDX) policy that enables MLS members to display and use MLS data while respecting the rights of property owners and brokers to market their properties however they want. Basically, persons who want to make use of MLS data have to share their own data as well.

They can opt out of the sharing policy so that competitors cannot post their properties on competing websites, but then they cannot post competitors' properties on their own sites.

There are a number of websites that provide consumers with the capability to search through listings all over the country and even the world. Of course, it is always wise to recognize that information posted on the internet is not necessarily reliable and that the source of the information should be considered carefully.

Email and texting. Frequent and virtually instantaneous contact between real estate practitioners and consumers is possible via email and texting. As both these forms of communication fall under the category of advertising, practitioners need to carefully observe their state's advertising regulations. In brief, be truthful, direct, and concise. Provide the information required by law, and do not violate prohibitions against unsolicited emails and messages.

Social media. Social media websites allow rapid exchange of information, documents, photos, messages and data with a select group of contacts. They also represent another form of advertising and so are subject to real estate commission advertising regulations in most states.

Smartphones. Smartphones facilitate the use, not only of email, texting, and social media, but also of immediate internet access, document review, photo and document sharing, data storage, and video conferencing. They offer, in fact, an almost complete mobile office.

Managing information. The ability to satisfy the needs of clients and customers is largely dependent on a broker's ability to obtain, organize, and manage information. Information is a cornerstone of the broker's perceived value in the marketplace and a major reason why buyers and sellers seek a broker out. Systematic collection and updating of relevant information is therefore a business priority.

Property data. Most brokerages maintain two categories of property data: available properties, and all properties in the market area. In residential brokerage, available property basically consists of the listings in the MLS and for-sale-by-owner properties. Records for all properties in an area are accessible in tax records. Commercial brokerages usually keep track of available and occupied commercial properties in a proprietary database.

Buyer data. Buyer information is usually compiled and maintained, often informally, by each agent in a brokerage. An agency's base of prospects who are looking for property at any given time is valuable for marketing new listings.

Tenant data. In residential and commercial leasing companies, information is compiled and maintained on all tenants in an area, by property type used. Such files contain a tenant's lease expiration, property size, and rent.

Client data. It is important to keep track of both current and former clients. Former clients are likely prospects to become clients again or customers. They are also a source of referrals. Current clients, of course, should be the broker's primary concern.

Market data. Today's clients and customers expect a broker to know the market intimately. It is often the broker with the best market knowledge who dominates business in the market. Knowing a market includes keeping up to date on:
- pricing and appreciation trends
- financing rates and terms
- demographic patterns and trends
- construction trends
- general economic trends

Advertising regulations. Advertising is an important tool in marketing properties and procuring buyers. It is, however, subject to regulation and restrictions. In general, state laws and regulations require that:
- advertising must not be misleading
- the sponsoring and managing broker is responsible for the content of advertising done by agents
- all advertising must reveal the identity of the brokerage firm; licensee may not use blind ads that conceal their identities

- brokers selling their own property through the brokerage must disclose the brokerage identity
- licensees must include the broker's business identity in any advertising; they may not advertise in their own name solely (unless selling their own property through channels other than the agency)

Telephone Consumer Protection Act The TCPA (Telephone Consumer Protection Act) addresses the regulation of unsolicited telemarketing phone calls. Rules include the following:
- telephone solicitors must identify themselves, on whose behalf they are calling, and how they can be contacted
- telemarketers must comply with any do-not-call request made during the solicitation call
- consumers can place their home and wireless phone numbers on a national Do-Not-Call list which prohibits future solicitations from telemarketers.

CAN-SPAM Act. Formally, Controlling the Assault of Non-Solicited Pornography and Marketing Act of 2003. This legislation supplements the Telephone Consumer Protection Act (TCPA). Key points of the law are that it
- bans sending unwanted email 'commercial messages' to wireless devices
- requires express prior authorization
- requires giving an 'opt out' choice to terminate the sender's messages

Seller's closing expenses. The following are typical expenses which a seller usually pays
- mortgage payoff and/or any secondary mortgage loans (if any)
- brokerage fee (per listing agreement)
- attorney fee
- transfer tax/stamps
- prorated property taxes
- title fee
- survey (if stipulated in the sales contract)

Buyer's closing costs. Typical expenses incurred by the buyer include
- loan application and/or other fees related to the loan
- appraisal fee
- attorney fee
- title fee
- home inspection fee
- homeowner's insurance

THE LISTING AGREEMENT

- listing agreement secures the licensee's employment and compensation.

- listings governed by agency law and contract law; identify roles, duties, scope of authority – listing establishes the agency relationship

- principals are the listing broker and the client buyer, seller, landlord or tenant; parties on other side are customers

- listing types: exclusive, exclusive agency, and opens; exclusives assure compensation for one's efforts, predominate brokerage practice – broker gets paid if property sells or buyer buys during the listing period regardless of who is procuring cause

- net listings: legal in Florida but frowned on – broker gets all proceeds above a previously stated net number for the seller; leads to pricing distortions

- licensees must undertake due diligence to generate accurate statements regarding the property; should assure accuracy of property condition, title marketability, material defects' disclosure

OBTAINING LISTINGS

- listings are the traditional and critical source of brokerage revenue since listing broker gets paid when property sells – licensees not assured of compensation working with buyers

- must prospect among homeowners to generate listings; direct selling supported by Web and MLS advertising, yard signs, open houses and community involvement to create referral channels; ultimately leads to obtaining listing presentations with sellers

- listing presentation elements: associate's marketing plan; personal expertise; company strengths; aim is to complete, sign the listing

- key to listing is identifying the optimum price where seller gets top dollar <u>and</u> property sells within reasonable time frame; accomplished via accurate CMA

MARKETING LISTINGS

- goal is to obtain signed sale contract; must design, execute marketing plan and selling actions directed at targeted prospects

- prospects must subsequently be qualified financially and personally; matched with properties that meet needs; must also communicate progress with principal; licensee must also make timely disclosures regarding property condition

- if buyer is interested, associate must obtain best possible offer including price and down payment, closing date, and financing requirements; all offers must be promptly presented to seller; then help seller counteroffer if necessary

PRE-CLOSING ACTIONS

- once buyer is contracted; transaction enters pre-closing phase where all closing requirements and contingencies must be met. Include survey, appraisal, loan approval, repairs

- licensee responsibilities include assisting with locating inspectors, attorneys, title companies; appraisers; facilitating communications, and distributing documents

- broker involvement includes trust fund handling; overseeing associate's activities, and maintaining proper accounting – broker must be careful not to commingle or convert transaction trust funds

**COMMUNICATION &
TECHNOLOGY**

- marketing responsibilities include managing MLS involvements with listing; how exposures and showings are handled; controlling data flow and co-brokerage activities and open houses; must optimize listing's website exposure and maintain accuracy of information presented on web pages

- must maintain email and texting information flow with client and customers while complying with FREC regulations; engage in social media exposure and response flows

- key to marketing plan execution is to manage flows of data: property, buyer, tenant, client, and market data

- observe advertising regulations including proper identifications, TCPA, CAN-SPAM, and disclosures where appropriate

SECTION SIXTEEN QUIZ: Elements of the Listing Process

1. The unique legal aspect about a listing agreement is that it

   a. confers a broad scope of authority to the agent in representing the client.
   b. is the instrument that grants the agent the power to contract on behalf of the client.
   c. is governed by both agency law and contract law.
   d. enables the licensee to sidestep fiduciary duties.

2. Residential brokers prefer the exclusive listing because

   a. they will get paid regardless of who sells the property.
   b. they can let other brokers undertake the lion's share of the marketing effort.
   c. they will receive the difference between the seller's desired net and the selling price.
   d. the preferred listing, the net listing, is illegal in Florida.

3. The more experienced the sales associate, the more such associate is able to rely on

   a. referrals to generate listings.
   b. the effectiveness of web advertising.
   c. his or her credibility in representing the firm.
   d. market conditions and interest rates to maximize income.

4. Which of the following best expresses the goal of prospecting for listings?

   a. To get a signed offer to purchase
   b. To get a listing presentation
   c. To negotiate a fair price for the property
   d. To find someone who is selling his or her property

5. Which of the following is a high-priority activity in marketing listings?

   a. Conducting weekly open houses
   b. Showing prospects as many properties as possible in a given time period
   c. Showing only your listings to buyers to maximize your income
   d. Showing properties that match the customer's requirements

6. How would you go about determining the value of the seller's property?

   a. By identifying the net proceeds the seller must receive from the sale
   b. By arriving at a price based on amount of the mortgage payoff
   c. By determining how much the property has appreciated in value since it was purchased
   d. By relying on an analysis of comparable properties which have recently sold in the same neighborhood

7. Once a buyer's offer is received, it is the sales associate's responsibility to

    a. Determine whether the offer is sufficient to be presented to the seller.
    b. Determine the best time during the work week to present the offer.
    c. Determine whether it is in the seller's best interest to reject or accept the offer.
    d. Determine the earliest possible time to present the offer regardless of its merits.

8. Which of the following brokerage agreement offers the brokerage firm the fullest protection regarding the payment of compensation in the event that the seller sells to a neighbor?

    a. Open listing
    b. Exclusive right to sell
    c. Net listing
    d. Non-listing

9. The primary responsibility of the sales associate, once a signed contract is received, is to

    a. file the contract and deposit the earnest money in the trust account.
    b. give the contract and deposit to the broker.
    c. get the property into the MLS
    d. obtain the commission for selling the property.

10. The licensee's principal responsibilities during the pre-closing period are to

    a. handle trust funds and facilitate pre-closing activities.
    b. manage the marketing plan and all advertising.
    c. complete the title search and property inspection.
    d. arrange for the buyer's mortgage loan.

11. An important practice in the electronic dissemination of listing information is that

    a. the firm's listing data can only be shared by the local MLS.
    b. IDX policy enables MLS members to display and use MLS data on their websites.
    c. brokerage firms must pay to display and disseminate property listing data on their own websites.
    d. MLS data users are not compelled to share their data despite their ability to use other broker's data.

12. Email and texting as forms of communication fall under which of the following brokerage categories?

    a. Prospecting
    b. Pre-closing activities
    c. Social media
    d. Regulated advertising

13. A distinct advantage of smartphone usage in real estate marketing is that the smartphone enables associates to
    a. operate as mobile offices.
    b. increase their overall prospect conversion rates.
    c. improve their ability to communicate effectively.
    d. increase their degree of reliability and persuasiveness.

14. The most central of all themes in advertising regulation is

   a. that advertising not be misleading or deceptive.
   b. to minimize property condition misrepresentations.
   c. to minimize the use of unauthorized signage.
   d. to minimize misrepresentations by real estate teams.

15. Which of the following is NOT a provision of the Telephone Consumer Protection Act?

   a. Solicitors must identify themselves.
   b. Telemarketers must comply with do-not-call requests.
   c. Marketers are restricted from sending unwanted faxes.
   d. Advertising emails must offer an opt-out alternative available by paying a one-time fee.

17 Inside the Sales Contract

Legal Characteristics
Contract Mechanics and Processes
Primary Sales Contract Provisions
Secondary Sales Contract Provisions

The conventional transfer of real estate ownership takes place in three stages. First, there is the negotiating period where buyers and sellers exchange offers in an effort to agree to all transfer terms that will appear in the sale contract.

Second, when both parties have accepted all terms, the offer becomes a binding sale contract and the transaction enters the pre-closing stage, during which each party makes arrangements to complete the sale according to the sale contract's terms.

Third is the closing of the transaction, when the seller deeds title to the buyer, the buyer pays the purchase price, and all necessary documents are completed. At this stage, the sale contract has served its purpose and terminates.

LEGAL CHARACTERISTICS

Executory contract. A sale contract is executory: the signatories have yet to perform their respective obligations and promises. Upon closing, the sale contract is fully performed and no longer exists as a binding agreement.

Signatures. All owners of the property should sign the sale contract. If the sellers are married, both spouses should sign to ensure that both spouses release homestead rights to the buyer at closing. Failure to do so does not invalidate the contract but can lead to encumbered title and legal disputes.

Enforceability criteria. To be enforceable, a sale contract must:
- be validly created (mutual consent, consideration, legal purpose, competent parties, voluntary act)
- be in writing
- identify the principal parties
- clearly identify the property, preferably by legal description
- contain a purchase price
- be signed by the principal parties

Validity and enforceability. The statute of frauds requires that the following contracts be in writing to be enforceable in court:
- contracts for the sale of land
- leases that will not be completed within one year

Written vs. oral form. A contract for the sale of real estate is enforceable only if it is in writing. A buyer or seller cannot sue to force the other to comply with an oral contract for sale, even if the contract is valid.

Assignment. Either party to a sale transaction can assign the sale contract to another party, subject to the provisions and conditions contained in the agreement.

Who may complete a sales contract? A broker may assist buyer and seller in completing an offer to purchase. It is advisable, and legally required in most states, for a broker to use a standard contract form promulgated by state agencies or real estate boards, as such forms contain generally accepted language. This relieves the broker of the dangers of creating new contract language, which can be construed as a practice of law for which the broker is not licensed.

Real estate licensees may fill in the blanks on contract forms customarily used in the area if the forms have been prepared by an attorney.

Unauthorized practice of law. Real estate licensee drafting of contracts, riders, or addenda to contracts constitutes the unauthorized practice of law. Licensees are prohibited from preparing any legal document regarding the transaction, such as deed, title, or mortgage documents; conducting real estate closings; and providing legal advice. Offers to purchase, listing agreements, and addenda should be prepared by the local association as approved by an attorney.

Licensees are prohibited from having a party sign a contract with blanks to be completed later. Changes or deletions in a contract should be only made at the direction of the party signing the contract and must be initialed or signed and dated. A licensee should advise a party who is unsure regarding any legal issue or language to use in adding information to a contract to contact an attorney.

CONTRACT MECHANICS AND PROCESSES

Offer and acceptance. A contract of sale is created by full and unequivocal acceptance of an offer. Offer and acceptance may come from either buyer or seller. The offeree must accept the offer without making any changes whatsoever. A change terminates the offer and creates a new offer, or counteroffer. An offeror may revoke an offer for any reason prior to communication of acceptance by the offeree.

Equitable title. A sale contract gives the buyer an interest in the property that is called equitable title, or ownership in equity. If the seller defaults and the buyer can show good faith performance, the buyer can sue for specific performance, that is, to compel the seller to transfer legal title upon payment of the contract price.

Earnest money and escrow. The buyer's earnest money deposit fulfills the consideration requirements for a valid sale contract. In addition, it provides potential compensation for damages to the seller if the buyer fails to perform. The amount of the deposit varies according to local custom. It should be noted that the earnest money deposit is not the only form of consideration that satisfies the requirement.

The sale contract provides the escrow instructions for handling and disbursing escrow funds. The earnest money is placed in a third-party trust account or escrow. A licensed escrow agent employed by a title company, financial institution, or brokerage company usually manages the escrow. An individual broker may also serve as the escrow agent.

The escrow holder acts as an impartial fiduciary for buyer and seller. If the buyer performs under the sale contract, the deposit is applied to the purchase price.

Strict rules govern the handling of earnest money deposits, particularly if a broker is the escrow agent. For example, state laws direct the broker when to deposit the funds, how to account for them, and how to keep them separate from the broker's own funds.

Trust fund handling. Florida law prescribes how licensees must handle any escrow or earnest money deposits they receive. In Florida, a broker must hold money received in connection with the purchase or lease of real property in a trust fund account. The broker must record receipt of the money and place that money in the trust account within a specified time period.

Trust fund handling requirements include:
- the broker named as trustee of the account
- maintenance of records in a particular accounting format
- separate records kept for each property or transaction
- records of funds received and paid out reconciled with bank statements every month
- withdrawals only by the broker-trustee or other specifically authorized person

Deposits. Escrow money accepted by a sponsoring broker must be placed in the escrow account in a timely manner. The broker must notify all principals in writing if a party to the transaction fails to provide escrow moneys, if a principal's payment is dishonored by the financial institution, or if the amount of escrow money deposited is insufficient.

Withdrawals and disbursements. Earnest money must be kept in the account until a transaction is consummated or terminated once the payor's financial institution honors the deposit of the funds. The actual terms of the contract regarding release of the funds must be adhered to by the sponsoring broker. The funds may also be disbursed at the written direction of all parties.

If the sponsoring broker receives an order from a court providing for disbursement, the sponsoring broker must disburse escrow funds according to the court order.

Broker-owned funds. Commissions and fees earned by the sponsoring broker must be disbursed from the account no earlier than the day the transaction is consummated or terminated and no later than the next business day, or according to the written direction of the principals. Brokers may not withhold escrow funds because of a claim for commission or compensation.

Funds other than commissions and other funds owed to the broker may be transferred to the closing agent in a specified time frame prior to the scheduled closing.

Recordkeeping. Brokers must maintain a bookkeeping system that includes a journal showing chronological sequence of funds received and disbursed, a ledger for each transaction, a monthly bank statement, a master account log identifying all escrow accounts and banks holding accounts, and a monthly reconciliation statement that insures agreement between escrow account, journal and master escrow account log. Escrow records must be maintained for five years.

Commingling and conversion. Mixing of personal or company funds with client funds is grounds for the revocation or suspension of a real estate license. Depositing client funds in a personal or business account, or using them for any purpose other than the client's business, is also grounds for suspension or revocation of a license. It is important for the broker to remove commissions, fees or other income earned by the broker from a trust account within the period specified by law to avoid committing an act of commingling.

Contract contingencies. A sale contract often contains contingencies. A contingency is a condition that must be met before the contract is enforceable. The most common contingency concerns financing. A buyer makes an offer contingent upon securing financing for the property under certain terms on or before a certain date. If unable to secure the specified loan commitment by the deadline, the buyer may cancel the contract and recover the deposit. An appropriate and timely loan commitment eliminates the contingency, and the buyer must proceed with the purchase.

It is possible for both buyers and sellers to abuse contingencies in order to leave themselves a convenient way to cancel without defaulting. To avoid problems, the statement of a contingency should:
- be explicit and clear
- have an expiration date
- expressly require diligence in the effort to fulfill the requirement

A contingency that is too broad, vague, or excessive in duration may invalidate the entire contract on the grounds of insufficiency of mutual agreement.

Default. A sale contract is bilateral, since both parties promise to perform. As a result, either party may default by failing to perform. Note that a party's failure to meet a contingency does not constitute default, but rather entitles the parties to cancel the contract.

Buyer default. If a buyer fails to perform under the terms of a sale contract, the breach entitles the seller to legal recourse for damages. In most cases, the contract itself stipulates the seller's remedies. The usual remedy is forfeiture of the buyer's deposit as liquidated damages, provided the deposit is not grossly in excess of the seller's actual damages. It is also customary to provide for the seller and broker to share the liquidated damages. The broker may not, however, receive liquidated damages in excess of what the commission would have been on the full listing price. If the contract does not provide for liquidated damages, the seller may sue for damages, cancellation, or specific performance.

Seller default. If a seller defaults, the buyer may sue for specific performance, damages, or cancellation.

Types of conveyance contracts. Sale contracts can vary significantly in length and thoroughness. They also vary according to type of transaction is involved. Types of sales contracts include:

- Residential Contract of Sale
- Commercial Contract of Sale
- Foreclosure Contract of Sale
- Contract of Sale for New Construction
- Contract of Sale for Land
- Exchange Agreement

As the most common sale transaction is a residential sale, a Residential Contract of Sale is the type with which a licensee should first become familiar.

PRIMARY SALE CONTRACT PROVISIONS

A typical residential sale contract contains the following provisions.

Parties, consideration, and property. One or more clauses will identify the parties, the property, and the basic consideration, which is the sale of the property in return for a purchase price. There must be at least two parties to a sale contract since one cannot convey property to oneself. All parties must be identified, be of legal age, and have the capacity to contract.

The property portion of the clause identifies fixtures and personal property included in the sale. Unless expressly excluded, items commonly construed as fixtures are included in the sale. Similarly, items commonly considered personal property are not included unless so stated specifically.

Legal description. A legal description must be sufficient for a competent surveyor to identify the property.

Price and terms. A clause states the final price and details how the purchase will occur. Of particular interest to the seller is the buyer's down payment, since the greater the buyer's equity, the more likely the buyer will be able to secure financing. In addition, a large deposit represents a buyer's commitment to complete the sale.

If seller financing is involved, the sale contract sets forth the terms of the arrangement, the amount and type of loan, its rate and term, and how the loan will be paid off.

It is important for all parties to verify that the buyer's earnest money deposit, down payment, loan proceeds, and other promised funds together equal the purchase price stated in the contract.

Loan approval. A financing contingency clause states under what conditions the buyer can cancel the contract without default and receive a refund of the earnest money. If the buyer cannot secure the stated financing by the deadline, the parties may agree to extend the contingency by signing next to the changed dates.

Earnest money deposit. A clause specifies how the buyer will pay the earnest money. It may allow the buyer to pay it in installments. Such an option enables a buyer to hold on to the property briefly while obtaining the additional deposit funds. For example, a buyer who wants to buy a house makes an initial deposit of $200, to be followed in twenty-four hours with an additional $2,000. The sale contract includes the seller's acknowledgment of receipt of the deposit.

Escrow. An escrow clause provides for the custody and disbursement of the earnest money deposit, and releases the escrow agent from certain liabilities in the performance of escrow duties.

Closing and possession dates. The contract states when title will transfer, as well as when the buyer will take physical possession. Customarily, possession occurs on the date when the deed is recorded, unless the buyer has agreed to other arrangements. The closing clause generally describes what must take place at closing to avoid default. A seller must provide clear and marketable title. A buyer must produce purchase funds. Failure to complete any pre-closing requirements stated in the sale contract is default and grounds for the aggrieved party to seek recourse.

Conveyed interest; type of deed. One or more provisions will state what type of deed the seller will use to convey the property, and what conditions the deed will be subject to. Among common "subject to" conditions are easements, association memberships, encumbrances, mortgages, liens, and special assessments. Typically, the seller conveys a fee simple interest by means of a general warranty deed.

Title evidence. The seller covenants to produce the best possible evidence of property ownership. This is commonly in the form of title insurance.

Closing costs. The contract identifies which closing costs each party will pay. Customarily, the seller pays title and property-related costs, and the buyer pays financing-related costs. Annual costs such as taxes and insurance are prorated between the parties. Note that who pays any particular closing cost is an item for negotiation.

Damage and destruction. A clause stipulates the obligations of the parties in case the property is damaged or destroyed. The parties may negotiate alternatives, including seller's obligation to repair, buyer's obligation to buy if repairs are made, and the option for either party to cancel.

Default. A default clause identifies remedies for default. Generally, a buyer may sue for damages, specific performance, or cancellation. A seller may do likewise or claim the earnest money as liquidated damages.

Broker's representation and commission. The broker discloses the applicable agency relationships in the transaction and names the party who must pay the brokerage commission.

Seller's representations. The seller warrants that there will be no liens on the property that cannot be settled and extinguished at closing. In addition, the seller warrants that all representations are true, and if found otherwise, the buyer may cancel the contract and reclaim the deposit.

A sale contract may contain numerous additional clauses, depending on the complexity of the transaction. The following are some of the common provisions.

Inspections. The parties agree to inspections and remedial action based on findings.

Owner's association disclosure. The seller discloses existence of an association and the obligations it imposes.

Survey. The parties agree to a survey to satisfy financing requirements.

Environmental hazards. The seller notifies the buyer that there may be hazards that could affect the use and value of the property.

Compliance with laws. The seller warrants that there are no undisclosed building code or zoning violations.

Due-on-sale clause. The parties state their understanding that loans that survive the closing may be called due by the lender. Both parties agree to hold the other party harmless for the consequences of an acceleration.

Seller financing disclosure. The parties agree to comply with applicable state and local disclosure laws concerning seller financing.

Rental property; tenants rights. The buyer acknowledges the rights of tenants following closing.

FHA or VA financing condition. A contingency allows the buyer to cancel the contract if the price exceeds FHA or VA estimates of the property's value.

Flood plain; flood insurance. Seller discloses that the property is in a flood plain and that it must carry flood insurance if the buyer uses certain lenders for financing.

Condominium assessments. Seller discloses assessments the owner must pay.

Foreign seller withholding. The seller acknowledges that the buyer must withhold 15% of the purchase price at closing if the seller is a foreign person or entity and forward the withheld amount to the Internal Revenue Service. Certain limitations and exemptions apply.

Tax deferred exchange. For income properties only, buyer and seller disclose their intentions to participate in an exchange and agree to cooperate in completing necessary procedures.

Merger of agreements. Buyer and seller state that there are no other agreements between the parties that are not expressed in the contract.

Notices. The parties agree on how they will give notice to each other and what they will consider to be delivery of notice.

Time is of the essence. The parties agree that they can amend dates and deadlines only if they both give written approval.

Fax transmission. The parties agree to accept facsimile transmission of the offer, provided receipt is acknowledged and original copies of the contract are subsequently delivered.

Survival. The parties continue to be liable for the truthfulness of representations and warranties after the closing.

Dispute resolution. The parties agree to resolve disputes through arbitration as opposed to court proceedings.

C.L.U.E. report. CLUE (Comprehensive Loss Underwriting Exchange) is a claims history database used by insurance companies in underwriting or rating insurance policies. A CLUE Home Seller's Disclosure Report shows a five-year insurance loss history for a specific property. Among other things, it describes the types of any losses and the amounts paid. Many home buyers now require sellers to provide a CLUE Report (which only the property owner or an insurer can order) as a contingency appended to the purchase offer. A report showing a loss due to water damage and mold, for instance, might lead a buyer to decide against making an offer because of the potential difficulty of getting insurance. A report showing no insurance loss within the previous five years, on the other hand, is an indication that the availability and pricing of homeowner's insurance will not present an obstacle to the purchase transaction, and also that the property has not experienced significant damage or repair during that time period.

Addenda. Addenda to the sale contract become binding components of the overall agreement. The most common addendum is the seller's property condition disclosure. Examples of other addenda are:

- agency disclosure
- asbestos / hazardous materials
- radon disclosure
- liquidated damages
- flood plain disclosure
- tenant's lease

17 Inside the Sales Contract
Snapshot Review

LEGAL CHARACTERISTICS

- executory contract – must complete certain actions in order to fulfill; after closing contract is extinguished; all principals should sign to facilitate title transfer and maintain marketability

- for enforceability, contract must meet validity criteria and be in writing; validity = mutual consent; consideration; legal purpose; competent parties; voluntary act; additionally contract must identify principals, identify property with legal description, contain price, be signed

- must be completed by principal and legal counsel; licensees may fill in blanks of pre-printed forms

CONTRACT MECHANICS AND PROCESSES

- offer and acceptance necessary to create binding agreement; cannot make any changes to an offer to create acceptance – if change, offer becomes counteroffer

- equitable title acquired by buyer upon execution = buyer can acquire title under certain conditions or upon contract fulfillment

- earnest money fulfills consideration component of valid contract; amount varies by custom; contract contains instructions for handling, disbursing deposit and other trust funds; broker and sale associates must abide by strict trust account handling requirements

- broker must keep trust funds in trust account until closing unless otherwise authorized by all parties; must also maintain trust account records showing all deposit and withdrawal activity; must retain for five years

- contract contingencies such as financing must be satisfied prior to closing. Contingencies should be specific in nature and duration as they can trigger a right to cancel the contract by either party

- if buyer defaults, seller typically retains the deposit as liquidated damages or seller can opt for other remedies if stated in the agreement; broker may receive portions of liquidated damages; seller may also sue for damages or specific performance (e.g., buyer must buy property)

- seller default: typical buyer remedy is to sue for specific performance which compels the seller to sell

PRIMARY SALES CONTRACT PROVISIONS

- Parties, consideration, property – consideration is the property in exchange for the price; must be at least two principals of legal age capacity to contract; property provision includes fixtures and personal property to be included

- price and terms clause covers how property will be paid for; includes amount of down payment and all specifics of the loan; loan approval provision details any financing contingency and what happens if buyer is not approved

- earnest money includes the deposit plus the eventual down payment, both of which are escrowed and for which there are deadlines for receipt.

- closing, possession and deed: stipulates date of closing, move-in date, and what deed seller will use to convey; seller must deliver clear, marketable title at closing with no unwanted encumbrances; deed should be general warranty deed

**SECONDARY CONTRACT
PROVISIONS**

- inspections; homeowner's association disclosures; survey; environmental hazard disclosures; building code compliance; due-on-sale clause; seller-financing disclosures; flood plain disclosure requiring flood insurance; condo assessments disclosures; foreign seller withholding requirement;

- CLUE report indicating property's history of insurance claims; five-year look-back period

SECTION SEVENTEEN QUIZ: INSIDE THE SALES CONTRACT

1. What happens if the sellers of a home are married, but the husband does not sign the sale contract?

   a. The contract becomes invalid.
   b. This can lead to an encumbered title and/or legal disputes.
   c. The buyers must acknowledge that they understand the husband failed to sign and the transaction can then carry on smoothly.
   d. Nothing happens.

2. A legal description must be sufficient for a competent _____ to identify the property.

   a. surveyor
   b. title agent
   c. escrow agent
   d. lender

3. Which property types are eligible to participate in tax deferred exchanges?

   a. Industrial properties
   b. Commercial and residential properties
   c. Income properties only
   d. Any property type

4. Which of the following is the most common addendum to a sale contract?

   a. Seller's property condition disclosure
   b. Radon disclosure
   c. Flood plain disclosure
   d. Tenant's lease

5. If _____ is involved, the sale contract sets forth the terms of the arrangement, the amount and type of loan, its rate and term, and how the loan will be paid off.

   a. conventional financing
   b. FHA financing
   c. VA financing
   d. seller financing

6. How long must escrow records be retained?

   a. For 7 years
   b. For 5 years
   c. For 10 years
   d. For 3 years

7. A sale contract confers to the buyer an interest in the property called _____.

    a.   prospective title.
    b.   an ownership option.
    c.   equitable title.
    d.   legal title.

8. A sale contract is _____ if the signatories have yet to perform their respective obligations and promises.

    a.   fully performed
    b.   a non-binding agreement
    c.   completed
    d.   executory

9. Which items are commonly included in the sale of a home?

    a.   Personal property
    b.   Furniture
    c.   Items commonly construed as fixtures
    d.   Patio sets and exterior furnishings

10. What happens if a buyer fails to perform his or her duties in a contract?

    a.   A sale contract is unilateral and requires that only the seller perform.
    b.   The contract may go into default.
    c.   The seller cannot seek legal recourse for damages.
    d.   The seller cannot sue for specific performance.

11. Which costs are typically covered by the buyer?

    a.   The buyer's financing-related costs
    b.   Title-related costs
    c.   Property-related costs
    d.   The total annual property tax amount

12. If the seller is a foreign person, the buyer must withhold ____ of the purchase price at closing and forward the withheld amount to the IRS.

    a.   5%
    b.   15%
    c.   20%
    d.   25%

13. A CLUE Home Seller's Disclosure Report shows a(n) ____ insurance-loss history for a specific property.

    a.   180-day
    b.   one-year
    c.   three-year
    d.   five-year

14. Which of the following is the most common type of contingency?

    a. Inspection contingency
    b. Appraisal contingency
    c. Financing contingency
    d. Sale of buyer's property contingency

15. What is the most common type of deed used in residential sales transactions?

    a. General warranty deed
    b. Trustee deed
    c. Special warranty deed
    d. Quitclaim deed

18 Real Estate Mathematics

Real Estate Applications

REAL ESTATE APPLICATIONS

Legal descriptions
Listing agreements
Brokerage business
Sales contracts
Appraisal
Finance
Investments
Taxation
Closings

Legal descriptions

Fractions of sections, acres, and linear dimensions

Fraction	# Acres	Feet X Feet
1 section	640 acres	5280 X 5280
1/2 section	320 acres	5280 X 2640
1/4 section	160 acres	2640 X 2640
1/8 section	80 acres	2640 X 1320
1/16 section	40 acres	1320 X 1320
1/32 section	20 acres	660 X 1320
1/64 section	10 acres	660 X 660

Calculating area in acres from the legal description

1. Formula:

    (1)   First multiply all the denominators of the Section fractions in the legal description together

    (2)   Then divide 640 by the resulting product.

2. Examples:

N 1/2 of the SW 1/4 of Section 6:

$$\frac{640}{(2 \times 4)} = \frac{640}{8} = 80 \; acres$$

W 1/2 of the NW 1/4 of the NE 1/4 of Section 8

$$\frac{640}{(2 \times 4 \times 4)} = \frac{640}{32} = 20 \; acres$$

Problem 1:   Calculate the acreage of the following:

SW 1/4 of the N 1/2 of the E 1/2 of Section 14

SE 1/4 of the NW 1/4 of the SE 1/4 of Section 20

Listing agreements

Co-brokerage commission

1. Formulas: sale price x commission rate = total commission

total commission x split rate = co-brokerage commission

2. Example: A house sells for $600,000. The commission is 6%, and the co-brokerage split is 50-50.

$600,000 x 6% = $36,000 total commission x 50% = $18,000 co-broker's commission

Agent's commission

1. Formula: broker's commission x agent's split rate = agent's commission

2. Example: Assume an $18,000 broker's commission and a 60% - 40% agent-broker split rate.

$18,000 x .6 = $10,800 agent's commission ($7,200 to broker)

Problem 2:   A property is co-brokered by listing broker Schroeder and selling broker Hobson for $425,000. The co-brokerage split is 50-50. Schroeder's agent, Joachim, is on a 65% split schedule. Hobson's selling agent, Wallace, splits 50-50 with her broker. If the total commission rate is 7%, what are the participants' commissions?

Broker Schroeder:	$
Broker Hobson:	$
Schroeder's agent, Joachim:	$
Hobson's agent, Wallace:	$

Brokerage business

Goodwill calculation

1. Formula: Goodwill = Price - Value of assets

2. Example: A seller wants $1 million for a business. Assets in the business, including inventory, furniture, equipment, leasehold improvements, and working capital, have a total value of $750,000. The goodwill is:

    $1,000,000 - 750,000 = $250,000 goodwill

> **Problem 3:**   A prospective purchaser complained to a seller that the selling price had far too much goodwill: $200,000. After all, the assets only totaled $352,000. What was the price?

Sales contracts

"Percentage of listing price" calculation

1. Formula: Percentage of listing price = offer divided by listing price

2. Example: A property listed for $400,000 receives an offer for $360,000. The percentage of listing price is:

    $360,000 divided by 400,000 = 90%

> **Problem 4:**   A seller receives an offer of $674,000 on a property listed at $749,000. How much is the offer as a percent of the listing price?

Earnest money deposit calculation

1. Formula: Deposit = Listing price x required percentage

2. Example: A seller requires a 2% deposit on a property listed for $320,000. The required deposit is:

    $320,000 x 2% = $6,400

Rent escalations

1. Formula: New rent = current rent x (100% + escalation rate)

2. Example: An apartment's rent is scheduled to increase by 6%. If the current rent is $1,800, the new rent is:

$1,800 x (100% + 6%) = $1,800 x 106% = $1,908

FIRPTA withholding

1. Formula: FIRPTA withholding = gross proceeds from sale x 15%

2. Example: Gross proceeds on a FIRPTA-regulated property sale are $340,000. The required withholding amount is:

$340,000 x 15% = $51,000

Appraisal

Adjusting comparables

1. Rules:
   a. NEVER adjust the subject!

   b. If the comparable is better than the subject, subtract value from the comparable

   c. If the comparable is **worse** than the subject, **add** value to the comparable

2. Examples:
   a. A comparable has a pool and the subject does not. The appraiser estimates the value contribution to be $25,000. Adjust the comparable by entering -25,000 in the CMA.

   b. A comparable has 3 bedrooms and the subject as 4. The appraiser estimates the value contribution of a bedroom to be $15,000. Adjust the comparable by entering +15,000 in the CMA.

Problem 7: Identify the proper adjustments for the following:

(a) The subject has a two-car garage, while the comparable does not. Value of garage is $33,000.

Adjustment:

(b) A comparable has a fireplace, and the subject does not. Value of fireplace is $8,000.

Adjustment:

(c) The subject has 1,500 square feet. The comparable has 1,600 square feet. The value of extra square feet is $200/SF.

Adjustment:

Income capitalization

Gross rent multiplier (GRM)

1. Formula: gross rent x multiplier = value

2. Example: $200,000 x 9 = $1,800,000

Net income capitalization

1. Formula: net income (NOI) ÷ capitalization rate = value

$$\frac{net\ income\ (\ NOI\ )}{capitalization\ \ rate} = value$$

2. Example: $50,000 ÷ 10% = 50,000 ÷ .10 = $500,000

Problem 8: A property grosses $450,000, nets 350,000, and has a capitalization rate of 9%. Prevailing GRMs are 8.

(a) What is the property value using the GRM?

(b) What is the property value using net income capitalization?

Interest only loans

1. Formulas: interest payment (I) = principal (P) x interest rate (R)

   annual interest payment ÷ 12 = monthly interest payment

   monthly interest payment x 12 = annual interest payment

   $$I = P \ x \ R$$
   $$R = \frac{I}{P}$$
   $$P = \frac{I}{R}$$

2. Examples: A $300,000 interest-only loan @ 10% has annual payments of $30,000 and monthly payments of $2,500.

   Annual interest = $300,000 x 10% = $30,000
   Monthly interest = $30,000 ÷ 12 = $2,500

   The loan amount of an interest-only loan that has an annual interest rate of 8% and a monthly interest payment of $700 is $105,000.

   Annual interest = $700 x 12 = $8,400
   Loan amount = $8,400 ÷ .08 = $105,000

Problem 9:

(a) A $250,000 loan carries a 7% rate. What is the monthly interest payment?

(b) A $300,000 loan has monthly payments of $2,000. What is its annual interest rate?

(c) A 12% loan has annual payments of $15,000. What is the loan amount?

Loan-to-value (LTV) ratio

1. Formulas:

    loan amount = market value x LTV

    LTV = loan amount ÷ market value

2. Example:

    A 75% LTV will allow a lender to make a loan of $375,000 on a $500,000 property.

    loan amount = $500,000 x 75% = $375,000

    LTV = $375,000 ÷ $500,000 = 75%

Problem 10:

(a) A lender requires $90,000 down on a $400,000 property. Calculate the lender's required LTV.

(b) A property is valued at $600,000. The lender will allow a maximum LTV of 75%. How much can the buyer borrow on the property?

Income underwriting ratio calculation

1. Formulas:

    Conventional:

    monthly PITI = (25-28%) x monthly gross income

    FHA:

    monthly PITI = 31% x monthly gross income

2. Examples:

    A borrower has monthly gross income of $2,000. Conventional lenders are using a ratio of 28%. The borrower can afford the following monthly PITI payments:

    Conventional:

    PITI = 28% x $2,000 = $560

    FHA:

    PITI = 31% x $2,000 = $620

Problem 11: A borrower earns $4,000/month and pays $600/month in debt repayments. A conventional lender requires a 26% income ratio, and an FHA lender requires 31%. What monthly PITI can this person afford based on the income ratio?

Conventional: $

FHA: $

Debt underwriting ratio calculation

1. Formulas: Conventional:

Expense = (36% x gross income) – monthly debt

FHA:

Expense = (43% x gross income) - monthly debt

2. Example: An individual has a monthly gross income of $6,000, and has monthly debt payments of $900. The borrower can afford the following monthly housing expense:

Conventional:

Expense = (36% x $6,000) - 900 = $1,260

FHA:

Expense = (43% x $6,000) – 900 = $1,680

Problem 12: A borrower earns $4,000/month and makes monthly debt payments of $600. What monthly payment for housing can this person afford based on the debt ratio?

Conventional: $

FHA: $

Points

1. Formula: 1 point = 1% (.01) of loan amount

2. Example: A lender charges 3 points (3%) on a $350,000 loan. The points charges are:

   3 points = 3%
   .03 x $350,000 = $10,500

> **Problem 13:** A lender is charging 2.75 points on a $240,000 loan. How much must the borrower pay for points?

Investments

Appreciation

1. Formulas: total appreciation = current value – original price

   total appreciation rate = total appreciation ÷ original price

   one-year appreciation rate = one-year appreciation / prior-year value

2. Example: A house bought for $500,000 appreciates $50,000 each Year for 3 years.

   total appreciation = $650,000 - 500,000 = $150,000

   total appreciation rate = $150,000 ÷ $500,000 = 30%

   first- year rate = $50,000 ÷ $500,000 = 10%

> **Problem 14:** A property is purchased for $360,000. A year later it is Sold for $410,000. What is the amount of appreciation, and what is the appreciation rate?

Equity

1. Formula: equity = current value – current loan amount

2. Example: A buyer bought a property for $600,000 with a loan of $450,000. The house has appreciated $60,000 and the buyer has reduced the original loan by $30,000. The buyer's current equity is:

Equity = ($600,000 + 60,000) - ($450,000 - 30,000) = $240,000

Problem 15: A property is purchased for $450,000 with a $75,000 downpayment. Five years later the property is worth $540,000, and the loan balance has dropped $12,500. What is the owner's new equity?

Pre-tax cash flow

1. Formula and example:

potential rental income	$50,000
- vacancy and collection loss	3,000
= effective rental income	47,000
+ other income	2,000
= gross operating income (GOI)	49,000
- operating expenses	20,000
- reserves	3,000
= net operating income (NOI)	26,000
- debt service	15,000
= pre-tax cash flow	11,000

Problem 16: An apartment building has a potential income of $300,000 and vacancy of $12,000. Its bills total $128,000, and $12,000 has been reserved for repairs. Payments on the loan total $88,000. What is the property's pre-tax cash flow?

Tax liability

1. Formula
   and example:

	net operating income (NOI)	26,000
+	reserves	3,000
-	interest expense	15,000
-	cost recovery expense	5,000
=	taxable income	9,000
x	tax rate (28%)	
=	tax liability	2,520

> **Problem 17:** The property from the previous problem has annual cost recovery of $28,000. Out of the annual debt service, $8,000 is non-interest principal payback. The property owner's tax rate is 28%. What is the property's annual tax?

Annual depreciation (cost recovery) expense

1. Calculation:
   a. identify improvements-to-land ratio

   b. identify value of improvements: ratio x property price

   c. divide value of improvements by total depreciation term

2. Example: A property was bought for $400,000. 75% of the value is allocated to the improvement. The property falls in the 39-year depreciation category.

   (1) improvements-to-land ratio = 3:1, or 75%

   (2) improvement value = $400,000 x 75% = $300,000

   (3) annual depreciation = $300,000 ÷ 39 = $7,692

> **Problem 18:** A property is purchased for $400,000. Improvements account for 80% of the value. Given a 39-year depreciation term, what is the annual depreciation expense?

Capital gain

1. Formula
   and example: (residential property)

Selling price of property	$300,000
- Selling costs	24,000
= Amount realized (ending basis)	$276,000
Beginning basis (price) of property	$250,000
+ Capital improvements	10,000
- Total depreciation expense	0
= Adjusted basis of property	260,000
Amount realized (ending basis)	$276,000
- Adjusted basis of property	260,000
= Capital gain	$ 16,000

Problem 19:   A principal residence is bought for $360,000. A new tile roof is added, costing $15,000. Five years later the home sells for $440,000, and the closing costs $35,000. What is the homeowner's capital gain?

Return, rate of return, and investment amount

1. Formulas:

$$\frac{net\ operating\ income}{price} = return\ on\ investment\ (ROI)$$

$$\frac{cash\ flow}{cash\ invested} = cash\text{-}on\text{-}cash\ return\ (C\ on\ C)$$

$$\frac{cash\ flow}{equity} = return\ on\ equity\ (ROE)$$

2. Example: A property is bought for $200,000 with a $50,000 down payment and a $150,000 interest-only loan. The property has a net income of $20,000 and a cash flow of $8,000. In addition, the property has appreciated $30,000.

   ROI   = $20,000 ÷ $200,000 = 10%
   C on C = $8,000 ÷ $50,000 = 16%
   ROE   = $8,000 ÷ $80,000 = 10%

Problem 20: A multi-unit rental property was bought four years ago for $1,200,000 with a $200,000 down payment. The property now rents for $8,500 per month. Expenses and debt service are $1,000/month and $6,500/month respectively. An appraiser estimates the property's current value at $1,450,000. The investor pays off her principal balance at a rate of $5,000 per year. Compute the following investment returns for the investor:

ROI   =
C on C =
ROE   =

Taxation

Tax rate calculation

1. Formula:

$$\text{tax rate (millage rate)} = \frac{\text{tax requirement}}{\text{tax base}}$$

2. Example: A municipality has a revenue requirement of $10,000,000 after accounting for its revenues from sale of utilities. This requirement has to be covered by property tax. The real estate tax base, after homestead exemptions, is $300,000,000. The tax rate will be:

$$\frac{10,000,000}{300,000,000} = .0333 \quad 33.33 \text{ mills}$$

Problem 21: Barrington has an annual budget of $25,000,000 to be paid by property taxes. Assessed valuations are $300,000,000, and exemptions total $25,000,000. What must the tax rate be to finance the budget?

Homestead exemption calculation

1. Formula and
   example

	assessed value	$360,000
-	homestead exemption	50,000
	taxable value	$310,000

Taxing the property

1. Formulas: taxable value of property x tax rate (mill rate) for each taxing authority in jurisdiction

   total tax = sum of all taxes by taxing authority

2. Example: The taxable value of a property after exemptions is 400,000 and tax rates are as shown. The property's tax bill will be:

School tax:	$400,000 x 10 mills	= $4,000
City tax:	$400,000 x 4 mills	= 1600
County tax:	$400,000 x 3 mills	= 1200
Total tax:		$6,800

Problem 22:   A homeowner's assessed valuation is $225,000. The homestead exemption is $25,000. Tax rates for the property are 8 mills for schools; 3 mills for the city; 2.5 mills for the county; and .5 mills for the local community college. What is the homeowner's tax bill?

Special assessments calculation

1. Formula: a. Identify total costs to be assessed

                b. Calculate prorated share for each property impacted

                c. Multiply cost x prorated share

2. Example: A canal will be dredged at a cost of $200,000. The improvement affects 30 properties with a total canal frontage of 4,000 feet. One property has 200' of frontage. Its assessment bill will be:

                (1) 200' ÷ 4,000' = 5% share

                (2) $200,000 x 5% = $10,000 assessment

> **Problem 23:** A street beautification project is to cost $25,000. The project affects 20 properties having a total of 2,000 front feet. One owner's lot has 75 front feet. What will this owner's special assessment be?

Closings

Prorations

1. Formulas and rules:

Accounting for common items paid (or received) in advance vs arrears

	arrears	advance	debit	credit
real estate taxes	x		seller	buyer
rents received by seller		x	seller	buyer
utilities	x		seller	buyer

Whose share is charged to whom?

- if buyer pays taxes in arrears: charge seller, credit buyer for seller's portion

- if seller received rents in advance: charge seller, credit buyer for buyer's portion

- if seller pays utilities in advance: credit seller, charge buyer for seller's portion

Calculating the proration: 360-day method and 365-day method

1. **Calculate the daily proration amount**

   a. 360-day method: divide the annual amount by 360 or monthly amount by 30

   b. 365-day method: divide the annual proration amount by 365, or monthly amount by # days in that month

2. **Calculate # of seller's days**

   a. 360-day method: use 30 days for each month; actual number of seller days within the month, counting (or not counting) the day of closing

   b. 365-day method: use actual number of days for each month and partial month

3. **Calculate the seller's share**

   Multiply the daily amount times the number of seller's days – both methods

4. **Calculate buyer's share (both methods)**

   Subtract seller's share (from #3) from total share

2. Example: A rental property closes on January 25 and the closing day is the seller's. The 365-day method will be used for the prorations. Monthly rent already received by seller is $2,400. Annual real estate taxes to be paid in arrears by buyer are $4,000. Round to the nearest cent.

   1. **Rent proration**: (monthly; 365-day method)

Daily amount:	$2,400 monthly rent ÷ 31 days in January = $77.42
# Seller's days:	25
Seller's share:	$77.42 x 25 = $1,935.50
Buyer's share:	$2,400 – 1,935.50 = $464.50

      Credit buyer and debit seller for buyer's share of $464.50

   2. **Tax proration**: (annual; 365-day method)

Daily amount:	$4,000 ÷ 365 = $10.96
# Seller's days:	25
Seller's share:	$10.96 x 25 = $274
Buyer's share:	$4,000 – 274 = $3,726

      Credit buyer and debit seller for seller's share of $274

Problem 24: A rental property closes on March 15th. Proratable income and expenses are: rental income of $1,800/month, received in advance by seller, March 1; annual taxes of $4,800/year, to be paid in arrears by buyer, January 1 of the year after sale. The day of closing is the seller's. February has 28 days. Prorate the items using the 365-day method, and assign debits and credits.

rent:
seller's share	$
buyer's share	$
debit seller/credit buyer	$
-- or --	
debit buyer/credit seller	$

taxes:
seller's share	$
buyer's share	$
debit seller/credit buyer	$
-- or --	
debit buyer/credit seller	$

SECTION 18 WORKSHOP ANSWER KEY

Problem 1: 40 acres
10 acres

Problem 2:
Schroeder:	$5,206.25
Hobson:	$7,437.50
Joachim	$9,668.75
Wallace:	$7,437.50

Problem 3: $552,000

Problem 4: 90%

Problem 5: $4,680

Problem 6: $716.63

Problem 7:
(a) +33,000 to comparable
(b) - 8,000 to comparable
(c) - 20,000 to comparable

Problem 8:
(a) $3,600,000
(b) $3,888,888

Problem 9:
(a) $1,458
(b) 8%
(c) $125,000

Problem 10:
(a) 77.5%
(b) $450,000

Problem 11: Conventional: $1,040/month
FHA & VA: $1,240/month

Problem 12: Conventional: $840
       FHA: $1,120

Problem 13: $6,600

Problem 14: $50,000; 13.89%

Problem 15: $177,500

Problem 16: $60,000

Problem 17: $14,560

Problem 18: $8,205

Problem 19: $30,000

Problem 20:   (a)   ROI= 7.5%
       (b)   C on C = 6.0%
       (c)   ROE = 2.55%

Problem 21: 90.9 mills, or 9.09%

Problem 22: $2,800

Problem 23: $937.50

Problem 24:

	rent:	seller's share	$870.96
		buyer's share	$929.04
		debit seller/credit buyer	$929.04
	taxes:	seller's share	$973.16
		buyer's share	3,826.84
		debit seller/credit buyer	$973.16

SECTION EIGHTEEN QUIZ: Real Estate Mathematics

1. Homeowner Theresa owns the Northwestern ¼ of the Northwestern ¼ of the Northwestern ¼ of Section 4. How many acres is that property?

   a. 4 acres
   b. 40 acres
   c. 10 acres
   d. 8 acres

2. Spenser, who works for selling broker Smith, sells a house listed by listing broker Adams. The house sells for $425,000. The co-brokerage split between Smith and Adams is 50-50. Spenser is on a 65% commission schedule with Smith. If the total commission rate is 7%, what is Spenser's commission?

   a. $9,669
   b. $13,812
   c. $14,875
   d. $19,338

3. Seller Andy requires a 3.5% deposit on all offers. Buyer Josh wants to offer $312,000 for the property. The property was appraised at $325,000. What must the earnest money deposit be if Josh presents his current offer?
   a. $10,920
   b. $11,375
   c. $9,500
   d. $10,538

4. A house is being appraised using the sales comparison approach. The house has three bedrooms, two bathrooms, and a patio. The appraiser selects a comparable house that has three bedrooms, 2.5 bathrooms, and no patio. The comparable house just sold for $100,000. A half-bath is valued at $5,000, and a patio at $1,000. Assuming all else is equal, what is the adjusted value of the comparable?

   a. $100,000
   b. $104,000
   c. $96,000
   d. $106,000

5. An apartment building that sold for $450,000 had monthly gross rent receipts of $3,000. What is its monthly gross rent multiplier?

   a. 12.5
   b. .01
   c. .08
   d. 150

6. A $300,000 loan has monthly interest-only payments of $2,000. Its annual interest rate is:

   a. 4%
   b. 6%
   c. 8%
   d. 10%

7. A lender determines that a homebuyer can afford to borrow $1,200,000 on a mortgage loan. The lender requires an 80% loan-to-value ratio. How much can the borrower pay for a property and still qualify for this loan amount?

a. $960,000
b. $1,060,000
c. $1,500,000
d. $1,600,000

8. A loan applicant has an annual gross income of $36,000. How much will a lender allow the applicant to pay for monthly housing expense to qualify for a loan if the lender uses an income ratio of 28%?

a. $2,160
b. $840
c. $1,008
d. $720

9. Greg recently obtained an 80% loan on his $320,000 home, and he had to pay $4,480 for points. How many points did he pay?

a. 1.4 points
b. 1.75 points
c. 4.48 points
d. 3.584 points

10. A homeowner paid $1,850,000 for a house three years ago. The house sells today for $2,390,000. How much has the property appreciated?

a. 23 %
b. 77 %
c. 29 %
d. 123 %

11. A property has a net income of $50,000, interest payments of $35,000, principal payments of $3,000, and annual cost recovery of $7,000. The property's tax rate is 28%. What is the property's annual tax on income?

a. $4,200
b. $3,360
c. $2,240
d. $1,400

12. A property is purchased for $200,000. Improvements account for 75% of the value. Given a 39-year depreciation term, what is the annual depreciation expense?

a. $3,846
b. $5,128
c. $6,410
d. $8,294

13. A homeowner sold her house and had net proceeds of $191,000. Her adjusted basis in the home was $176,000. She immediately bought another house for $200,000. What was her capital gain?

a. $191,000
b. $9,000
c. $15,000
d. None

14. The village of Parrish has an annual budget requirement of $20,000,000 to be funded by property taxes. Assessed valuations are $400,000,000, and exemptions total $25,000,000. What must the tax rate be to finance the budget?

a. 4.70%
b. 5.33%
c. 5.00%
d. 11.25%

15. Aaron finally found a buyer for his six-plex and closing is set for June 20th. At closing, four of his tenants have paid their $650 rent and two of the units remain unoccupied. What will the proration be assuming the 365-day method and that the closing day belongs to the seller?

a. Debit seller, credit buyer $1,733.30.
b. Debit seller, credit buyer $866.70.
c. Credit seller, debit buyer $866.70.
d. Credit seller, debit buyer $1,733.30.

16. A town is replacing a sidewalk that serves five homes. The length of the sidewalk is 200 feet. Mary's property has 38 feet of front footage. If the cost of the project to be paid by a special assessment is $7,000, what will Mary's assessment be?

a. $1,400
b. $1,330
c. $184
d. $1,840

Practice Examination

1. What are the two principal types of real estate managers who oversee groups of properties?

   a. Property managers and asset managers
   b. Staff managers and management managers
   c. Property managers and management managers
   d. Lead managers and asset managers

2. Paula is a member of the U.S. Air Force. What must she do to renew her real estate license?

   a. Complete continuing education and apply for renewal
   b. Apply for renewal and pay the renewal fee
   c. Complete continuing education, apply for renewal, and pay the renewal fee
   d. Paula is exempt from renewal requirements.

3. If a licensee does not renew an active license by the expiration date, what happens?

   a. The license becomes voluntarily inactive.
   b. The license becomes null and void.
   c. The license becomes involuntarily inactive.
   d. Nothing, the licensee is automatically given 2 years to renew the license.

4. If Ursula changes employing brokers, she must notify the FREC of the change

   a. immediately.
   b. within 30 days of the change.
   c. within 10 days after the change.
   d. There is no need to notify the FREC of an employing broker change.

5. Designated sales associates are used when

   a. the brokerage wants to represent both the residential buyer and the residential seller.
   b. the nonresidential buyer and seller have assets of $1 million or more.
   c. any client requests the designation.
   d. the broker is handling any nonresidential sale.

6. Which of the following statements is true?

   a. Transaction brokers owe fiduciary duties to their clients.
   b. The duty of limited confidentiality prevents the transaction broker from disclosing known material facts.
   c. Transaction brokers have no duty of undivided loyalty.
   d. Transaction brokers and single agents owe the same duties to their clients.

7. Brokerage relationship disclosure records must be retained

   a. until the transaction closes.
   b. for 2 years.
   c. for 5 years.
   d. only if related to a legal proceeding.

8. What is an agent's duty regarding inspections?

   a. Personally conduct a detailed inspection of all major structures and systems
   b. Accompany all inspectors as they inspect the agent's listed property
   c. Disclose the result of any inspection, if known to the agent
   d. Interview and hire inspectors for clients.

9. Under what circumstances may a licensee offer an opinion of title?

   a. When the licensee develops the opinion of title with assistance from his employing broker
   b. When the licensee obtains the opinion of title from an attorney and passes the information on to the client
   c. When the licensee uses the abstract of title completed by the title company to develop the opinion of title
   d. When the client does not wish to consult an attorney

10. In Florida, the unlicensed practice of law is a

   a. misdemeanor of the third degree.
   b. first-degree felony.
   c. civil violation.
   d. third-degree felony.

11. What should a licensee be aware of if they are conducting cold calls?

   a. That they are exempt from complying with the Do-Not-Call list
   b. Phone calls before 8 a.m. and after 9 p.m. are prohibited.
   c. That cold calls by two or more licensees are illegal.
   d. That auto-dialers are only allowed if they are used for text messages.

12. What is mediation?

   a. A legal procedure used if parties do not agree to arbitration.
   b. An informal conflict settlement procedure that is conducted by a qualified third party.
   c. A process conducted by one or more third party judges.
   d. A way for the broker to be removed from the dispute.

13. Which of the following is not a requirement of the Florida Americans with Disabilities Accessibility Implementation Act?

   a. Allowing a service dog to live in a no-pet apartment building
   b. Installing a ramp at the entrance to an apartment building where a wheel-chair-bound tenant lives
   c. Widening the bathroom doorways to 29 inches in a new apartment building
   d. Providing handicapped parking in an apartment building's parking lot

14. If a lease agreement does not indicate where a security deposit is to be held, the landlord must provide that information to the tenant

   a. prior to signing the lease.
   b. within 15 business days of signing the lease.
   c. within 30 days of receiving the deposit.
   d. That information must be in the lease.

15. A landlord has _____ to notify a vacated tenant of a claim against the tenant's security deposit.

   a. 7 days
   b. 15 days
   c. 30 days
   d. 45 days

16. Which of the following is a protected class by the Florida Fair Housing Act?

   a. Race
   b. Marital status
   c. Age
   d. Occupation

17. One difference between a cooperative estate and a condominium estate is that

   a. a default by a coop owner may cause a foreclosure on the entire property instead of just a single unit, as with a condominium.
   b. the condominium owner must pay expenses as well as rent.
   c. the coop owner owns stock and a freehold real estate interest whereas the condominium owner simply owns real estate.
   d. the condominium owner owns the common elements and the airspace whereas the coop owner only owns the apartment.

18. Which disclosure requirement is consistent for condominiums, cooperatives, and HOAs?

   a. Budget estimates
   b. Right to cancel
   c. Exchange program membership
   d. No guaranteed selling price

19. An important difference between a judicial foreclosure and a non-judicial foreclosure is

   a. there is no right to redeem the property in a non-judicial foreclosure.
   b. a judicial foreclosure forces a sale of the property.
   c. a non-judicial foreclosure ensures that all liens are paid in order of priority.
   d. the lienor receives title directly in a non-judicial foreclosure.

20. Four principal determinants of value underlying the price for a product are

   a. durability, quality, scarcity, and materials.
   b. desire, utility, scarcity, and purchasing power.
   c. popularity, utility, quality, and discount.
   d. desire, costs, convenience, and time.

21. Lakewood Ranch has a rapidly growing population, but there are no longer any vacant lots around the lake to build more houses. In this case, it is likely that the price of existing homes on the lake

a. will stabilize, since the population must stabilize.
b. will increase.
c. will decline, since no further building can take place.
d. will not show any predictable movement.

22. If there is a significant undersupply of homes in a market, construction will tend to increase. This is an example of

a. supply outstripping demand.
b. overpricing products.
c. the price mechanism.
d. the market tending toward equilibrium.

23. In appraisal, loss of value in a property from any cause is referred to as

a. deterioration.
b. obsolescence.
c. depreciation.
d. deflation.

24. The first two steps in the cost approach are to estimate the value of the land and the cost of the improvements. The remaining steps are

a. estimate depreciation, subtract depreciation from cost, and add back the land value.
b. subtract deterioration from cost, estimate land depreciation, and total the two values.
c. estimate depreciation of land and improvements, subtract from original cost.
d. estimate obsolescence, subtract from the cost of land and improvements.

25. The roof of a property cost $10,000. The economic life of the roof is 20 years. Assuming the straight-line method of depreciation, what is the depreciated value of the roof after 3 years?

a. $10,000
b. $8,500
c. $7,000
d. $1,500

26. The income capitalization approach to appraising value is most applicable for which of the following property types?

a. Single family homes
b. Apartment buildings
c. Undeveloped land
d. Churches

27. Which of the following is true of the tax treatment of a principal residence?

a. The owner may deduct the property's interest and principal from ordinary income.
b. The owner may depreciate the property and deduct depreciation expenses.
c. The owner can deduct any capital gain when the property is sold.
d. The owner may be able to exclude capital gain from taxable income when the property is sold.

28. An investment property seller pays $19,750 in closing costs. These costs

   a. may be deducted from personal income.
   b. may be deducted from the property's income.
   c. may be deducted from the sale price for gains tax purposes.
   d. may be deducted from the adjusted basis for gains tax purposes.

29. Capital gain tax is figured by multiplying one's tax bracket times

   a. the sum of the beginning basis plus gain.
   b. the difference between net sale proceeds and adjusted basis.
   c. the sum of net sale proceeds and capital gain.
   d. the difference between net sale proceeds and capital gain.

30. Which homeowners' policy is also known as renters' insurance?

   a. HO-0
   b. HO-2
   c. HO-4
   d. HO-7

31. Which of the following is a true statement about the "80% rule" for homeowner's policies?

   a. 80% of replacement value is the maximum an insurance company will pay.
   b. If insured for less than 80% of replacement cost, a home's coverage will include a deduction for depreciation.
   c. If insured for 80% of replacement cost, a home is covered for the full cost of replacement.
   d. Insurance companies will not insure residences for less than 80% of their replacement cost.

32. A limitation of coverage on an insurance policy is called a(n)

   a. deductible.
   b. condition.
   c. exclusion.
   d. package.

33. In what sense is the use of standardized forms a risk management procedure?

   a. It eliminates the risk of being unable to draft a contract correctly.
   b. It reduces the risk of losing a client by having to make a referral to an attorney.
   c. It reduces the risk of committing an unauthorized practice of law.
   d. It eliminates the risk of wasting valuable time in creating custom forms.

34. Keeping thorough records of every transaction is not only a risk management technique, it is

   a. good for company morale.
   b. helpful for business planning.
   c. a technique for discovering market trends.
   d. a legal requirement.

35. Which of the following communication records must (as opposed to should) be kept?

    a. Notes on every conversation.
    b. Copies of required communications to principals.
    c. Notes from company training sessions.
    d. Business cards of licensees one meets at open houses.

36. The standard E & O policy covers damages resulting from

    a. failure to disclose an environmental condition.
    b. antitrust violations.
    c. mishandling of earnest money deposits.
    d. negligence, error or omission in carrying out professional services.

37. Which of the following is a common risk relating to the agency relationship?

    a. Failing to inform and disclose properly.
    b. Failing to take a personal interest in a transaction.
    c. Acting as an exclusive agent without an oral agency agreement.
    d. Forgetting to record the listing agreement.

38. A _____ manages a property for one or more owners.

    a. building manager
    b. maintenance manager
    c. property manager
    d. rental agent

39. The Equal Credit Opportunity Act ensures that

    a. all property managers evaluate potential tenants fairly and equally.
    b. less-qualified tenants be given easier application guidelines.
    c. all real estate agents treat clients equally.
    d. applicants get different opportunities based on their credit score tiers.

40. If a landlord wants to evict a tenant, their first step is to _____.

    a. have a court issue a judgment for possession.
    b. serve notice on the tenant a specified number of days before beginning the eviction suit.
    c. require the tenant to vacate.
    d. have a sheriff forcibly remove a tenant.

41. A resident manager typically _____.

    a. lives on the property.
    b. manages a single large property.
    c. prepares retail leases for their tenants.
    d. manages commercial properties.

42. What is a tube that carries water away from the foundation footing called?

    a. Downspout
    b. Soil pipe
    c. Drain tile
    d. Vent pipe

43. An electrician is looking to insulate his electrical work, what should he use?

   a. Asbestos
   b. Vapor barrier
   c. Copper
   d. Plumber's tape

44. Which of the following is a high-priority activity in marketing listings?

   a. Conducting weekly open houses
   b. Showing prospects as many properties as possible in a given time period
   c. Showing only your listings to buyers to maximize your income
   d. Showing properties that match the customer's requirements

45. How would you go about determining the value of the seller's property?

   a. By identifying the net proceeds the seller must receive from the sale
   b. By arriving at a price based on amount of the mortgage payoff
   c. By determining how much the property has appreciated in value since it was purchased
   d. By relying on an analysis of comparable properties which have recently sold in the same neighborhood

46. What happens if a buyer fails to perform his or her duties in a contract?

   a. A sale contract is unilateral and requires that only the seller perform.
   b. The contract may go into default.
   c. The seller cannot seek legal recourse for damages.
   d. The seller cannot sue for specific performance.

47. Which costs are typically covered by the buyer?

   a. The buyer's financing-related costs
   b. Title-related costs
   c. Property-related costs
   d. The total annual property tax amount

48. Albert recently obtained an 80% loan on his $740,000 home, and he had to pay $8,880 for points. How many points did he pay?

   a. 1.2 points
   b. 1.5 points
   c. 2.1 points
   d. 5.1 points

49. Harry paid $800,000 for a house three years ago. The house sells today for $925,000. How much has the property appreciated (rounded to the nearest one tenth percent)?

   a. 5.8%
   b. 86.5%
   c. 15.6%
   d. 20.0%

50. A property has a net income of $450,000, interest payments of $125,000, and annual cost recovery of $80,000. The property's tax rate is 32%. What is the property's annual tax on income?

    a. $144,000
    b. $118,400
    c. $104,000
    d. $78,400

Section Quizzes: Answer Key

SECTION ONE: Real Estate Specializations

1. c. property managers handle day-to-day operations while asset managers manage portfolios of properties.
2. b. developers.
3. b. retail, office and industrial properties.
4. a. Brokers and agents
5. b. By geography
6. d. A broker who renders real estate services for a fee
7. b. state government.
8. a. Property managers and asset managers
9. c. Financial performance of an income property portfolio
10. a. Office leases

SECTION TWO: Florida License Law Review

1. b. Must disclose any criminal history
2. c. An applicant's fingerprints are sent to the FBI for a criminal background check
3. a. 90
4. c. are exempt from prelicense education but must take the state exam.
5. c. pass the state license exam with a score of 75% or higher.
6. a. Applicants who fail the state license exam may retake it only once within a year of failing it.
7. d. 2-year experience requirement
8. c. has resided in Florida continuously for 4 or more months within the previous year.
9. b. active duty military personnel who are licensed in another state.
10. d. Every licensed person or entity
11. a. 60
12. b. During the first license period prior to license expiration
13. c. 8 hours
14. c. Having a hardship
15. c. F.S. Chapter 120.
16. b. on March 31 or September 30.
17. c. September 30, 2030
18. d. Sally's license will become null and void.
19. d. Sally is exempt from renewal requirements.
20. c. The license becomes involuntarily inactive.
21. c. within 10 days after the change.

SECTION THREE: Florida Brokerage Relationships Review

1. c. provide sufficient information for the agent to complete the agent's tasks.
2. a. The agent has violated the duty of confidentiality.
3. b. the agent has not violated fiduciary duty.
4. d. inform the seller.
5. a. fairness, care, and honesty.
6. b. has an exposure to a charge of negligent misrepresentation.

7. d. practicing law without a license.
8. b. Bob and Sue are acting as transaction brokers.
9. a. may not represent any party's interests to the detriment of the other party in the transaction.
10. c. Whenever the licensee and principal agree to do so.
11. a. A sales associate designated by a broker to represent one party in a transaction while another associate of the broker is designated to represent the other party
12. c. Five years
13. b. at the time of signing a listing or representation agreement or before showing a property .
14. a. None
15 c. Dual agency
16. a. Disclosing facts that materially affect the property's value
17. b. the nonresidential buyer and seller have assets of $1 million or more.
18. c. Transaction brokers have no duty of undivided loyalty.
19. c. for 5 years.

SECTION FOUR: Property Disclosures and Professional Practices

1 c. disclose the information to others.
2. a. It may cause them to be held liable for improper disclosure of potential violations.
3. b. Conditions that pre-existed the coverage date of the warranty will not be covered.
4. c. Disclose the result of any inspection, if known to the agent
5. b. When the licensee obtains the opinion of title from an attorney and passes the information on to the client
6. d. third-degree felony.
7. b. Sue Stan for not paying Sarah her share of the commission.
8. c. They have to disclose it because it is a property defect.
9. a. It allows them to cancel the contract and regain their deposit.
10 b. Intentionally failing to disclose a material fact
11. d. Ones that RESPA or any other law does not prohibit
12. a. They should refer them to an attorney or title company.
13 c. Appraisal
14 b. Up to 5 years in prison
15. d. Licensees can share their commission with buyers or sellers as long as it is in writing and disclosed to everyone involved in the transaction.

SECTION FIVE: Brokerage Practice Regulations

1. c. the advertising must not be misleading.
2. b. .Separate enclosed offices for each broker and associate
3. d. The registration for a closed branch office may not be transferred to a new branch office.
4. c. considered blind advertising.
5. c. Turn the check over to the employing broker by end of the next business day.
6. b. No later than the end of the third business day following receipt of the funds
7. a. within 15 business days of the last demand.
8. c. .interpleader action.
9. a. Sales associates are not permitted to use a trade name.
10. d .removing records from the previous broker's office.
11. a. The words "licensed real estate broker"
12. b. Phone calls before 8 a.m. and after 9 p.m. are prohibited.
13. b. An informal conflict settlement procedure that is conducted by a qualified third party.
14. d. Only if the seller has a yard sign up and they are not on the do-not-call list.

15. c. The Adams Team
16. b. Telephone Consumer Protection Act
17. a. CAN-SPAM Act

SECTION SIX: Fair Housing and Landlord-Tenant Laws

1. b. prohibit discrimination in housing transactions.
2. c. the Civil Rights Act of 1968.
3. c. the Fair Housing Amendments Act of 1988
4. a. blockbusting.
5. c. steering.
6. a. providing unequal services.
7. a. discriminatory misrepresentation.
8. d. The prohibition may be legal.
9. c. The agent and the owner
10. b. public accommodations and employment.
11. c. any time before midnight on the seventh day after signing the contract.
12. b. Joe owns an apartment building and has just interviewed a prospective tenant on the phone. When the tenant arrived to sign the lease, Joe realized the individual is Hispanic. Consequently, Joe refused to rent to this individual.
13. a. Allowing a service dog to live in a no-pet apartment building
14. c. within 30 days of receiving the deposit.
15. c. 30 days
16. a. Race
17. b. There is no maximum.
18. d. removing garbage and cleaning plumbing fixtures.
19. a. By providing a written 7-day notice specifying the noncompliance and intention to terminate
20. c. Garbage removal

SECTION SEVEN: Condos, Co-ops, Timeshares, HOAs and CDDs

1. c. fee simple ownership of the airspace in a unit and an undivided share of the entire property's common areas.
2. b. The property is owned by tenants in common or by a freehold owner who leases on a time-share basis.
3. a. A cooperative may hold an owner liable for the unpaid operating expenses of other owners.
4. a. a default by a coop owner may cause a foreclosure on the entire property instead of just a single unit, as with a condominium.
5. b. Right to cancel
6. d. Timeshare
7. a. Condominium resales
8. b. HOA
9. c. proprietary
10. d. 15
11. b. Storm water management
12. a. 10 days
13. c. The co-op owner owns neither a unit nor an undivided interest in the common elements.
14. a. weeks or months.
15. d. owners who occupy the timeshare for their own use.

SECTION EIGHT: Foreclosures and Short Sales

1. c. foreclosure.
2. a. there is no right to redeem the property in a non-judicial foreclosure.
3. b. a deed in lieu of foreclosure.
4. c. mortgagor.
5. a. It establishes the level of lender risk.
6. b. short sale
7. a. Any time until the foreclosure sale is over
8. c. The lender gives the borrower official notice.
9. a. The lender determines the short sale price.
10. b. The listing agent

SECTION NINE: Real Estate Market Economics

1. c. the amount of money a buyer and seller agree to exchange to complete a transaction.
2. b. desire, utility, scarcity, and purchasing power.
3. b. will increase.
4. d. the market tending toward equilibrium.
5. c. the market is over-supplied.
6. a. The demand must literally come to the supply.
7. b. base employment.
8. a. have been increasing.
9. d. expanding the sewer system.
10. a. trade area population and spending patterns.
11. c. costs of occupancy and building efficiency.
12. a. The final price both buyer and seller agree to
13. b. equilibrium
14. d. Real estate is illiquid.
15. c. decreases.
16. b. Employment
17. c. differing values

SECTION TEN: Estimating Property Value

1. a. if two similar properties are for sale, a buyer will purchase the cheaper of the two.
2. a. is physically and financially feasible, legal, and the most productive.
3. d. the price that a willing, informed, and unpressured seller and buyer agree upon for a property assuming a cash price and the property's reasonable exposure to the market.
4. b. the broker may not be a disinterested party.
5. a. there may be no recent sale price data in the market.
6. c. select comparable properties, adjust the comparables, estimate the value.
7. b. the seller offers below-market seller financing.
8. b. weights the comparables.
9. b. market value is not always the same as what the property cost.
10. b. replacement cost.
11. d. functional obsolescence.
12. b. incurable economic obsolescence.
13. c. depreciation
14. a. estimate depreciation, subtract depreciation from cost, and add back the land value.

15. b. $8,500
16. b. Apartment buildings
17. c. estimate net income, and apply a capitalization rate to it.
18. c. potential gross income minus vacancy and credit loss minus expenses.
19. b. $400,000
20. a. numerous expenses are not taken into account.
21. b. $240,000
22. c. a poorer
23. b. contribution
24. d. When demand exceeds supply
25. c. Highest and best use principle

SECTION ELEVEN: Real Property Investment Analysis

1. b. the more the investor stands to gain, the greater the risk that the investor may lose.
2. a. income and tax benefits.
3. c. debt.
4. d. relatively illiquid.
5. b. a more management-intensive investment.
6. a. a general partnership.
7. d. gross income minus expenses minus building depreciation.
8. c. deduct interest payments from income.
9. d. The owner may be able to exclude capital gain from taxable income when the property is sold.
10. c. may be deducted from the sale price for gains tax purposes.
11. b. the difference between net sale proceeds and adjusted basis.
12. a. cost recovery expense.
13. c. dividing cash flow by the investor's equity.
14. d. Cost recovery
15. a. Depreciation
16. b. $250,000; $500,000
17. c. It is a percentage increase over the original price found by dividing the estimated total appreciation by the original price.
18. a. Starker 1031 exchange

SECTION TWELVE: Property Insurance

1. a. The mortgage lender will place coverage on the home.
2. d   flood insurance.
3. d. Offering coverage from a company who only employs its own agents
4. c. Package
5. d. HO-6
6. c. HO-8
7. c. HO-4
8. b. If insured for less than 80% of replacement cost, a home's coverage will include a deduction for depreciation.
9. c. exclusion.
10. d. Damage caused by earthquakes
11. d. is required in high risk flood hazard areas for properties finances by federally backed mortgage loans.
12. b. Flood insurance is sold by the NFIP.

13. b. omit information indicating a property is in a flood zone because it is the buyer's responsibility to discover during the DDP.
14. d. 60 days.
15. b. presence of a metal roof.
16. c. the property is furnished so the owners could return at any time.
17. b. goes back for up to seven years listing both personal property and personal auto claims.
18. d. purchase a landlord's policy.
19. b. monoline
20. a. 1%

SECTION THIRTEEN: Risk Management

1. b. reduction.
2. c. risk outsourcing.
3. a. It deflects and reduces risk by preventing others from claiming they were misled.
4. c. It can be a guide to compliance with the law.
5. c. It reduces the risk of committing an unauthorized practice of law.
6. d. a legal requirement.
7. b. Copies of required communications to principals.
8. d. negligence, error or omission in carrying out professional services.
9. a. Failing to inform and disclose properly.
10. b. failing to disclose known adverse facts.
11. d. avoid creating a false impression that the licensee is a certified appraiser.
12. b. exceeding the authority of the agreement.
13. a. use a checklist of all items, contingencies, dates and responsibilities that must be met.
14. d. the principals may make changes as long as they sign or initial each change.
15. b. obtain education in the content and intent of the laws.
16. a. being present at a conversation where the setting of commission rates is discussed.
17. a. License discipline, fines, and possible incarceration.
18. c. stating that a client should seek legal counsel.
19. d. avoid statements of opinion and speculation in all reports.
20. b. It reduces the chance of presenting an offer from an unqualified buyer.
21. a. professional liability.
22. c. workers' compensation.
23. d. criminal
24. b. Forever
25. a. Because of the "time is of the essence" clause

SECTION FOURTEEN: Property Management

1. c. fiduciary
2. b. financial reporting to the principal.
3. d. revenue from all sources minus losses from uncollected rents, vacancies, and evictions.
4. a. cost per tenant prospect generated per lease.
5. b. raise rental rates.
6. d. High tenant turnover increases expenses and reduces profits.
7. b. Routine, preventive, and corrective
8. a. ensure that disabled employees have the same level of access to facilities that all employees have.

9. c. A court may hold the manager responsible for the physical safety of tenants in leased premises.
10. a. replacement value.
11. b. cash for the management firm's operating expenses.
12. c. General
13. a. apportioned under the terms of the management contract.
14. b. The tenant pays a fixed rent, and the landlord pays all operating expenses.
15. d. the property manager does not have to maintain it.
16. b. deliver a habitable property.
17. c. A tenant declares a landlord in default and vacates the leased premises.
18. a. the competitive market for the property.
19. c. property manager
20. a. all property managers evaluate potential tenants fairly and equally.
21. b. serve notice on the tenant a specified number of days before beginning the eviction suit.
22. a. lives on the property.
23. c. The lease will be terminated if it was leased under a life estate.
24. d. Use the property and the rooms only for their intended purposes
25. b. 30-day

SECTION FIFTEEN: Construction Terminology

1. d. Bungalow
2. a. Flat
3. a. heat pump
4. b. Lead
5. c. Facade
6. b. beam.
7. a. Bifold door
8. b. Spanish mission
9. a. Outlet box
10. c. Drain tile
11 a. Asbestos
12. a. Trap
13. c. Stucco
14. a. truss
15. b. Return

SECTION SIXTEEN: Elements of the Listing Process

1. c. is governed by both agency law and contract law
2. a. they will get paid regardless of who sells the property
3. a. referrals to generate listings
4. b. To get a listing presentation
5. d. Showing properties that match the customer's requirements
6. d. By relying on an analysis of comparable properties which have recently sold in the same neighborhood
7. d. Determine the earliest possible time to present the offer regardless of its merits.
8. b. Exclusive right to sell
9. b. give the contract and deposit to the broker.
10. a. handle trust funds and facilitate pre-closing activities.
11. b. IDX policy enables MLS members to display and use MLS data on their websites.

12. d. Regulated advertising
13. a. operate as mobile offices.
14 a. that advertising not be misleading or deceptive.
15 d. Advertising emails must offer an opt-out alternative available by paying a one-time fee.

SECTION SEVENTEEN: Inside the Sales Contract

1. b. This can lead to an encumbered title and/or legal disputes.
2. a. surveyor
3. c. Income properties only
4. a. Seller's property condition disclosure
5. d. seller financing
6. b. For 5 years
7. c. equitable title.
8. d. executory
9. c. Items commonly construed as fixtures
10. b. The contract may go into default.
11. a. The buyer's financing-related costs
12. b. 15%
13. d. five-year
14. c. Financing contingency
15. a. General warranty deed

SECTION EIGHTEEN: Real Estate Mathematics

1. c. 10 acres
2. a. $9,669
3. a. $10,920
4. c. $96,000
5. d. 150
6. c. 8%
7. c. $1,500,000
8. b. $840
9. b. 1.75 points
10. c. 29%
11. c. $2,240
12. a. $3,846
13. c. $15,000
14. b. 5.33%
15. b   Debit seller, credit buyer $866.70
16. b $1,330

PRACTICE EXAMINATION

1. a. Property managers and asset managers
2. d. Paula is exempt from renewal requirements.
3. c. The license becomes involuntarily inactive.
4. c. within 10 days after the change.
5. b. the nonresidential buyer and seller have assets of $1 million or more.
6. c. Transaction brokers have no duty of undivided loyalty.
7. c. for 5 years.
8. c. Disclose the result of any inspection, if known to the agent
9. b. When the licensee obtains the opinion of title from an attorney and passes the information on to the client
10. d. third-degree felony.
11. b. Phone calls before 8 a.m. and after 9 p.m. are prohibited.
12. b. An informal conflict settlement procedure that is conducted by a qualified third party.
13. a. Allowing a service dog to live in a no-pet apartment building
14. c. within 30 days of receiving the deposit.
15. c. 30 days
16. a. Race
17. a. a default by a coop owner may cause a foreclosure on the entire property instead of just a single unit, as with a condominium.
18. b. Right to cancel
19. a. there is no right to redeem the property in a non-judicial foreclosure.
20. b. desire, utility, scarcity, and purchasing power.
21. b. will increase.
22. d. the market tending toward equilibrium.
23. c. depreciation
24. a. estimate depreciation, subtract depreciation from cost, and add back the land value.
25. b. $8,500
26. b. Apartment buildings
27. d. The owner may be able to exclude capital gain from taxable income when the property is sold.
28. c. may be deducted from the sale price for gains tax purposes.
29. b. the difference between net sale proceeds and adjusted basis.
30. c. HO-4
31. b. If insured for less than 80% of replacement cost, a home's coverage will include a deduction for depreciation.
32. c. exclusion.
33. c. It reduces the risk of committing an unauthorized practice of law.
34. d. a legal requirement.
35. b. Copies of required communications to principals.
36. d. negligence, error or omission in carrying out professional services.
37. a. Failing to inform and disclose properly.
38. c. property manager
39. a. all property managers evaluate potential tenants fairly and equally.
40. b. serve notice on the tenant a specified number of days before beginning the eviction suit.
41. a. lives on the property.
42. c. Drain tile
43 a. Asbestos
44. d. Showing properties that match the customer's requirements
45. d. By relying on an analysis of comparable properties which have recently sold in the same neighborhood
46. b. The contract may go into default.

47. a. The buyer's financing-related costs
48. b. 1.50 points
49. c. 15.6%
50. d. $78,400

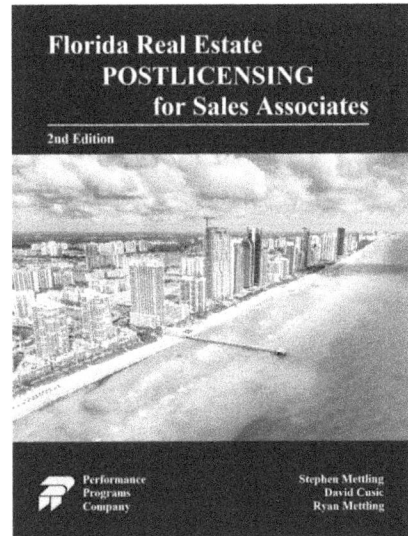